Praise for the first title in The Book Lover's Guide Series

"...you are apt to find dozens of bookstores here that you may never have heard of but clearly will have just what you're looking for, no matter how arcane."

Chicago Tribune

"A must!"

Chicago Live, NBC

"Book of the Week"

WFMT Chicago, *The Storytellers.*

"She (the author) has sought out the obscure and unique and you'll make some delightful discoveries."

Illinois School Library Media Association

The Book Lover's Guide

To Washington, D.C.

Lane Phalen

Brigadoon Bay
Books

Hoffman Estates, Illinois

The publisher and author of this book assume no legal responsibility for the completeness or accuracy of the contents of this book nor any legal responsibility for any increase or decrease in the value of any enterprises, whether for profit or non-profit, by reason of their inclusion or exclusion from this work. Contents are based on information believed to be accurate at the time of publication.

Neither Brigadoon Bay Books nor the author have accepted payment from any firms or organizations as a condition for inclusion in this book.

Publisher's Cataloging in Publication
(Prepared by Quality Books Inc.)

Phalen, Lane.
    The book lover's guide to Washington, D.C. / by Lane Phalen.
    p. cm. -- (Book lover's guide series)
    Includes index
    Preassigned LCCN: 93-072986.
    ISBN 1-88033-909-9

        1, Booksellers and bookselling.--Washington (D.C.)--Directories.
I. Title.

Z478.6.W37B74 1993   381'.45002025'753
                           QBI93-21592

9 8 7 6 5 4 3 2 1

To my dear sisters
who have always been and will be
my best friends,

Lori Meadows

&

Cindy Schlesinger

Table of Contents

Alexandria

A Likely Story Children's Bookstore

Children's books
1555 King St.
Alexandria, VA 22314
703-836-2498
Hours: Mon.-Sat. 10-6; Sun. 1-5

Children will love the delightful storybooks sold at A Likely Story Children's Bookstore. They'll also enjoy the many craft workshops, story telling time, author's autographing sessions, and contests. Luckily a newsletter is published so parents and kids can mark their calendars. The little ones in your family won't want to miss any of their special events. Most of the workshops are free.

Of special note is a program that A Likely Story coordinated during the Christmas holidays. As a result of the generosity of clients, they were able to provide gift-wrapped books to more than 650 needy children during the holidays.

A Likely Story Children's Bookstore holds approximately 20,000 titles of children's books, books about parenting, and cookbooks. Books are targeted for infants through their teenage years. The staff are ex-librarians and ex-teachers and therefore provide vital assistance to clients when choosing gift books.

Also for sale in the store are video tapes, rubber stamps, stickers, educational games, and stuffed characters found in books. Free gift wrapping is available. Because of the ramp, the store is easily accessible for wheelchairs, strollers, and the occasional wagon.

A Likely Story Children's Bookstore is so popular that they ship books daily. Some addresses are overseas. When you are in the area, you're sure to be impressed with their commitment to children's learning and development of their imaginations.

Aftertime Comics Inc.

Science Fiction/Fantasy

1304 King St.
Alexandria, VA 22314
703-548-5030
Hours: Sun.-Thurs. 12-6;
Fri. & Sat. 11-7

Whether you're a dedicated comic book collector or hooked on a continuing comic book story, you don't want to miss the latest issue. Aftertime Comics has a Hot Line just for you: (703) 548-4486. By calling the number, you'll be able to find out what comic books arrive at the store weekly.

Aftertime Comics receives approximately 2,000 titles each month. If that isn't enough, they will search for specific titles to complete your comic book collection. They also stock many rare and out-of-print comic books in the store. After checking out the comic books, you'll also want to browse through the science fiction and games that are sold in the store. The store is not wheelchair accessible.

A life-time comic book collector himself, owner David Erskine says that his staff is knowledgeable and friendly. He has plans to open a second store.

Air, Land & Sea

Aviation

1215 King St.
Alexandria, VA 22314
703-684-5118
Hours: Mon.-Fri. 10-6;
Sat. & Sun. 9-5

Primarily stocked with aviation books, Air, Land & Sea also sells nautical and warfare books. From one-third to one-half of the small store is devoted to books. Approximately 80% of the books are used, "not rare and not collectible," said store owner Buzz Polistak.

"Air, Land & Sea is an enthusiasts store," said Buzz whose hobby of building model airplanes led him to opening the store in 1971.

Along with the books and models, Air, Land & Sea sells paintings, prints, and aviation memorabilia. You can mail order items and Buzz will keep an eye out to find used books on your want lists. The store is open daily but is not wheelchair accessible. Air, Land & Sea is located in the Colonial part of Alexandria.

Aquarius Metaphysical Center

Metaphysics
1210 King Street
Alexandria, VA 22314
703-836-0616
Hours: Wed.-Sun. 1-7

"A spiritual oasis in the District of Columbia area," is the description given by Aquarius Metaphysical Center owner, Carroll Miles. "It is a friendly, congenial, peaceful atmosphere."

If metaphysics and New Age draws pictures of wart-nosed witches and gypsies reading palms, one trip with an open mind to Aquarius Metaphysical Center will show you a different world.

According to Carroll, "the New Age heralds mankind's evolution into a higher consciousness, spirituality and a better world."

You see the results and the acceptance of the New Age everywhere. Physicians report the success of creative visualization or mind over matter, business men preach the power of positive thinking, coaches tell athletes to see themselves scoring. Who today hasn't heard of near-death experiences in which the person sees a bright white light? How is it that people feel that they have been someplace before?

Answers and explanations to these topics can be found in the nearly 3,000 titles of new and used books sold at Aquarius Metaphysical Center. Topics include, of course, New Age and Metaphysics, but also philosophy, self-help, psychology, recovery, nature, alternative life styles, religion, science, occult, meditation, and magic. You'll even find fantasy and science fiction books to enjoy in your spare time.

Supplemental items sold include crystals, candles, musical tapes, herbs, jewelry, tarot cards, incense, magazines, games, and so much more. Fortunately, the store is completely accessible to everyone.

Carroll has developed the bookstore into a complete metaphysical center offering astrological charting, personality reports, past-life readings, and more. You'll find experts who have studied many fields of metaphysics and will educate and explain conscious power and help you access the strength within your self.

Aquarius has created a bulletin board system for computers that allows computer buffs access to metaphysical discussions through 125 networks and local conferences. Four international echomail networks include TrekkerNet (the Star Trek only network), Dune Network (based upon Frank Herbert's Dune Chronicles), SmartNet (a general conference network), and TTN (the triBBS network). Call Aquarius for more information.

A popular event happening at Aquarius takes place every other Sunday: Mystic Sunday. Ordained ministers and licensed spiritual counselors meet with people individually to discuss self-exploration, mini-mystical consultations, and problem-solving.

Carroll is always open and energetic in making Aquarius Metaphysical Center a unique meeting place giving personalized attention and service to clients. Experience the Age of Aquarius.

11

Ark & The Dove

Religious-Christian   6122 Rose Hill Dr.
Alexandria, VA 22310
703-971-7000
Hours: Mon.-Fri. 10-8; Sat. 10-6

    A full Christian bookstore, The Ark & The Dove offers you peace and a wide selection of books and items. The books total 25,000 titles and a catalog is available. Approximately 400 of the books have been written by Christian authors. They do place special orders. The store is wheelchair accessible.

Blue & Gray Books and Prints

Civil War   210 King Street
Alexandria, VA 22314
703-739-9849
Hours: Sun.-Thurs. noon-6;
Fri. & Sat. noon-9

    No one can visit the Washington area without being aware of the Civil War influence. At Blue & Gray Books and Prints, the Civil War of yesterday comes alive today. In addition to books about the Civil War, Blue & Gray sells fine art prints depicting scenes from the war.
    The quality of selections at the bookstore is ensured by the owner, Raymond G. LePage, PhD. A true family business, Blue & Gray is also owned by Raymond's wife, Claire, and managed by their children Melissa and Marc.
    Old Alexandria proves the perfect setting for this bookstore. They are located on the second floor of a historic townhouse. Unfortunately, the store is not wheelchair accessible.
    With a second location in North Carolina, Blue & Gray Books and Prints prove to be excellent resources for information about the Civil War.

Boat Owners Assoc. of the US-Book Dept.

Nautical   880 S. Pickett St.
Alexandria, VA 22304
703-823-9550
800-937-2629
FAX 703-461-2854
Hours: Telephone & mail orders only

    The Boat Owners Association wants to make your boating experience a fun and safe one. They sell more than 300 titles through mail order.

Topics include instruction and maintenance of sail and motor boats. They also have books discussing cruising and charts for all parts of the nation. An annual catalog is published.

With a toll free voice and fax numbers, it is easy to contact them. Be safe, have fun, and be sure to contact them if you own or plan to buy a boat.

The Book Niche & Capital Comics Center

Comics & Misc.

2008 Mount Vernon Ave.
Alexandria, VA 22301
703-548-3466
Hours: Mon.-Fri. noon-7;
Sat. noon-6:30

There is a little niche in Alexandria that successfully combines new and used books with comic books to create a bookstore for everyone.

Book Niche & Capital Comics, owned by Dennis Webb, sells books highlighting the classics, mystery, science fiction, the American West, biographies, and television and movie related books. Of course, they wouldn't live up to their name if they didn't have such a fine collection of comics and comic strips.

Established almost twenty years ago, the store employees are happy to place special orders and maintain client's "want lists." Because many of the store's customers are collectors, the store sells a wide selection of collector's supplies.

There is one step at the entrance for wheelchairs to jump in order to enter. In a store as unique as Book Niche & Capital Comics, you're sure to find items not sold in any other Washington stores.

The Book Rack

Used-General

7001 J Manchester Blvd.
Alexandria, VA 22310
703-780-2325
Hours: Mon.-Thurs. 11-7;
Fri. & Sat. 10-6; Sun. noon-5

Owner Ellen Betts says that The Book Rack in Alexandria stocks "a little bit of everything." In addition to selling, buying, and trading paperbacks, the store also sells new children's books and Cliff Notes.

The Book Rack is wheelchair accessible. Although Ellen listed the above hours that the store is open, she recommends calling ahead to make sure that she is there.

Book Stop

Used-Music
3640-A King St.
Alexandria, VA 22302
703-578-3292
<u>Hours:</u> Mon.- Wed., Fri. noon-6;
Sat. 11-6; Sun. 1-5

You're welcome to stop by the Book Stop seven days per week where you can find 12,000 used books and sheet music. Owner Toby Cedar is pleased to search for book titles on your want list. She also will do appraisals on used books.

The store is wheelchair accessible but Toby courteously reports that wheelchair users may need a bit of assistance to open the front door. She is always happy to help all customers and sees to the comfort of browsers by providing seating in the store.

Established in 1982, Book Stop has a general interest stock of books that will make you stop here often.

Brentano's

General
Landmark Center
5801 Duke Street
Alexandria, VA 22304
703-914-0254
<u>Hours:</u> Mon.-Sat. 10-9:30; Sun. 11-6

The area surrounding Washington played a crucial role during the Civil War and the Brentano's bookstore located in Landmark Center, Alexandria sells a large selection of books covering all aspects of the war. They also have a large travel department. In addition to a wealth of general interest books, Waldenbooks and Brentano's, which are owned by the same company, sell magazines, audio and video tapes, calendars, and posters.

Special services abound at both Waldenbooks and Brentano's. Each store has the capability to track down and quickly place in the hands of customers those books in print that are not stocked in the store.

Top selling hardcover books are sold at a discount. A great way to receive an extra ten percent discount is to join the Preferred Reader Program. As a member, you are entitled to receive an extra ten percent off the price of everything in the store except magazines. So just think, for an annual fee of $10, you can purchase all the books you want at a discount including the bestsellers and even bargain books. But, Brentano's and Waldenbooks don't stop there. For every $100 worth of merchandise that a Preferred Reader customer buys, he or she receives a $5.00 store coupon.

If you're in the market for a Bible, Waldenbooks and Brentano's can have the family keepsake imprinted. Ask staff members about the details of this service.

Landmark Center stores are all wheelchair accessible. It's clear that Waldenbooks and Brentano's can please both your book appetite and your wallet.

Cardinal Images

Metaphysics

50 S. Pickett St.
Alexandria, VA 22304
703-370-5228
Hours: Mon.-Sat. 11-7; Sun. noon-6

When you hear the word "cardinal," you may think of a red bird, a baseball team, or a Catholic dignitary, but Cardinal Images uses another meaning to "cardinal." Webster's Dictionary states cardinal means "of prime importance." Cardinal Images stands up to Webster's definition.

With a main focus on new age and metaphysical books, Cardinal Images also brings you a variety of books about holistic health, recovery programs, occult and magic, women's studies, and same-sex relationships. You can also enjoy their collection of audio books, video tapes, magazines, T-shirts, posters, games, and a variety of items.

Employees at Cardinal Images believe in bringing quality service to customers and will place special orders or even gift wrap your purchases. Telephone and mail orders are no problem.

As a wonderful special program, Cardinal Images sponsors a reading group and invites authors to visit the store for autographing sessions. A bulletin board in the store keeps customers informed of local activities.

The store is open everyday and is completely accessible to wheelchair-users, stroller-pushers, and the able-bodied. If you drive, an off-street parking lot is available and if you prefer mass-transit, that is nearby as well.

Established in 1988, Cardinal Images continues to develop a fine stock of books guaranteed to please.

Cokesbury Virginia Theological Seminary Book Service

Religious, Christian

3737 Seminary Rd.
Alexandria, VA 22314
703-370-6161
800-368-3756
FAX 703-370-1429
Hours: Mon.-Sat. 10-5

Cokesbury is a name most Christians associate with fine quality products that all have a religious accent. The Virginia Theological Seminary bookstore is now owned by Cokesbury and customers can now take full advantage of the products.

Owned by Cokesbury since 1992, the bookstore is developing the store to include many more items than they previously sold. Clothing and children's books were two of the targeted areas for expansion.

The bookstore is on the lower floor of the Addison Academic Building. Shoppers in wheelchairs should use the Quaker Lane entrance and follow the signs. You can also shop by catalog using their fax and toll free numbers. They have added a TDD/TT toll-free service: 1-800-227-4091.

Cokesbury publishes a complete yearly catalog as well as many specialty catalogs including choir apparel, handbells, clergy robes, vacation Bible school resources, and more. Items are sold to the clergy and to lay-people.

At the bookstore of the Virginia Theological Seminary, you can purchase items and obtain catalogs. The Vice-President of Product Management of Cokesbury, Marc Lewis, says: "You can count on Cokesbury, year after year. Your satisfaction is always guaranteed."

Comics Center & Book Niche

Comics
2008 Mt. Vernon Ave.
Alexandria, VA 22301
703-548-3466
Hours: Mon.-Thurs. 11:30-7;
Fri. noon-8; Sat. noon-6:30

If you are not a fan of comic books, give yourself a second chance by visiting Comics Center & Book Niche. Owner Dennis Webb will introduce (or re-introduce) you to comic books featuring Little Lulu, Donald Duck, the Lone Ranger, or a few of the Super Heros.

If you don't enjoy the story lines, you will definitely admit that the artwork is superb. Dennis has artistic panels of comic books that are suitable for framing.

If you still don't feel right in reading the thin comic books, Dennis has the solution for you. Some of the older comic books and newspaper comic strips have been bound in hardback covers.

OK, comics still aren't your thing. Comics Center & Book Niche lives up to its name and offers you a fine collection of science fiction, Westerns and mystery books. Among the selections offered are Star Trek, Star Wars, and Indiana Jones.

In addition to collector supplies, Comics Center & Book Niche sells "little selections of many things that other bookstores don't have," said Dennis. Those selections include black & white and color television and movie photographs, magic tricks, gadgets, novelty items, and even houseplants!

The store is wheelchair accessible from the outside, but, as you can imagine, the aisles are narrow. Employees are happy to assist customers.

Dennis points to his mother as the person giving him a start in selling comic books. While Dennis was in college, his mother owned an antique shop that sold books and magazines. She allowed him to develop the business which has grown into the unique place that it now is.

Crown Books

General   3676 King St.
                                   Alexandria, VA 22310
                                   703-379-0944
                                   <u>Hours:</u> Mon.-Sat. 10-9; Sun. 11-5

   Read about the discounts and services that Crown Books gives to customers by referring to the Alexandria SuperCrown store located on Little River Turnpike.

Crown Books

General   500 King St.
                                   Alexandria, VA 22314
                                   703-548-3432
                                   <u>Hours:</u> Mon.-Sat. 10-10; Sun. 10-6

   Crown Books gives you great discounts. For a full description of those discounts, please see the write-up for the Alexandria SuperCrown on Little River Turnpike.

Crown Books

General   1716 Duke St.
                                   Alexandria, VA 22314
                                   703-548-9548
                                   <u>Hours:</u> Mon.-Sat. 9-7; Sun. 11-5

   To learn about the terrific discounts and services that Crown Books offers you, see the write-up of the SuperCrown store on Little River Turnpike in Alexandria.

Crown Books

General   6230 N. Kings Hwy.
                                   Alexandria, VA 22303
                                   703-765-1858
                                   <u>Hours:</u> Mon.-Sat. 10-9; Sun. 11-5

   See the description of the Alexandria SuperCrown bookstore on Little River Turnpike to read about the discounts offered by Crown Books.

Donna Lee's Books

General

206 Queen St.
Alexandria, VA 22314
703-548-5830
<u>Hours:</u> Mon.-Fri. 11-3;
Sat. & Sun. 10-4

If you are interested in genealogy, history, antique maps, or Americana, Donna Lee's Books is a place you will enjoy visiting. As an antiquarian bookstore, you will find approximately 8,000 quality books in those categories.

You can also discuss the books you are looking for, and they will conduct a search for the title. They also expertly appraise books. A unique feature, book repairs are done by the book masters at Donna Lee's Books.

Conducting business since 1980, Donna Lee's Books is open daily. Because the store is not wheelchair accessible, you can contact them and discuss other possible ways to obtain the books you want.

Eastern Front Military Distributors

Militaria

2507 Randolph Ave.
Alexandria, VA 22301
703-836-2690
<u>Hours:</u> Telephone and Mail order only

Strictly a mail order business, Eastern Front Military Distributors sells books to the public through a catalog. As the name of the book business indicates, they sell books relating to the military, in particular military history of the U.S. Air Force and German military on air, land, and sea during World War II.

They sell new titles as well as rare out-of-print books. Eastern Front has approximately 2,000 in stock. The business has been in operation since the late 1980's.

Eastern Mountain Sports, Inc.

Outdoor Sports

Landmark Plaza
6178F Little River Tpk.
Alexandria, VA 22312
703-354-8664
<u>Hours:</u> Mon.-Sat. 10-9; Sun. noon-5

Whether the great outdoors is your playground or you prefer to observe nature, you'll find books to suit your needs at Eastern Mountain Sports.

The chain store has three stores in local malls in the Washington area. In addition to this one, Eastern Mountain Sports has stores in Gaithersburg, MD, and McLean, VA.

For a more complete description of Eastern Mountain Sports, see the write-up for the Gaithersburg store.

Family Bookstores

Religious-Christian   Landmark Center
                                          5801 Duke Street
                                          Alexandria, VA 22304
                                          703-642-0508
                                          <u>Hours:</u> Mon.-Sat. 10-9:30

Serving Alexandria's Christian community, Family Bookstores offers a fine selection of books and gifts. The store at Landmark Center is wheelchair accessible. Please refer to the more complete description of Family Bookstores for the Fredricksburg, VA store.

From Out of the Past

Antiquarian-General   6440 Richmond Hwy.
                                          Alexandria, VA 22306
                                          703-768-7827
                                          <u>Hours:</u> Tues.-Sat. 11-6

Writers and those that write journals usually protectively guard their works as if they were their own children. Why? Giving birth to books is to give a bit of immortality to the author.

Since 1968, many words from days gone by find places on the shelves of Mylo C. Keck at his used and antiquarian bookstore appropriately called From Out of the Past.

Described by radio personality Paul Harvey as "the man who is buried in his work," Mylo tenderly cares for more than 200,000 books and keeps 50,000 books in the store which is open daily except Sunday and Mondays. He also sells a million out-of-print back issues of a variety of magazines that Mylo describes as a "volcano explosion of magazines."

From Out of the Past is easy to reach. There is off-street parking nearby, a bus stops at the door, and the subway is only three-quarters of a mile away. The store is wheelchair accessible and seating within the store makes browsing a delight. Telephone and mail orders are accepted.

Mylo doesn't discriminate among the topics of the books. They reach a broad range of interests. All books are hardbacks. Whatever you're looking for, talk to Mylo, he may have just the old book for you.

Milo has conducted research for law firms dealing with advertising and copyright cases and movie studios who need specific ephemera for their sets.

How did he become such an expert? Mylo says he was a "Dagwood Bumstead who attended an auction twenty-five years ago" and found collecting books to be a perfect recreation. He opened From Out of the Past bookstore in 1968.

If you're looking for the unique or old beloved best-seller, call Mylo at From Out of the Past. No doubt you'll find what you have been looking for and make a friend in the process.

Gilpin House Books & Gifts, Inc.

General

208 King St.
Alexandria, VA 22314
703-549-1880
Hours: Mon.-Thurs. 9am-10pm;
Fri. & Sat. 9am-11pm

Located in a historical townhouse in Old Alexandria, Gilpin House Books & Gifts is a quaint store that has a general interest supply of books with particularly large travel, gardening, and children's book departments.

With four steps at the entrance, there is really no way that they can make the bookstore wheelchair accessible.

In addition to books, Gilpin House sells beautiful needlepoint pillows, afghans, and clocks. You'll enjoy browsing here.

Hearthstone Bookshop

Genealogy & Local History

Potomac Square
8405-H Richmond Hwy.
Alexandria, VA 22309
703-360-6900
Hours: Mon.- Wed., Fri., Sat. 10-5;
Thurs. 10-8

When you visit Washington's only bookstore devoted to genealogy and local history, you'll feel like you stepped into history. Hearthstone Bookshop, "The Genealogy Store," is located in Potomac Square which is designed with colonial architecture.

With a stock of approximately 3,000 titles, Hearthstone Bookshop sells all the books and supplies you need to trace your family tree. They have family trees ready for you to fill out that go up to 16 generations. In addition, they are specialists in local history and maintain a healthy selection of books to make your visit to Washington, D.C. fact-filled fun.

Proprietor Stuart Nixon, who conducts searches and places special orders for requested titles, reports that the shop is located just a few miles from Mount Vernon, home of George Washington. Hearthstone Bookshop is completely wheelchair accessible and the wheelchair ramp for the strip mall is directly in front of the store. Off-street parking and mass transit are nearby.

The bookshop, established in 1981, has extended hours on Thursdays. Mail and telephone orders are happily accepted and keep employees busy. A catalog is available for a nominal charge. Members of the Ancestry Research Club and teachers of genealogy classes or workshops are given a 10 percent discount. Ask for more details in the store.

Blue-blood or Yankee stew, you'll enjoy Hearthstone Bookstore for the unique books sold and the charming atmosphere.

Jennie's Book Nook

Antiquarian-Americana

15 W. Howell Ave.
Alexandria, VA 22301
703-683-0694
Hours: Mail order only

A charming southern lady, Virginia Vruch operates a used bookstore specializing in history, biography, poetry, literature, children's books. She has large selections about the Civil War, Virginia history, and Robert E. Lee. A volunteer at the boyhood home of Robert E. Lee, Jennie is the research curator and trains the volunteer staff at the house.

A retired librarian at the Pentagon, Jennie says that books have always had a special place in her heart. She has written two books and is working on a third. Her first book is a two volume genealogy of her family called "Proud Wanderers." Her second book, "Beneath the Oaks of Ivy Hill" is a record of those buried in Ivy Hill Cemetery where some graves date back to the late 1700's. Currently she's working on a book of newspaper excerpts from the small town of Hickman, Kentucky which lies on the Tennessee border. The book is titled "Once Long Ago." In the little spare time that Jenny has, she is working on her husband's genealogy.

Selling books for approximately twenty years, Jennie's business is conducted primarily through mail orders. It is a business that sprang from her hobby of book collecting. She does conduct elaborate searches for the books you request.

Jennie believes in the philosophy that "there is a special charm to all things old," and she certainly lives to ensure that the past is not lost.

Jesus Bookstore of Mount Vernon

Religious, Christian

7700 Richmond Hwy.
Alexandria, VA 22306
703-780-3200
Hours: Mon., Wed., & Fri. 10-9;
Tues., Thurs. & Sat. 10-6

Affiliated with the Jesus Bookstore in Dale City, MD, Jesus Bookstore in Alexandria also carries a full stock of Christian books and related item. The store is wheelchair accessible.

Kay's Bookshelf

Antiquarian & Used

8727-D Cooper Road
Alexandria, VA 22309
703-360-3202
Hours: Mon., Wed., Fri. 10-8; Tues.
& Thurs. 10-6; Sat. 10-5; Sun. noon-5

When asked what special categories of books Kay Kilgus sells at Kay's Bookshelf, she replied that there is no special category. Kay's is a general interest, something-for-everyone used bookstore. Children can play with toys in the playroom while adults browse.

Kay prefers to call the books "recycled" instead of used. So many of the books look as if they have never been read. If you are a romance book collector, Kay's offers many titles in the older series romances so you can complete your collection.

Every week Kay receives new recycled books. She buys books as well as offering an exchange for titles. Kay's Bookshelf also rents hardcover books. They do free gift wrapping and will mail books anywhere in the world. The store itself is wheelchair accessible.

Kay's Bookshelf is such a popular store that they are opening a second location in Morton. The store was not opened at the time that this book went into publication so you'll want to call the Alexandria location for details. You won't want to miss it.

Listen 2 Books

Books on cassette tape

3111 Duke Street
Alexandria, VA 22314
703-823-5004
800-AUDIO BOOKS
FAX 703-823-0861
Hours: Mon.-Fri. 10-8;
Sat. 10-6; Sun. noon-5

People are listening more now than ever! Listening to books, anyway. The books-on-cassette-tape industry has boomed and now you can visit a store that deals exclusively with audio books.

Since 1990, Listen 2 Books has sold new and used tapes, rented them, bought them, and even traded them. You can buy or rent audio books by mail order. Ask them for details. Listen 2 Books sells books-on-cassette-tape under 22 categories. Business books-on-cassette-tape top the best seller and rental lists.

"People used to think that books-on-cassette-tape are only for the blind. A large group of customers are craftsmen, such as artists and printers, who listen to the tapes while they are working," partner Debbi Parrish said. Other people who enjoy the tapes instead of printed material are commuters, people exercising, and children.

Joe Andahazy and partners Debbi Parrish and Kim Kuntavanish pride themselves in the personal service offered by Listen 2 Books.

Employees listen to tapes and someone in each of their two stores has listened to all the tapes in the store. The staff is invaluable when choosing tapes. Most tapes are read by actors but some are read by the authors. Some tapes are available in abridged and unabridged editions.

Listen 2 Books is one of only twenty or so such stores in the country. The two locations in Alexandria and Arlington are both popular places. The store in Alexandria has between 3,500 and 4,000 titles while the Arlington branch has approximately 2,000 titles.

The store publishes a yearly catalog and issues quarterly updates through their newsletter. Both stores are wheelchair accessible. A toll free number and gift certificates are other client services that Listen 2 Books offers.

With the tiny tape players available now, books-on-cassette-tape have established a whole new medium for literature that enables people to learn and enjoy books while their hands and eyes are free.

Maranatha Christian Bookstore & Supply

Religious-Christian

1607 Commonwealth Ave.
Alexandria, VA 22301
703-548-2895
Hours: Mon.-Fri. 10-6;
Thurs. 10-8; Sat. 10-5

A complete religious bookstore, Maranatha Christian Bookstore and Music sells more than 5,000 titles of Christian books and books for children. They do beautiful imprinting on Bibles.

Maranatha Christian Bookstore does accept mail orders but does not publish catalogs. Music comprises an important department at this bookstore. They sell music cassettes and will sell and rent video tapes for family entertainment. Also for sale are Christian jewelry, greeting cards, wall plaques, bookcovers, etc.

The store does have a small section reserved for used books which is continuously growing. Not many religious bookstores sell choir robes but you will find a nice selection of robes here.

Established in 1971, Maranantha Christian Bookstore and Music is wheelchair accessible. The whole family will enjoy this bookstore.

NTL Institute

Business

1240 N. Pitt St., Ste. 100
Alexandria, VA 22314
703-548-1500
Hours: Telephone & Mail order only

Do you feel like you hit a brick wall every time you deal with employees and co-workers? NTL (National Training Laboratory) Institute for Applied Behavioral Science should be the next telephone call you make.

Since 1947, NTL Institute offers you books, training products, and workshops concerning human resources, organizational development, and personal and professional development. Faculty at the workshops include leading educators, consultants, administrators and business professionals from around the world.

To obtain a catalog and informational brochure from NTL Institute stop by their office or call them. If you need to enhance your management style, contact NTL Institute now. They have the book or workshop to help you.

Old Mill Books

Antiquarian-General

PO Box 21561
Alexandria, VA 22320
703-683-1831
Hours: Mail order

Many non-book lovers think that we bibliophiles are loners and live vicariously through the books we read. Book lovers can secretly smile at their misconception. We know that the love of books can lead to terrific friendships.

George Loukides, owner of Old Mill Books, knows this is true and has made many friends due to a shared interest in books. A retired playwright, George travels the world and offers fabulous used books to clients. Constantly turning over, his stock of books feature the South Pacific, Southeast Asia, Australia, New Zealand, and the Antarctic. Prices range from $5.00 to the thousands. George is more than happy to conduct searches on his specialized field. All sales are conducted by mail order and George even conducts informal appraisals of books by mail.

George stumbled into the book business by purchasing a box of old books at a New York auction. He researched their value, continued reading and learning about the book business and opened a used bookstore in New Jersey. Fortunately for Washington, he moved to this area. George says that the book business is "a lot of fun" and you'll have fun and make a new friend when you meet him through Old Mill Books.

Old Town News

News & Magazines

721 King Street
Alexandria, VA 22314
703-739-9024
Hours: Mon.-Sat. 9am-10pm; Sun. 8-6

Old Town News is a bustling shop featuring newspapers and magazines. They also sell a few bestselling paperbacks. The store is wheelchair accessible.

Olsson's Books & Records at Old Town

General   106 S. Union St.
                              Alexandria, VA 22314
                              703-684-0077
                              Hours: Mon.-Thurs. 10-10;
                              Fri. & Sat. 10-midnt; Sun. 11-6

Located in Old Alexandria, Olsson's Books & Records fills two stories. Wheelchair clients can visit the first floor where Olsson's sells records and a small number of sale books. The main stock of books are located on the second story and are not wheelchair accessible.

For a more detailed description of the Olsson's chain, see the description for the Dupont Circle Olsson's in Washington.

One Good Tern Ltd.

Nature & Birds   1710 Fern St.
                             Alexandria, VA 22302
                             703-820-8376
                             800-432-8376
                             Hours: Mon., Wed., Fri. 10-6; Tues.
                             & Thurs. 10-8; Sat. 9-6; Sun. noon-5

Upon seeing the name of this bookstore, you might thing that they misspelled the name "turn." I did until I discovered that One Good Tern Ltd. is a wonderful nature store highlighting many books about birds. The word "tern" means "little seagull." Now it makes sense.

The approximately 2,000 titles of books in the store focus on nature, gardening, and the environment. Many are children's books. The store is accessible to everyone and open everyday. A catalog is published to make telephone and mail orders simple. Employees will conduct searches and place special orders.

So many more items other than books are available at this delightful store. They sell bird food, bird feeders, and binoculars to make bird watching possible. They also have nature and bird related items such as video tapes, magazines, stationery, T-shirts, children's games, and calendars.

One Good Tern Ltd. works hard to enhance customer's understanding of birds and nature. On Saturday mornings, they conduct bird walks to catch sight of both rare and common birds in the area. A bulletin board in the store informs customers of the bird walks and other activities in the area. The store publishes a newsletter three times per year.

Established in 1986, One Good Tern Ltd. is a wonderful creation of owner Mark Farmer. He continually develops a nature and bird-loving bookstore for the whole family.

Professional Book Center

Professional & Scholarly   607 S. Washington Street
                                              Alexandria, VA 22314
                                              703-519-6117 (SAT. only)
                                              <u>Hours:</u> Open Saturday 10-6 or by mail
                                              order or appointment

When you read the slogan of the Professional Book Center, you'll find that the slogan has many meanings. The slogan: "Washington's One of a Kind Bookstore." The first meaning is that the bookstore sometimes receives only one or two copies of the extremely unique professional topics.

The other meaning relates to the fact that the bookstore truly is one of a kind. Owner Mark Trocchi says that the store is a "Browser's Paradise." The topics are incredibly specialized and customers include PhD's in scrappy parkas to librarians buying for professional associations, universities, and colleges. In fact, if a librarian buys $10,000 worth of merchandise, the Professional Book Center will pay for their round-trip airfare. Ask them about it.

A third meaning to their slogan is attributed to the incredibly unique stock of books they sell.

"They're the cream of the crop, all new books, no used or second hand books," said Mark describing the stock.

All of the books are for the academician in medical science, biological science, ageing and gerontology, international studies, environmental sciences, law, psychology, music and arts, social sciences, economics, political science, business, and more. Mark reports that books relating to physics leave the store almost as fast as they arrive. Books are published by the leading publishers, university and college presses, and unusual small publishers.

Back to their slogan: a fourth reason that it fits the book business is because of the hours they operate. They are open only on Saturdays or by appointment for serious book buyers. Call (703) 519-3909 for appointments or to talk with store manager Michael Armah.

A fifth reason why the store lives up to its slogan is the location. The business has no sign! To visit the store, you must enter Smith's of Bermuda women's clothing and gift store, go to the back of the store, and climb a flight of stairs. Shoppers unable to climb the stairs are welcome to call the bookstore and shop by catalog through the mail.

All-in-all, the Professional Book Center is an unusual, funky, independent bookstore. Mark said he likes that the store is covered "in a bit of a shroud of mystery" and that it is "a fun place" to book browse.

In business since 1977, the Professional Book Center stocks 15,000 titles which are quickly growing. The store maintains a list of new arrival schedules. Books are organized and categories are easy to find. Even though all books are discounted 40% everyday, they do have special sales. A Christmas Egg Nog party offers egg nog and a 50% discount on books.

When you are looking for books aimed toward scholarly, scientific technological, or medical fields, look to the Professional Book Center.

Ptak Science Books

Science-Technology

810 N. Fairfax
Alexandria, VA 22314
Mail: PO Box 25852
Alexandria, VA 22313
703-683-6837
FAX 703-684-6843
Hours: Wed.-Sat. noon-5

"Very solid, high protein and little fat," is how John Ptak described the antiquarian, out-of-print, and used books he sells. Ptak Science Books offers antiquarian, out-of-print, and used scientific books.

With more than 50,000 titles in stock, you will, no doubt, find just the science books you want. However, if you don't, John does search for scientific books and appraisals of the books you do own.

John also sells antique American maps, including geological maps, dated from the 17th-mid 19th century. You'll also be able to purchase scientific prints and portraits.

Most business is conducted by mail but if you would like to view the stock, call John first. He usually keeps hours from "noon to tea time."

While this book was in production, Ptak Science Books moved from Washington to this address in Alexandria, one block west of the Potomac River. He is now part of the Internet and his number is: JFPtak2access.digex.net

Saint Paul Book & Media Center

Religious-Catholic

1025 King St.
Alexandria, VA 22314
703-549-3806
FAX 703-683-2568
Hours: Mon.-Fri. 10-6; Sat. 10-5:30

Located in Olde Town Alexandria on the corner of Route 7 and Route 1 south, Saint Paul Book & Media Center is a charming store that sells academic Catholic, spiritual, and philosophical books, many which they publish themselves.

There is one step at the entrance but the store does have wide aisles inside. Off-street parking and nearby mass transit add to the convenience of the bookstore. Shopping at home is easy with a copy of their catalog.

The Scottish Merchant

Scottish-Irish

215 King St.
Alexandria, VA 22314
703-739-2302
Hours: Mon.-Thurs. 10-10;
Fri. & Sat. 10-11; Sun. 11-9

With hundreds of titles in stock, The Scottish Merchant specializes in Scottish and Irish books. Manager Ken Grant also conducts searches and welcomes special orders.

In addition to books, The Scottish Merchant offers imported gift items from Scotland and Ireland, clothing, jewelry, music, and yes, kilts.

"We have our kilts custom tailored in Scotland ensuring the best quality," Ken said. "A kilt should last a lifetime."

Established in the late 1980's, The Scottish Merchant unfortunately is not wheelchair accessible due to the four steps at the entrance. It is open everyday. Shopping by telephone is no problem.

The store reflects the needs and supports the area Gaelic clubs. If you are Celtic (no, not a basketball player), you will certainly sing a toast to the long life and health of The Scottish Merchant. Slainte!

Spinnaker & Spoke

Nautical Sports & Bicycle

Washington Sailing Marina
George Washington Memorial Pkwy.
Alexandria, VA 22314
703-548-9027
Hours: Daily 9-6

Just two miles south of the Washington National Airport is Washington's sailing marina where you can picnic, rent and take lessons in sailing and windsurfing, rollerblade on the trails, or rent a bicycle to speed along the waterfront.

According to Marina Manager, Steve LeVel, the shop, Spinnaker & Spoke has "the finest marine collection of books in the area."

You'll find the books in a corner of the crowded marina shop that is wheelchair accessible. Topics of books include yachting, cruising, water safety and first aid, boat repairs, boat building, windsurfing, charts and guides to the local area, and bicycling maintenance and trail maps.

The shop also sells boating needs, clothing, and assorted nautical gifts. The marina shop is the place to rent sailboats, wind-surfing boards, and bicycles.

The full service marina is open to the public and has a snack bar and restaurant with a nautical theme bar. On sunny days, this is a great place to enjoy Washington.

SuperCrown

General   6244-O Little River Turnpike
                                  Alexandria, VA 22312
                                  703-750-3553
                                  Hours: Mon.-Sat. 10-10; Sun. 10-8

Crown Books maintains 55 very busy branches in the Washington, D.C. area. All stores stock the same fine general interest books. The difference between Crown Books and SuperCrown is merely a matter of numbers. SuperCrown stocks more than 50,000 titles. Most stores are open the same hours and all are wheelchair accessible. If they don't have a particular title in stock, employees are happy to place special orders which are quickly filled. Gift certificates are available at all branches.

When you shop at Crown Books, you know that you will be getting terrific discounts regardless of which store you visit. Crown Books shook the bookstore world in the 1970's by starting to offer discounts everyday. They are as follows: New York Times best-selling hardbacks: 40% off; all other hardbacks: 20% off; New York Times best-selling paperbacks: 25% off; all other paperbacks: 10% off; Best-selling computer books: 25% off; Audio books-on-cassette-tape: 20% off; video tapes, magazines, and CD-Rom: 10% off. Crown Books also have tables with stacks of hardback books that are greatly discounted and are sold for $1.00-$5.00.

With headquarters in Landover, Maryland, Crown Books and SuperCrown can be found nationwide. Everyone knows of the fine reputation of Crown Books. Find the branch closest to you.

Sutton Place Gourmet Inc.

Cooking   600 Franklin St.
                                  Alexandria, VA 22314
                                  703-549-6611
                                  Hours: Mon.-Sat. 9-9; Sun. 9-8

Gourmets or those who have only cooked dinner straight out of the can will find Sutton Place Gourmet a fine place to visit. They stock more than 100 titles of cookbooks and reference guides and sell the food you will need in order to make treats for the taste buds.

This branch of Sutton Place Gourmet has a few steps at the street-level entrance. However, those shoppers using wheelchairs can park in the garage and take the elevator to the first floor and you'll be able to roll right into the store with no problem.

Thistle & Shamrock Books

Scottish & Irish

600 N. Henry
Alexandria, VA 22314
703-548-2207
FAX 703-548-6162
Hours: Mail order or Appt. only

Even if you can't Irish step-dance or Highland fling, you are sure to enjoy the 500 new selections offered by Thistle & Shamrock Books.

It's difficult to find Irish and Scottish books here in the United States but Dr. Roderick W. Clarke has succeeded. He operates Thistle & Shamrock Books by appointment and accepts telephone and mail orders from his catalog.

You'll find books about Irish and Scottish fiction, the Gaelic language and history of the two countries. Ask Dr. Clarke about any current publications because he does place special orders.

Contact Thistle & Shamrock Books before taking your vacation to Scotland and Ireland. You'll enhance your trip with the many books Dr. Clarke sells.

Tools of the Trade—Books for Communicators

Communications

3148-B Duke St.
Alexandria, VA 22314
703-823-1919
800-827-8665
FAX 703-823-8948
Hours: Mon.-Sat. 10-5 & by
appointment or mail order

When you were a kid in high school were you the one who groaned loudest when the teacher said your next exam would include essay questions? No doubt today you're faced with communicating on paper or by computer with everyone from your co-workers to your housekeeper. When you want to get your point across, start by looking to Tools of the Trade—Books for Communicators.

With a catalog of more than 1,400 titles, Tools of the Trade offers you books focusing on writing, computers, desktop publishing, graphic design, typography, print production, editing, publishing, journalism, and communications. Tools of the Trade will search for books you want and special order them for you.

Although the business was established in 1984, Tools of the Trade was purchased in 1992 by Richard E. Farkas and Julie B. Glass who brought a wealth of knowledge with them since they both had worked in publishing. They immediately set out to develop the business into a valuable resource both for the publishing community and for anyone else who communicates by computer. Today, that encompasses almost everyone in business.

Some of the things Richard and Julie immediately did was to bring to the business many changes including the installation of electronic ordering to expedite orders; the installation of Books in Print on CD-ROM, enabling them to find the book you want in a flash; obtaining a toll free telephone line for your benefit; expanding the hours of operation to include appointments at times the business is closed; and regularly issued newsletters to clients informing them of the newest books in the field of communication.

Located in Alexandria, the store is wheelchair accessible. The store is located on the lower level of a business that used to be a private home. Richard and Julie said that they would be placing a larger sign in the front yard to make the store more visible from the street. The parking lot is on a steep hill. Telephone and mail orders are always accepted.

Many titles that are not listed in the catalog are carried in the store. The owners are continuously developing the stock and have plans to conduct workshops in the store. Their plans include making the store a haven for writers.

Whether you need to make your presentations at work look professional, or if you publish your club's newsletter, or even if you want to make your letters to relatives special, contact Tools of the Trade—Books for Communicators today. They are there for you.

Voyages Books & Art

Antiquarian & Used-General

209 Madison Ave.
Alexandria, VA 22304
703-739-2484
Hours: Daily 11-6

To most people the word "voyages" brings images of magnificent ships slowing gliding across an ocean. To William Claire, "Voyages" is the name of the national and international award winning literary magazine he published and edited in the 1960's and 70's. His advisory editors for "Voyages" included Mark Van Doren and Anais Nin. The magazine featured work by Nobel laureates and young writers who have since become famous. If William Claire's name sounds familiar, it should. He is a widely published poet and editor.

Understandably, William has a passion for books and since 1985 owns and coordinates Voyages Books and Art. This is an antiquarian and used book business that has five branches in antique centers.

"The ambiance at these places are wonderful," says William, "and I attract endless customers who usually do not go into old book stores."

The closest and largest branch located at the Washington Antique Center in Alexandria's Old Town section is open daily and is wheelchair accessible.

Clients also see William's collection by appointment. A majority of his books feature fine art, fiction, and poetry. He also conducts searches and appraisals.

You'll be pleased that you included a stop at any of the five Voyages Books and Art. Call for addresses of the other four locations.

Waldenbooks

General

Landmark Center
5801 Duke Street
Alexandria, VA 22304
703-658-9576
Hours: Mon.-Sat. 10-9:30; Sun. 11-6

Located in busy Alexandria, Waldenbooks makes for a calm oasis among the bustling crowds. This branch has large romance and children's sections but you'll also find a broad collection of general interest books. Waldenbooks and Brentano's are owned by the same company and also sell magazines, audio and video tapes, calendars, and posters. The store is wheelchair accessible.
To read about the special services that Waldenbooks and Brentano's offer to their customers, please see the write-up for the Brentano's store in Landmark Center.

WaldenSoftware

Computers

Landmark Shopping Center
5889 Duke Street
Alexandria, VA 22304
703-354-8502
Hours: Mon.-Fri. 10-9:30; Sun. 11-6

In addition to software, WaldenSoftware sells books and magazines. They can introduce you to the newest software and direct you to the correct books to help you sort out your old software programs. This branch of WaldenSoftware is wheelchair accessible.

Why Not

Children's books

200 King St.
Alexandria, VA 22317
703-548-4420
Hours: Mon. 10-5; Tues.-Sat. 10-9; Sun. noon-5

Why not bring your children to Why Not? They'll love it. Located in Old Alexandria, Why Not sells books, clothing, toys based upon books, and music on tape.
Owners Jeanne Graef and Kate Schlabach have been in business for more than thirty years and bring their expertise to create an atmosphere enjoyed by adults and children.

There is one step at the entrance for strollers and wheelchairs to jump. If you can't visit the store, why not call them?

Woodlawn Plantation Museum Shop

Museum-History   9000 Richmond Hwy
                                    Alexandria, VA 22309
                                    703-780-4000
                                    Hours: Everyday 9:30-4:30

Built on land bequeathed by George Washington to his adopted daughter, Nelly Parts Custis, and his nephew, Maj. Lawrence Lewis, as a wedding gift, Woodlawn Plantation is a beautiful Georgian mansion with formal gardens. The house and grounds which overlook Mount Vernon and the Potomac River, are open for tours to the public.

The Museum Shop is located in the mansion's basement features history books, most with a strong Civil War emphasis, architectural books, and books for children as well as unique gift, handcrafted items, and Virginia food products. The shop is not wheelchair accessible but Guides are helpful.

Along with the annual events of concerts, teas, antique car and coaching day, 19th-century Festival Days, Halloween Happenings, a Fall Quilt Exhibition, and performances of "A Woodlawn Christmas," a celebrated Needlework Exhibition is held at the site for three weeks each March.

Located on the same site is the 1940's Usonian Home, the Pope-Leighey House, featuring all of the original Frank Lloyd Wright-designed furnishings. This museum shop features Wright-related books and gifts.

Woodlawn Plantation and the Pope-Leighey House are properties of the National Trust for Historic Preservation. It is open everyday except during the month of January and Thanksgiving, Christmas, and New Year's Day.

Woodlawn Saddlery Ltd.

Equestrian   Potomac Square
                                    8405-J Richmond Hwy.
                                    Alexandria, VA 22309
                                    703-360-2288
                                    Hours: Sun. 1-5; Mon.-Wed. 10-6;
                                    Thurs. 10-8; Fri. closed; Sat. 9-5

Remember pony rides when you were a child? If riding horses never got out of your system, you should head toward the stables in Alexandria. Before you go, you must visit Woodlawn Saddlery Ltd. store.

The shop sells everything for the rider including saddles, boots, clothing, and books. The books address riding and jumping, discussions of the different breeds of horses, how to show horses in competition, veterinarian and first aid for horses, as well as books written about horses specifically for children.

While at Woodlawn Saddlery, you'll tap into the expertise of the employees who are riders themselves. A stable is located just one and a half miles south of the store.

Washington, D.C.

Adams Bookstore

New & Used Nonfiction

2912 M St. NW
Washington, D.C. 20037
202-337-2665
Hours: Daily noon-6 (or sundown)

At Adams Bookstore you will find a variety of used nonfiction books including old and unusual books. Located near the Foggy Bottom Metro Stop and one block away from the Four Seasons Hotel, the Adams Bookstore has five stairs at the entrance.

Ag-Connection Bookstore

Agriculture/textbooks

14th St. & Indy Ave. SW
South Bldg, Rm AM-8
Washington, D.C. 20250
202-720-6070
Hours: Mon.-Fri. 8:30-3

With approximately 2,000 titles, the Ag-Connection Bookstore sells textbooks for USDA courses. They also sell gift items such as T-shirts, sweatshirts, coffee mugs, and caps sporting the USDA logo. The bookstore is open weekdays and is wheelchair accessible.

Agape Christian Bookstore

Religious-Christian

1001 Connecticut Ave. NW
Washington, D.C. 20036
202-223-3282
Hours: Mon.-Fri. 10:30-6:30

Agape Christian Bookstore also is a publisher of Christian books which are sold in the store. You'll find approximately 1,000 titles among the wide variety of other items including audio books, books with large print, video tapes, T-shirts, games, calendars, greeting cards, posters, and stationery.

Be sure to check the in-store bulletin board while you visit Agape Christian Bookstore. Announcements of activities for Christians are regularly posted. The store is open weekdays and is completely wheelchair and stroller accessible.

Alexander Graham Bell Association for the Deaf

Speech for the Deaf   3417 Volta Place NW
                                         Washington, D.C. 20007
                                         202-337-5220
                                         Hours: Mon.-Fri. 9-4

Alexander Graham Bell knew that the only reason that children with hearing impairments did not speak was that they were not taught to talk. The famous scientist and inventor of the telephone devoted a great portion of his life to helping children with hearing impairments develop their potential for listening, speaking, and speechreading.

Using the prize money awarded from the French government's prestigious Volta Award for his invention of the telphone, this great teacher of the deaf founded the Volta Bureau in 1890 which is now the home of the Alexander Graham Bell Association for the Deaf.

Books sold by the Association include auditory training, language, listening and talking, speech, oral interpreting, speech reading, identification of hearing loss in young children, teaching aids, mainstreaming deaf children into public schools, and reference books. Videos can be purchased or rented from their library audiovisuals.

Revenue from the sale of items goes to fund many programs relating to the goals of the Alexander Graham Bell Association for the Deaf. When you contact the Association, you will also learn of the many benefits of supporting the Association and how to become a membership of the Association.

The Association is located in an ancient building in Georgetown which is not wheelchair accessible. Most book and support materials are sold by mail order through the catalog.

American Institute of Architects Bookstore

Professional Association   1735 New York Ave. NW
                                         Washington, D.C. 20006
                                         202-626-741275
                                         Orders 800-365-ARCH (2724)
                                         FAX 202-626-7420
                                         Hours: Mon.-Fri. 8:30-5

The American Institute of Architects (AIA) Bookstore stocks over 5,000 titles specifically devoted to architecture, architectural practice, architects, architectural history, landscape design, construction, and the building arts. Among the books for the general audience are professional volumes on Building Codes, Environmental/Green Architecture, and the Americans with Disabilities Act. They also have a children's section.

The attractive AIA Bookstore sells many gift items. A catalog is available. Wheelchair access is gained via the courtyard entrance on 18th Street.

American Management Association Store

Business/Management 440 First St. NW
Washington, D.C. 20001
202-347-3092
FAX 202-347-4549
Hours: Mon.-Fri. 8:30-5

Approximately 800 titles published by the American Management Association and other titles are offered by the American Management Association in their store. The store is a part of the management training center in Washington and offers self-study guides as well as audio and video tapes. A catalog is published four times per year.

For browsing through the titles, clients will find the store on the second floor of the building. But wheelchair users, do not fret, there is an elevator available.

With headquarters in New York, the American Management Association store in Washington is small but thorough.

American Society of Landscape Architects

Landscape Architecture 4401 Connecticut Ave. NW
Fifth Floor
Washington, D.C. 20008
202-686-2752
FAX 202-686-1001
Hours: Mon.-Fri. 8:30-5:Telephone & Mail order only

Professionals and backyard designers all enjoy the book selections offered by the American Society of Landscape Architects. They offer approximately 350 titles touching on gardening design, the environment, urban design, and, of course, landscape architecture.

The books are available to everyone, professional or novice, through telephone, mail orders and FAX orders by using their catalog. Send for a copy of their catalog today and turn your yard into the beauty spot on your block.

Ambia, Inc.

African & Other Cultures

900 Brentwood Rd. NE
PO Box 90872
Washington, D.C. 20090
202-546-3539
<u>Hours:</u> Mail order only

"Open your mind or your child's to a world more vast than you can imagine," Ambia's literature states. "African-American literature remains an undiscovered treasure for many people...not because it is scarce, but because most people simply do not know that these books exist."

Although Ambia is not currently a bookstore, they are a Washington based mail order book club. They are a book club that does not inconvenience you with frequent mailings or by sending you books that you did not order. There is no minimum purchase required. Join for a $19.95 membership fee and choose a quality book for a higher retail value free of charge. Video tapes are also available. A catalog is published twice per year.

Ambia offers the ultimate source of Afrocentric literature for all ages and suited to all interests. Categories include bestsellers, fiction, nonfiction, biography, civil rights, Africa, history, poetry, sociology, business, education, politics, sports, music, and more.

Contact Ambia and, as they say, "Embark on a journey that's magical."

American Psychiatric Press (Health Matters)

Health

1400 K Street NW
Washington, D.C. 20005
202-789-7303
<u>Hours:</u> Mon.-Fri. 10-6; Sat. 11-5

A new specialty bookstore is scheduled to open in the spring of 1994 and you won't want to miss it. Named "Health Matters," the store will be open to the general public. They project that many people interested in wellness, medicine, fitness, nutrition, and parenting as well as psychiatrists, psychologists, and social workers will be delighted with the store.

Health Matters will carry titles published by the American Psychiatric Press and books offered by many other publishers. A catalog of the American Psychiatric Press will still be available for telephone orders. The store is wheelchair accessible.

Anacostia Museum

African-American Museum   1901 Fort Place SE
                                   Washington, D.C. 20560
                                   202-287-3414
                                   Hours: Daily 10-5 (except Dec.25)

Associated with the Smithsonian Museums, the Anacostia Museum was one of the first smaller, community-based museums in the Washington area. Established in 1967, the Anacostia Museum features African American history through art exhibits and educational programs.

Located in southeastern Washington, D.C., the museum features items from Maryland, Virginia, and the Carolinas which tell the story of the African American experiences in this country.

The museum shop sells books about African-American history and crafts. They also sell an assortment of children's toys. The museum and shop are wheelchair accessible.

The Anacostia Museum is open daily and one that should not be missed, especially if your roots are founded in Africa.

Another World

Comics   1504 Wisconsin Ave. NW
                                   Washington, D.C. 20007
                                   202-333-8651
                                   Hours: Summer: Daily 11-8;
                                   Other seasons: Sun.-Thurs. 11-7;
                                   Fri. & Sat 11-8

Another World is ready to whisk you away or beam you up. They sell new comic books and paperbacks such as the Star Trek series. In addition, you'll be able to buy games and accessories, such as Dungeon & Dragons, sports cards, posters, T-shirts, comic book collecting supplies, and even models to put together. Imagine owning your very own USS Enterprise.

Scott Steeno, Manager of Another World, reports that the store is wheelchair accessible.

If you think Another World doesn't sell something of interest to you, look again. They have a whole rack devoted to humorous books. Now who couldn't use a good laugh?

Arthur M. Sackler Gallery Shop

Oriental Arts Museum   950 Independence Ave. SW
                                   Washington, D.C. 20560
                                   202-357-4880
                                   Hours: Daily 10-5:30 (except Dec. 25)

The Arthur M. Sackler Gallery is a showcase to the Smithsonian's extensive collection of Eastern art. Special exhibitions are held year-round. The gallery was named for Dr. Arthur M. Sackler who donated more than 1,000 masterpieces of art.

The museum shop is particularly special. They carry a great number of books about the shows in the gallery, beautiful coffee-table books, and books about calligraphy, travel, philosophy, history, literature, and cooking. They also sell some children's books. All of the books are related to Middle Eastern art. The gifts for sale are exquisite and reasonably priced.

The museum and shop are completely wheelchair and stroller accessible. The Arthur M. Sackler Gallery is located near other branches of the fine Smithsonian museums.

Arts & Industries Building

Museum-Arts

900 Jefferson Dr. SW
Washington, D.C. 20560
202-357-1369
Hours: Daily 10-5:15 (except Dec. 25)

If the Victorian period intrigues you, the Arts & Industries Building of the Smithsonian Museum, is the place you must visit. The building houses the most extensive collections of American Victoriana in existence. This building is the second oldest of the museums and was restored in 1976.

The museum shop offers you many books about the Victorian period and lifestyles of the people who lived then. They also sell replicas of Victorian jewelry and picture frames, paper-doll cutouts, toys, and more. This is the shop that has a copy of the Smithsonian's official catalog just waiting for you.

Wheelchair users or stroller pushers, have no fear. The museum and shop are accessible.

Audubon Naturalist Bookshop

Natural history

1228 Connecticut Ave. NW
Washington, D.C. 20036
202-296-0646
FAX 202-296-4060
Hours: Mon.-Sat. 10-6

A Washington branch of the wonderful Audubon Naturalist Society's bookshop which has headquarters in Maryland, this store is actually larger and offers more items than the shop in Maryland.

To read about Audubon's life and about the society and the books and items they sell, please refer to the write-up for the main branch of the store.

B'nai B'rith Klutznich National Museum Shop

Judaica
1640 Rhode Island Ave. NW
Washington, D.C. 20036
202-857-6583
FAX 202-857-1099
Hours: Sun.-Fri. 10-4:30; closed Sat.

Emphasizing the contribution of Jewish-Americans in our history, the museum features twenty centuries of Jewish history. The permanent collection is one of the largest in the U.S.

The bookstore sells more than 200 Judaic books covering history, cooking, religion, reference, and children's books. Sale items also include gifts and religious items, Judaica jewelry, greeting cards for Jewish holidays, and more.

The museum is wheelchair accessible. It is open everyday except Saturday and Jewish holidays.

Whether you are Jewish or not, this museum is a beautiful introduction to the history and culture of Jews.

B. Dalton Bookseller

General
1776 K Street NW
Washington, D.C. 20006
202-872-0863
FAX 202-457-0599
Hours: Mon.-Fri. 9-7; Sat. noon-6

Located in the heart of Washington's business district, B. Dalton brings you a magnificent two-story bookstore in which every department is thorough. This store has an unbelievable 200,000 titles in 8,000 square feet of shopping space!

At the corner of K Street and 18th Street, the store's numerical address is "1776" which, B. Dalton headquarters note, is a landmark number in our nation's history and is fitting for B. Dalton's landmark store.

Inside the marbled entrance, you are sure to wonder where to begin. The store is surprisingly accessible so you can quickly find just the book you're looking for or you can spend the day browsing. To quickly shop for bestsellers, they have one shelf dedicated exclusively to the top ten listed by the Washington Post and the New York Times. They also include new arrivals here. The fiction, business, and computer sections are particularly large.

The store, which is carpeted throughout and decorated with soft colors, has departments clearly marked. They also have many sales people strolling through the store, ready to answer any questions the shopper may have. The combination of tall and short bookcases makes the store feel airy and filled with little niches. Shoppers using wheelchairs can maneuver in the store but must use an elevator in the next-door office building to access the other floor.

Authors visit the store for autographing sessions and the store offers charge accounts and a booksavers membership which allows members to receive a 10% discount on all books.

Other items for sale in the store include audio books, magazines, greeting cards, post cards, and calendars.

"1776" K Street NW is the location of a bookstore every book lover will love.

B. Dalton Bookseller

General
112 Union Station
50 Massachusetts Ave NE
Washington, D.C. 20002
202-289-1724
Hours: Mon.-Fri. 9-9;
Sat. 10-9; Sun. noon-6

Once just an old train station, Union Station has been transformed into a fantastic shopping mall with three stories filled with boutiques, high class restaurants, major clothing stores, snack shops, unique little stores, and, oh yeah, trains that come and go.

One of the busiest stores, B. Dalton focuses on fiction and travel. An entire back wall is covered with new titles. They also have a complete travel and regional section featuring every type of book imaginable about Washington.

Every traveller, whether coming or going via train or car, disabled or not, can delight in the books offered at B. Dalton.

B. Dalton Bookseller

General
Chevy Chase Pavilion
5345 Wisconsin Ave.
Washington, D.C. 20015
202-686-6542
Hours: Mon.-Thurs. 10-8; Fri. 10-9;
Sat. 10-8; Sun. noon-5

Opened in 1991, the Chevy Chase Pavilion is anchored by many office buildings and an Embassy Suites Hotel and has a quality B. Dalton bookstore. The shopping area is just up from a street known as the Rodeo Drive of DC. Those shopping who use wheelchairs will find the Pavilion accessible.

This B. Dalton branch has fine collections of business, current events, history, magazines, and children's books. The store is located on the lower level and adjacent to the food court.

B. Dalton Bookseller

General

Shops at National Place
1331 Pennsylvania Ave. NW
Washington, D.C. 20004
202-393-1468
Hours: Mon.-Fri. 10-9;
Sat. 10-7; Sun. noon-5

Actually located inside the lobby of the Marriott on the corner of 14th Street and Pennsylvania Avenue, B. Dalton has established a fine bookstore catering to visitors to Washington and also to workers in the nearby buildings which includes the National Press Building, The National Theater, and many political offices.

Find this B. Dalton and you can purchase books and a great spot to observe all of the events taking place on Pennsylvania Ave such as parades and protest marches.

A well-known general interest bookstore, this branch of B. Dalton has strong departments covering history, business, current affairs, and biographies. The store has a wall, floor-to-ceiling, of windows which certainly gives the store a bright atmosphere.

Because of their location in a major hotel, B. Dalton sells a fine group of Washington, D.C., guidebooks, maps, and coffee-table photography books.

B. Dalton, along with many other shops in the same area, is wheelchair accessible.

Backstage Books & Costumes

Performing Arts

2101 P St. NW
Washington, D.C. 20037
202-775-1488
FAX 202-296-3430
Hours: Mon.-Sat. 10-6; Thurs. 10-8

You might not look like Demi Moore, Tom Hulce, or Kelly MacGillis but you can purchase the same stage make-up they use at Backstage Books and Costumes. They actually shop at Backstage too.

Make-up is only one of the many items available. Half of the store contains books and the other half is filled with costumes and theater-related items.

The books (a few are used) focus on theater, performance, staging and directing techniques, scripts, screenplays, writing guides and musical scores. In addition, they sell dialect audio tapes and acting and make-up videos.

Professionals and closet thespians across the nation turn to Backstage for renting and/or buying costumes and masks. Many costumes are custom-made to suit specific needs. Backstage also sells picture frames, jewelry, and assorted "star" paraphernalia.

43

Catering to the needs of theater folk, Backstage Books and Costumes should be in the address books of everyone involved with the performing arts in any capacity. Located in an historical building in Washington, the store is not wheelchair accessible. Much business is conducted by mail order. Call and talk over your specific needs; they're sure to have just what you want.

Bartleby's Books

Antiquarian-Americana
1531 33rd Street NW
Washington, D.C. 20007
301-686-3367
FAX 202-686-3367
Hours: Everyday 11-6:30 (except Wed. closed) Call ahead

Wave the red, white, and blue and finish Mom's apple pie while browsing through the catalog from Bartleby's Books. You'll find a whole library of American books you missed the first time around.

Since 1984, John Thomson and Karen Griffin have been selling antiquarian books about all facets of American life. A bonus is that you can shop at home. Business is conducted through the catalog of more than 20,000 titles specializing in art and fiction in and about America. You can see Bartleby's Books in the wheelchair accessible store that they share with Fuller & Saunders.

Bethune Museum & Archives Shop

Black Women Studies
1318 Vermont Ave. NW
Washington, D.C. 20005
202-332-1233
Hours: Mon.-Fri. 10-4:30;
June-Aug. also open Sat. 10-4

Mary McLeod Bethune should be a name that is familiar to everyone in America. She holds a proud place in the history of African-American women and was honored with a museum dedicated in her name. Born to freed slaves in 1875, Mary worked in the developing days of the civil rights struggle, became a counselor to four presidents, worked for the National Child Welfare Commission, founded Bethune-Cookman College, advised the Roosevelt administration on minority affairs, was the director of the Division of Negro Affairs in the National Youth Administration, founded the National Council of Negro Women, organized black officials into the Black Cabinet, and lobbied for a fair share in New Deal programs.

Most people do not contribute a fraction of what Mary did during her lifetime. The Victorian townhouse that served as headquarters for the National Council of Negro Women from 1943 to 1966 is now a museum and active center dedicated to African-American women's history.

The small shop sells approximately ten books that discuss the contribution and history of African-American women with regard to social change in America. Also sold are jewelry, coffee mugs, T-shirts, and postcards. The museum is free but not wheelchair accessible. However, the shop, on the first floor, is wheelchair accessible.

Far too many people who have shaped America are forgotten and it's wonderful that this strong woman, Mary McLeod Bethune, is being recognized.

Bicks Books

General

2309 18th St. NW
Washington, D.C. 20009
202-328-2356
Hours: Mon.-Thurs. 10-8; Fri. & Sat. 10-midnight; Sun. noon-8

"Bick's Books exists to serve all those communities the chain stores slight," said Robby Bick, President. "We feel our job is to connect our customers with the books they need, whatever extra effort that takes on our part."

That extra effort includes special ordering of books, telephone and mail ordering, and gift wrapping. Of the approximately 40,000 titles in the store, there are new and used books, all with a general interest theme. Also sold are magazines, newspapers, video tapes, greeting cards, stationery, calendars, T-shirts, and assorted children's toys.

At times authors visit the store for autographing sessions. A bulletin board is kept to remind customers of special events. A newsletter is published quarterly.

Unfortunately, there are six steps at the front door. Off-street parking and mass transit is available nearby.

Robby says, "We also do our best to provide a comfortable and interesting browsing atmosphere where our clients can find books in all areas of interest."

Bird in Hand Bookstore & Gallery

Fine Art, Architecture

323 Seventh St. SE
Washington, D.C. 20003
202-543-0744
800-872-3685
FAX 202-547-6424
Hours: Wed.-Sun. 11-5; Tues. & Thurs. 11-8

For art, design and architecture books you must visit the small store Bird in Hand Bookstore & Gallery. The staff is extremely knowledgeable and pleased to provide personal service to all who enter the door. Approximately 1,000 titles are kept within the store.

Special events make Bird in Hand Bookstore & Gallery an extraordinary bookstore. Monthly they conduct an in-house art exhibit. The store also sponsors a writing group, something that many bookstores do not do.

Open everyday except Monday, Bird in Hand Bookstore & Gallery publishes a catalog of their wonderful books in stock and accepts telephone and mail orders. There are four steps at the entrance so those who can't climb the stairs will enjoy shopping through the catalog. A newsletter is published yearly. The bookstore will search for those special titles on your want list and place the special orders.

Whether you're an artist or an art aficionado, you'll enjoy Bird in Hand Bookstore & Gallery.

Blue Nile Books

New Age
2826 Georgia Ave. NW
Washington, D.C. 20001
202-232-3535
Hours: Daily 11-7

To travel to the Blue Nile you won't have to go any farther than right here in Washington, D.C. Blue Nile Books brings you new books featuring metaphysics, new age, self-help, health and nutrition, and cookery. Owner Duku Allen places special orders if the book you want isn't in stock.

Blue Nile Books has three steps at the entrance which makes it difficult to visit for shoppers with strollers and impossible for wheelchair users.

The store was established in 1977 and is open daily. Check the bulletin board at Blue Nile Books for community events.

Book Market

Used-Economics
2603 Connecticut Ave.
Washington, D.C. 20008
202-332-2310
Hours: Sun.-Thurs. 11-10;
Fri. & Sat. 11-midnight

It's easy to find the Book Market. Just locate the Washington Sheridan and the Shore Hotels, look around, and there it is.

The Book Market is a general used bookstore that has large departments in economics, mystery, and natural science. The store has approximately 25,000 titles. The Book Market keeps extra-late hours. The store is not wheelchair accessible.

Books For Growing

Religious-Christian   1611 16th St. NW
                                         Washington, D.C. 20009
                                         202-265-0796
                                         Hours: Usually Mon.-Sat. 10:30-5,
                                         call ahead

Too often we think growing stops when we reach a specific age. Books For Growing knows that growth is an ongoing process and are in Washington to provide books for spiritual growth. Associated with the Church of Holy City, the religious bookstore sells Christian and Catholic-oriented books as well as Bibles. They offer approximately 100 titles.

The Church of Holy City was established in the late 1890's by Emmanuel Swedenborigan and welcomed among the worshipers, Helen Keller.

Books For Growing does not keep specific hours but generally is open Monday through Saturday from 10:30-5. The store is wheelchair accessible.

Bookworks/Washington Project for the Arts

Fine art   400 Seventh St. NW
                                         Washington, D.C. 20004
                                         202-347-4590
                                         FAX 202-347-8393
                                         Hours: Tues.-Sat. 11-6

You don't need to be an artist to appreciate art. After admiring the works at the Washington Project for the Arts gallery, visit Bookworks. They offer more than 4,000 titles of art and photography books which include many books reasonably and inexpensively priced. Not only does Bookworks highlight American artists, they also have books about international artists.

Call before visiting if you need handicap access information.

Borders Book Shop

General   1801 K Street NW
                                         Washington, D.C. 20006
                                         202-466-4999
                                         Hours: Mon.-Sat. 9-9; Sun. 11-6

As of the writing of this book, Borders Books & Music is set to open another of their amazing bookstores in Washington, D.C. For the delight of patrons, this Borders has an Expresso Bar. The store is wheelchair accessible.

For a complete description of Borders Book Shops, please refer to the write-up for the Vienna, Virginia branch.

Brentano's

General

Mazza Galleria
5300 Wisconsin Ave. NW
Washington, D.C. 20015
202-364-2289
Hours: Mon.-Fri. 10-8;
Sat. 10-6; Sun. noon-5

Travel books comprise a large department of the Brentano's bookstore located on Wisconsin Ave. In addition to a wealth of general interest books, Waldenbooks and Brentano's (which are owned by the same company) sell magazines, audio and video tapes, calendars, and posters.

Special services abound at both Waldenbooks and Brentano's. Each store has the capability to track down and quickly place in the hands of customers those books in print that are not stocked in the store.

Top selling hardcover books are sold at a discount. A great way to receive an extra ten percent discount is to join the Preferred Reader Program. As a member, you are entitled to receive an extra ten percent off the price of everything in the store except magazines. So just think, for an annual fee of $10, you can purchase all the books you want at a discount including the bestsellers and even bargain books. But, Waldenbooks and Brentano's don't stop there. For every $100 worth of merchandise that a Preferred Reader customer buys, he or she receives a $5.00 store coupon.

If you're in the market for a Bible, Waldenbooks and Brentano's can have the family keepsake imprinted. Ask staff members about the details of this service.

It's clear that Waldenbooks and Brentano's can please both your book appetite and your wallet. The store is in the Mazza Galleria mall and is wheelchair accessible.

Bridge Street Books

General

2814 Pennsylvania Ave. NW
Washington, D.C. 20007
202-347-4590
Hours: Mon.-Thurs. 10-7; Fri. & Sat. 10-11; Sun. 1-6; longer summer hours

Located in an aged townhouse in Georgetown, Bridge Street Books specialized in politics, literature, poetry, and history books for the intellectual. Established in 1980, the bookstore is owned by Philip Levy who states that book buyers must visit the store to fully appreciate the stock. Bridge Street Books comprises two floors. It is not wheelchair accessible due to the three steps at the entrance.

The Brookings Institute Bookshop

World Economics & Politics   1775 Massachusetts Ave. NW
Washington, D.C. 20036
202-797-6258
Hours: Mon.-Fri. 9-4:30

A private nonprofit organization, the Brookings Institute is devoted to research, education, and publication in economics, government, foreign policy and the social sciences generally. In other words, it's the "think tank" known around the world.

All books sold in the book shop and catalog are those published by the Brookings Institute. Book orders are filled from around the world.

The small book shop is near the entrance of the Institute and is wheelchair accessible. The lone lady in the shop is responsive to visitors and telephone callers. She appreciates your patience when calling the shop. Telephone calls never seem to end.

Contact the Brookings Institute to be on the cutting edge of study by visiting the store, shopping for books by the catalog, or obtaining the quarterly newsletter.

The Capitol Gift Shop

Government   The Capitol
Washington, D.C. 20002
202-225-6827
Hours: Summer: Daily 9-6:30;
Winter: Daily 9-4:30

In the news nearly everyday and seen as a backdrop for broadcast reporters, the Capitol has been home to the Senate and the House of Representatives since November 22, 1800. Upon President John Adams' insistence, the House and Senate met for the first joint session of Congress in the building that was just a 2-story square structure. George Washington officiated at the cornerstone laying ceremony.

All Americans are welcomed to join guided tours of the building and from viewers boxes watch the government in action. When either the Senate or House is in session, you will see a flag flying over the side of the building where the legislative body meets.

One usually doesn't think of going to the Capitol to book shop but the giftshop does sell quite a few books. Topics are, of course, a history of the building and about this branch of our government, biographies of our past Presidents, and Washington guidebooks. Some books for children are available. In addition, they sell flags, replicas of our country's famous documents, photographs, posters, and even documentary video tapes. The giftshop is located on the first floor near the east front door. The shop and the tours accommodate wheelchair users.

49

Capitol Hill Books

Used-Classics

657 C Street, SE
Washington, D.C. 20003
202-544-1621
Hours: Mon.-Fri. 11-7;
Sat. 9-6; Sun. 11-5

A general interest used bookstore, Capitol Hill Books has strong departments in Latin, Greek, first editions and travel narratives. The store is not wheelchair accessible but if you call, you can arrange for books to be sent through the mail. Owner Bill Kerr has operated Capitol Hill Books since November of 1990.

Catholic Univ. of America Bookstore

College

620 Michigan Ave. NE
Washington, D.C. 20064
202-319-5232
FAX 202-832-4067
Hours: Mon. & Tues. 8:30-6:30;
Wed. & Thurs. 8:30-5:30; Fri. 8:30-5;
Sat. 11-2; Shorter summer hours

In addition to textbooks, Catholic University (CU) of America Bookstore also sells books published by CU authors through the CU Press. Books sold in the bookstore also include general trade bestsellers, travel, cooking, art, reference and children's books. They have a large selection of religious and philosophy books.

Belonging to a university, the bookstore sells a full line of clothes and gifts that sport the University's logo. A catalog is available for ordering these items.

Most employees at the Catholic University of America Bookstore work part-time because they are students at the University.

Chapters

General

1512 K Street NW
Washington, D.C. 20005
202-347-5495
Hours: Mon.-Fri. 10-6:30; Sat. 11-5

Chapters, A Literary Bookstore, is "an oasis of civility in downtown Washington, D.C.," as co-owner Robin Diener describes the bookstore.

You will rejuvenate yourself after a nice, quiet visit browsing through the interesting and diverse stock you find at Chapters. The books they stock are often the jewels that other stores do not carry. Chapters stocks many university press publications as well as many titles of cookbooks, gardening, and children's books. They have a huge poetry section. The design of Chapters makes for comfortable perusing of the more than 50,000 titles.

Owners Robin and Terri Merz established Chapters in 1985 and have developed fine programs of interest to the public. Authors, such as Amy Tan, visit the store to autograph and discuss their books. Chapters also brings experts to conduct lectures on a variety of topics. Every year on the anniversary of Marcel Proust's birth, Chapters celebrates with special activities.

On sunny days, Chapters has an adorable cart filled with sale books that is wheeled onto the sidewalk. Inside the entrance of the store there are a few stairs. If you use a wheelchair, a courteous employee will greet you and escort you through the back labyrinth entrance. The store has many levels inside and only half of the bookcases are wheelchair accessible. Employees are apologetic as they assist customers in wheelchairs.

Chapters does sell books by mail order and they do publish a Christmas catalog. They are truly a fine bookstore and a delight to do business with.

Cheshire Cat Bookstore

Children's books

5512 Connecticut Ave. NW
Washington, D.C. 20015
202-244-3956
Hours: Mon.-Sat. 10-6; Sun. 1-5

Charlotte Berman, one of the three owners, sees children's big smiles when they enter the store, Cheshire Cat Book Store. Like Lewis Carroll's Cheshire Cat, the children's smiles never do disappear.

The children may show up again in the Rabbit Hole play area while their adult escorts browse the children's and parenting books. Also sold in the store are cassettes, videos, and foreign language books.

Activities abound at Cheshire Cat Book Store. Check their newsletter, Cheshire Cat Chronicle, for the dates when authors, artists, and characters visit the store. Folk singers and an Irish fiddler have entertained at the store. In the spring and fall, adults are invited to a reception for local authors and illustrators whose books are to be published.

The Cheshire Cat Chronicle also includes descriptions of many children's books. Mail and telephone orders are welcomed. Fortunately, the store is completely stroller and wheelchair accessible.

It took the deliberation and discussion of four families to decide upon the name of the book store. They concluded that Cheshire Cat Book Store would remain on people's minds. Once a person visits the store, there is no doubt that he or she will remember this wonderful children's book store.

Cleveland Park Bookshop

Literary 　　　　　　　　3416 Wisconsin Ave., NW
　　　　　　　　　　　　　Washington, D.C. 20016
　　　　　　　　　　　　　202-363-1112
　　　　　　　　　　　　　FAX 202-362-9264
　　　　　　　　　　　　　Hours: Mon.-Sat. 10-10; Sun. 10-6

Because Cleveland Park Bookshop was located in a neighborhood filled with book lovers. Owner Janey Hulme made sure that when the bookshop moved in 1993 it stayed in the same neighborhood.

Fortunately for the residents of Cleveland Park, she was successful. With more space, the literary bookshop has grown in directions to please everyone. Topics with many titles include literature, biography, fiction, philosophy, poetry, cooking, nature, travel, and children's books.

With the move, Janie hopes that the shop will hold more special programs. The staff publishes a newsletter and maintains a bulletin board of announcements in the store so that everyone can mark their calendars and not miss any events.

Wheelchair accessible, Cleveland Park Bookshop is enjoyed by everyone. Special orders are filled quickly. The store also sells greeting cards, stationery, Christmas cards, posters, and gift wrapping.

The Corcoran Museum Shop

Museum 　　　　　　　　500 17th St. NW
　　　　　　　　　　　　　Washington, D.C. 20006
　　　　　　　　　　　　　202-638-3211
　　　　　　　　　　　　　FAX 202-737-2664
　　　　　　　　　　　　　Hours: Everyday 10-5 except Thurs.
　　　　　　　　　　　　　10-9; closed Tues.

The Corcoran Museum of Art was founded in 1869 as a place "dedicated to art, and used solely for the purpose of encouraging the American genius." The Corcoran is the largest privately-supported art museum.

The brochure for the museum states, "With its classrooms, galleries, cafe, shop and an array of informative and entertaining programs for visitors and members, the Corcoran is a living monument to art and American creativity."

Located only one block from the White House, the Corcoran entertains thousands of people with their collection of paintings, photography, drawings, sculpture, as well as musical concerts featuring chamber music and weekly jazz concerts.

Adjacent to the atrium on the main level, you'll find the Corcoran Shop selling a bounty of books featuring fine art, architecture, exhibition publications, and activity books for children. Also sold are magazines, posters, jewelry, puzzles, picture frames, and souvenirs. Gift products are adapted from items in the Corcoran collection. Your child won't want to leave without a lunch box shaped like the Corcoran and you won't want to pass on the scarves with art designs copied from items on exhibit.

The museum and shop are wheelchair accessible by using the elevator in the interior. A cafe in the middle of the atrium is a great spot for lunch, afternoon tea, or an evening dinner.

Since 1890, the Corcoran School of Art and continuing education programs have flourished to produce many of our fine artists. Students can earn a Bachelor of Fine Arts degree.

The Corcoran is Washington's first art museum and, with Boston and New York art museums, is one of the three oldest museums in the country. You sincerely will not want to miss a visit here and to the shop.

Crown Books

General   3131 M Street NW
                                         Washington, D.C. 20007
                                         202-333-4493
                                         Hours: Mon.-Thurs. 10-10;
                                         Fri. & Sat. 10-midnight;
                                         Sun. 11-8

Crown Books maintains 55 very busy branches in the Washington, D.C. area. All stores stock the same fine general interest books. The difference between Crown Books and SuperCrown is merely a matter of numbers. SuperCrown stocks more than 50,000 titles. Most stores are open the same hours and all are wheelchair accessible. If they don't have a particular title in stock, employees are happy to place special orders which are quickly filled. Gift certificates are available at all branches.

When you shop at Crown Books, you know that you will be getting terrific discounts regardless of which store you visit. Crown Books shook the bookstore world in the 1970's by starting to offer discounts everyday. They are as follows: New York Times best-selling hardbacks: 40% off; all other hardbacks: 20% off; New York Times best-selling paperbacks: 25% off; all other paperbacks: 10% off; Best-selling computer books: 25% off; Audio books-on-cassette-tape: 20% off; video tapes, magazines, and CD-Rom: 10% off. Crown Books also have tables with stacks of hardback books that are greatly discounted and are sold for $1.00-$5.00.

With headquarters in Landover, Maryland, Crown Books and SuperCrown can be found nationwide. Everyone knows of the fine reputation of Crown Books. Find the branch closest to you.

Crown Books

General

2020 K Street NW
Washington, D.C. 20006
202-659-2030
<u>Hours:</u> Mon.-Fri. 9-8;
Sat. & Sun. 9-6

See the write-up for the Washington M Street store to learn of the discounts that Crown Books offer to customers.

Crown Books

General

1155 19th St. NW
Washington, D.C. 20036
202-659-4172
<u>Hours:</u> Mon.-Fri. 9-9; Sat. 9-6

To read about the discounts and services that all Crown Books and SuperCrown offer, please refer to the description of Washington's M Street Crown Books.

Crown Books

General

1710 G Street NW
Washington, D.C. 20006
202-789-2277
<u>Hours:</u> Mon.-Fri. 9-7; Sat. 10-6

Please refer to the write-up for Washington's M Street Crown Books for a description of the discounts and services offered at Crown Books. This Crown Books store happens to be located across the street from the Executive Offices.

Crown Books

General

1200 New Hampshire Ave. NW
Washington, D.C. 20036
202-822-8331
<u>Hours:</u> Mon.-Sat. 9-8; Sun. 11-5

Read about Crown Books' discounts and services which are listed in the write-up for the M Street Crown Books in Washington.

Crown Books

General   3335 Connecticut Ave. NW
Washington, D.C. 20008
202-966-7232
Hours: Mon.-Sat. 10-9; Sun. 11-6

All SuperCrown and Crown Books extend the same discounts and services to customers. For details, see the write-up for Washington's M Street Crown Books.

Crown Books

General   4400 Jenifer St. NW
Washington, D.C. 20015
202-966-8784
Hours: Mon.-Sat. 10-9; Sun. 11-6

Please refer to the write-up for the M Street Crown Books in Washington for a complete description of the discounts and services offered at Crown Books.

Daughters of the American Revolution Museum Shop

History   1776 D Street NW
Washington, D.C. 20006
202-628-1776
Hours: Mon.-Fri. 8:30-4;
Sun. 1-5; closed Sat.

Located in the Headquarters of the National Society Daughters of the American Revolution (DAR), the museum is dedicated to collecting "materials for history, to preserve souvenirs of the Revolution, to study the manners and measures of those days, to devise the best methods of perpetuating the memories of our ancestors." The collection of more than 30,000 decorative and fine art objects on display includes silver pieces crafted by Paul Revere as well as items made or used in early America.

The DAR Museum shop sells books about history for adults and children. They also sell many more items including quilts, glassware, canvas bags, T-shirts, some toys, and more. The museum and shop are wheelchair accessible and it is recommended that you call ahead for instructions to the wheelchair access.

Decatur House Shop

Museum-Americana   748 Jackson Place NW
                                    Washington, D.C. 20006
                                    202-842-0920
                                    FAX 842-0030
                                    Hours: Mon.-Fri. 10-5;
                                    Sat. & Sun. noon-4

Located near the White House, Decatur House is one of the city's earliest important residences and one of the few which survives today. Visitors may tour this National Historic Landmark which reflects the Federal era lifestyle of the early 1800's.

Being a member of the Decatur House Friends, you are entitled to free admission to the properties, to receive an annual publication, a bi-monthly magazine, and a monthly newsletter, to participate in study tours and programs, and to receive a 10% discount on books and gifts in the museum shops located at National Trust properties.

At the shop in Decatur House, you will be presented with more than 700 titles highlighting architecture, history, cooking, regional and children's books. Gift items include beautiful book ends.

Wheelchair users rejoice! Decatur House is one of the few historic sites that is wheelchair accessible. The entrance is a round-about way and employees of the house appreciate a phone call before you arrive so they can be prepared to assist you. There are elevators to reach every floor of the house. The shop is also completely wheelchair accessible.

Decatur House is a landmark that most Washingtonians will recommend you put on your agenda in our capitol city.

Divine Science Metaphysical Bookstore

Metaphysical, Religious   Wisconsin at 35th St. NW
                                    Washington, D.C. 20007
                                    202-333-7631
                                    Hours: Mon.-Fri. 10-3, some seasonal
                                    variation

When visiting a bookstore, you expect to purchase the books you want to read. When you enter Divine Science Metaphysical Bookstore you can purchase books but also borrow books from their library.

Usually a lending library contradicts the purpose of a bookstore but the people at Divine Science Metaphysical Bookstore are committed to educating people about mystical and spiritual thoughts. In addition to metaphysical books, they also sell many books about Bible interpretation as well as greeting cards. Employees assist with you special orders for books.

Open weekdays, the bookstore shares a portion of the building with the Divine Science Church. The 100+ year old building provides an inspirational atmosphere for the type of books they sell. The bookstore is wheelchair accessible through a door which can be opened upon request.

You won't want to miss the quality of books you'll find at Divine Science Metaphysical Bookstore.

Editorial El Mundo

Spanish books, magazines   1796 Columbia Rd. NW
Washington, D.C. 20009
202-387-8716
Hours: Mon.-Fri. 9-7;
Sat. & Sun. 10-6

THE place in Washington, D.C. to purchase books, magazines, and newspapers written in Spanish is Editorial El Mundo. Manager Leonor Rodriguez is dedicated to bringing a variety of general interest books written in Spanish to Washingtonians.

She imports many books from a book distributor in Spain but she also travels to Venezula and Peru to search of stock for the store. She admitted that once she returned to Washington with three suitcases filled with books! She buys books written by Spanish authors as well as popular American authors whose works have been translated into Spanish. The store does sell a large number of children's books and cassette tapes.

If you speak English and want to learn Spanish or if you speak Spanish and want to learn English, you can find some study guides in Editorial El Mundo.

Fortunately, the store is street-level and wheelchair accessible. Some aisles may be tight but Leonor and her staff are more than happy to help customers.

The busy store also sells personalized social announcements, printed ribbons, greeting cards, gift wrapping, Washington maps and guides, party supplies, and a favorite of all children, pinatas.

Editorial El Mundo is connected with the Valdemar Travel Agency.

Fairy Godmother-Children's Books & Toys

Children's Books   319 7th Street SE
Washington, D.C. 20003
202-547-5474
Hours: Mon.-Fri. 10-6; Sat. 10-5;
in Fall open Sun. 1-5

Fairy Godmothers are supposed to be mystical, magical beings devoted to making children's dreams come true. Once you and the child in your life visit the bookstore named Fairy Godmother, you'll see the sparkle of magic in the little one's eyes. They see the magic of books which are in abundance here.

They sell books about all subjects for children from infancy through young adult ages. Some books are sold with stuffed toys or audio tapes to enhance the books. Fairy Godmother also sells some books in foreign languages. Adults can take advantage of the parenting books sold.

In addition to books, Fairy Godmother offers games and puzzles for sale. To delight children, the store sponsors story-telling time and invites authors to meet with the young readers.

When you want to relight that sparkle in a youngsters eye the way that only books can do, visit Fairy Godmother.

Farragut West Bookstore

General/Government pubs.   1510 H Street NW
Washington, D.C. 20005
202-653-5075
Hours: Mon.-Fri. 9-4:30

Farragut West Bookstore sells government publications and immigration forms. The store is wheelchair accessible and is open weekdays. They are able to supply you with catalogs of specific interests.

Folger Shakespeare Library Shop

Shakespeare   201 E. Capital St. SE
Washington, D.C. 20003
202-544-4600
FAX 202-544-4623
Hours: Mon.-Sat. 10-4; extra hours
during special events

Whether you are a Shakespearian expert or you needed the Cliff Notes to get through school, you'll appreciate the Folger Shakespeare Library. Founded in 1930, the library has a museum, theater, and a shop which are open to the public. Tours are conducted daily. The Reading Rooms are reserved for scholars by special appointment.

Although the museum shop is small, their selected stock is superb. Of course, you can find all the works of the Bard including editions published by the Folger Shakespeare Library. Other books discuss the Elizabethan period including biographies, fiction, mysteries, and cottages and gardens of Shakespeare's day. Some books are written especially for children. You are also offered a wealth of jewelry, miniature portraits, recordings of the Folger Consort, audio cassettes, video tapes, posters, pillows, hats, and so much more. For needle-crafters, cross-stitch patterns are available.

In addition to performances of Shakespeare's plays, at the Theater you can take acting lessons geared to professionals and non-professionals. The Shakespeare Theater at the Folger is a replica of a 16th-century theater.

The Library was recently awarded a large grant which they in part intend to use to make the building wheelchair accessible from the front and add an elevator inside. At the time that this book is being written, wheelchair users must call ahead and enter through the back of the building.

If you happen to be in Washington on the Saturday closest to April 23, the Folger Shakespeare Library comes alive with celebrations of the anniversary of Shakespeare's birth. A reborn Queen Elizabeth I oversees the medieval fair which includes actors, fire-eaters, and sword-swallowers. Guests are encouraged to join the acting troop on stage to perform scenes from the plays.

When you visit the museum shop, you are sure to leave feeling that you had discovered a shop that is the "be-all and the end-all" of Shakespearean shops. The quote, often said today, is from Shakespeare's play Macbeth.

Ford's Theatre Museum Bookshop

Americana   511 Tenth St. NW
Washington, D.C. 20004
202-426-0179
Hours: Daily 9-5

Probably the most famous theater in the country is Ford's Theatre because President Abraham Lincoln was shot here by John Wilkes Booth. The theater was closed in disgrace for 100 years.

Today the theater is open and managed by the National Park Service. The box where Lincoln and his wife sat remains empty and has a flag draped on it to honor Lincoln.

A small museum and museum shop are found in the basement of the building. The museum features such items as the suit of clothes in which Lincoln died, the flag that covered Lincoln's casket, the derringer Booth used that monumental day, and Booth's diary recording his plans.

The museum shop sells biographies of Lincoln, discussions of his assassination, books about the Civil War, and some books for children. They also sell Confederate money, replicas of the Gettysburg Address, Washington guidebooks, and a small assortment of souvenirs.

Although the museum and shop are in the basement of the theater, there is a lift for wheelchair.

After visiting Ford's Theatre you may want to tour the Peterson House, just across the street, where Lincoln died.

Fort Washington Park Bookshop

Nature   1900 Anacostia Dr. SE
Washington, D.C. 20042
202-763-4600
Hours: Daily 10-4:30

Fort Washington protected the nation's capital for more than 130 years. Volunteers in period costume give demonstrations of musket demonstrations and guide you through the fort. The fort is on 300 acres which provides many trails for hiking and areas for picnicking.

Inside the Visitor Center/Bookshop, which is wheelchair accessible, books about military history, nature, and those written for children are sold.

Francis Scott Key Book Shop

General

1400 28th St. NW
Washington, D.C. 20007
202-337-4144
Hours: Mon.-Sat. 9:30-6

Who is more American than the composer of our National Anthem? Francis Scott Key Book Shop brings you books as diverse as America herself, all sold with good old fashioned American practices. Three generations of customers can attest to that.

Co-owners Vivian Brown and Jennifer Herman provide their customers with personalized services that other bookstores wouldn't dream of providing. They keep a file of regular customers and their interests and buying is done with them in mind. For customers who shop by phone, Vivian and Jennifer are happy to describe books and recommend selections. After gift wrapping, they deliver books to addresses in the neighborhood or ship them by Parcel Post or United Parcel Service.

If you think that's special, wait. For neighbors, Vivian and Jennifer have been known to accept packages, walk dogs, hold keys for guests who arrive in the middle of the day, check alarms that ring, and the list goes on. The motto of Francis Scott Key Book Shop is "no request is too vague."

Located in a building built in 1865, the book shop is in a residential section of Georgetown. The quaint, old shop has two steps at the entrance and has tight aisles inside. Off-street parking and mass transit are available nearby.

Francis Scott Key Book Shop carries books in many categories and will special order and search for titles. They have large selections of fiction, history, politics, biography and children's books. Some books have large type print. Authors visit the store for autographing sessions.

Once you visit Vivian and Jennifer at Francis Scott Key Book Shop, you'll want to move to their neighborhood to enjoy their friendship as well as shopping at such a caring bookstore.

Franz Bader Bookstore

Fine Art
1911 I (eye) St., NW
Washington, D.C. 20006
202-337-5440
Hours: Mon.-Sat. 10-6

Make sure you go to I (eye) Street and not to 1 (first) Street because you won't want to miss Franz Bader Bookstore. The store specializes in five main fields of books: art and art history, architecture, design, photography, and the techniques of creating the arts. Also available are art related magazines and calendars. Books offered interest the general public as well as the academic community and artistic professionals. Imported books and foreign-language books are included.

Manager Sabine Yanul describes the store as "No muzak. No T-shirts. No Nonsense."

With 6,000 titles and a dedication to customer service, Franz Bader Bookstore does place special orders, maintains charge accounts, and will even gift wrap your purchases.

Established in 1954, Franz Bader Bookstore is completely wheelchair accessible. They also accept telephone and mail orders.

If you are skilled with the pen, brush, or camera, you'll enjoy this store. If you're an artistic wanna-be, you'll be inspired to begin your first masterpiece after a visit to this store.

Frederick Douglass Home Bookshop

Americana
1411 W St. SE
Washington, D.C. 20020
202-426-5960
Hours: Daily 9-5

The home of the nation's leading 19th century black spokesman, Frederick Douglass, is open to the public and serves as a museum and monument to this inspirational man. Douglass was an agent of the Massachusetts Anti-Slavery Society and was instrumental in organizing two regiments of blacks to fight on behalf of the Union. Douglass worked for human rights all of his life and had attended a women's suffrage convention on the day that he died.

In addition to the Douglass biographies sold at the bookshop, they sell biographies of other African-Americans who are prominent today and in our history. The shop also sells books about the Civil War. Many books are available for children.

Fortunately, the home and shop are wheelchair accessible.

Freer Gallery of Art Museum Shop

Asian Art Museum   Jefferson Dr. at 12th St. SW
                                      Washington, D.C. 20560
                                      202-357-2700
                                      Hours: Daily 10-5:30 (except Dec. 25)

Charles Lang Freer passionately collected Oriental art and American art that reflected a Far Eastern influence. His collection is the basis of the art found at the Freer Gallery. However, you'll also find works by Whistler and other major American artists. Freer and Whistler were friends and a bright "Peacock Room" that was painted by Whistler is a highlight of the Gallery. It's quite an eclectic collection.

The Freer Gallery is located next to the Sackler Gallery and there is an exhibition gallery which connects the two buildings. The Freer Gallery of Art went through extensive renovations and recently had been closed for quite a few years.

The museum shop reflects the art and exhibits of the Freer Gallery. The museum and shop are accessible to everyone.

Fuller & Saunders Books

Used-General   1531 33rd St. NW
                                      Washington, D.C. 20007
                                      202-337-3235
                                      Hours: Everyday (except closed Wed.)
                                      11-6:30 [call ahead]

"Our store is frequently closed when it's supposed to be open, and no matter how bad my attitude, people come back time after time. Go figure," said Alan Fuller, owner of Fuller & Saunders Books.

Aw, c'mon Alan, we all know that you're really a nice guy who sells a great selection of more than 4,000 used books featuring Americana, fiction, history, and militaria. A catalog is published and telephone and mail orders are accepted.

Fuller & Saunders Books shares a store with Bartleby's Books which is wheelchair accessible. Alan's goal for Fuller & Saunders Books is to be open everyday except Wednesdays. Alan suggests calling before visiting the store just to make sure that they're open.

Established in 1985 and going strong since then, Alan must be doing something right.

Gallaudet University Bookstore

College   800 Florida Ave. NE
                                         Washington, D.C. 20002
                                         202-651-5380
                                         FAX 202-651-5724
                                         Hours: Mon.-Fri. 9-4:30

Old Alexander Graham would ring his bell if he knew how vital his telephone has become to our society. First you had a telephone number. Then you were introduced to 800 and 900 numbers. Now you can reach people via their FAX numbers.

Until recently, the deaf were unable to tap into this valuable system. TDD, a telecommunications device for the deaf, enables hearing- and speech-impaired people to join the mainstream.

If you are deaf, if you know someone who is deaf, or if you would like to help persons who are deaf, the first place you should contact is Gallaudet University Bookstore. They offer both new and used books, videotapes, magazines, newspapers, and gift items relating to deafness and sign language.

The bookstore is open weekdays from 9 until 4:30 but they also publish a catalog for telephone and mail orders. If you can visit the store, you'll be pleased to find that the store is completely wheelchair accessible.

Be sure to contact Gallaudet University Bookstore to discover the most recent advancements in assisting the deaf.

George Washington Univ. Bookstore

College   Marvin Center
                                         800 21st Street NW
                                         Washington, D.C. 20052
                                         202-994-6870
                                         Hours: During school year:
                                         Mon.-Thurs. 9-7; Fri. 9-5; Sat. 11-4

Not only do students shop at George Washington University Bookstore; the surrounding neighborhood delights in their stock of more than 20,000 titles.

In addition to textbooks, they sell books to supplement studies or help readers to escape into fiction. They also place special orders. At times, the store sponsors author autographing sessions in the store.

George Washington University Bookstore also sells posters, calendars, stationery, and greeting cards. Everyone enjoys the T-shirts they sell, proclaiming the college's renowned patron, our first president.

Open when classes are in session, George Washington University Bookstore is open weekdays and Saturdays. There are seven steps to enter the store but they have made it accessible to wheelchair using patrons who can enter the building on the lower level and ring a buzzer. Someone will greet them and assist them with the building's elevator.

As with many college bookstores, they sell both new and used books. If you just stop here to pick up a college-logo T-shirt, you won't want to miss their selection of books.

Georgetown Univ. Law Center Bookshop

College

600 New Jersey Ave. NW
Washington, D.C. 20001
202-662-9458
FAX 202-662-9472
Hours: Mon.-Thurs. 9-6; Fri. 9-5

Like its other branches, the Georgetown University Law Center Bookshop is open to the public. By their name, you can guess that they sell textbooks for the Law School of Georgetown University. In 1993 they expanded their floor space and now offer more legal reference guides, newspapers, magazines, and a small selection of general interest reading. The bookstore is wheelchair accessible.

Georgetown Univ. Leavey Center Bookshop

College

3800 Reservoir Rd. NW
Washington, D.C. 20057
202-687-7482
800-548-5452
FAX 202-687-7925
Hours: Mon.-Fri. 9-8;
Sat. & Sun. 11-5

Some of the special books sold at Georgetown University Leavey Center Bookstore are the books written by instructors at the University.
Open to the public, the bookstore sells many general interest, reference, travel career guide books. For service to the University's School for Foreign Services, they stock many foreign language, English as a second language, and phrase books in stock. They estimate that they have over 20,000 titles.
Of course, you'll also be able to purchase T-shirts, sweats, and many gift items that carry the Georgetown University name and logo. A catalog is available.

Georgetown Univ. Medical Bookstore

College

3900 Reservoir Rd. NW
Washington, D.C. 20057
202-687-1268
FAX 202-687-3186
Hours: Mon.-Fri. 8:30-5; Sat. 10-4

The Medical Bookstore of Georgetown University strictly sells medical textbook and reference materials. However, it is open to the public and is wheelchair accessible. They do accept special orders.

Ginza Things Japanese

Orientalia

1721 Connecticut Ave. NW
Washington, D.C. 20009
202-331-7991
Hours: Mon.-Sat. 10-7; Sun. noon-6

If you haven't joined in the recent fascination with the martial arts and zen, now is your chance. At Ginza, "Things Japanese" you'll find a range of items from the land of the lotus blossom.

As far as books, Ginza stocks a large selection of books about architecture, gardening, art, fiction, health and nutrition, history, biographies, orientalia, philosophy, poetry and travel all with a Japanese flavor. The books about Japanese culture and language are particularly interesting. The delightful store also sells ceramics, bonsai supplies, art supplies, futons, woodblock prints, toys, games, and antiques.

Take the entire family to Ginza because there is something for everyone here. Parents and children together can learn origami, the ancient art of paper-folding to create charming little dragons and chickens.

Open everyday, Ginza has one step at the entrance and employees are happy to help customers in wheelchairs. Orders by telephone and mail are accepted. Books in stock include new and used titles. Special orders are no problem.

If you would like to expand beyond the martial arts or zen, contact Ms. Yoneyama at Ginza because she can put you in touch with new and wonderful items such as Go and Shogi.

Great Train Store

Trains

Union Station
50 Massachusetts Ave.
Washington, D.C. 20002
202-371-2881
Hours: Mon.-Fri. 8am-9pm;
Sat. 10-9; Sun. noon-6

Where do you expect to find a store called The Great Train Store? Inside Union Station, of course. And that's just where you will find one of the best specialty stores featuring trains in the nation.

You'll find enough books to fill a boxcar here. The books sold at The Great Train Store naturally focus on trains, railroad history, train models, magazines, train travelling, railroad cooking, novels, and children's books featuring Thomas the train of television's "Shining Time Station." Books are available in all price ranges.

Books are just one of the many types of items you'll find here. Hobbyists or kids of all ages will find everything they need to establish their own railroad model. Sizes of train sets go from miniature to those that require a little muscle to lift. Also available are video and audio tapes, railroad caps, patches, and items with railroad logos, children's little engineer overalls, games, framed artwork, and railroad memorabilia.

The Great Train Store is open everyday and is wheelchair accessible. The store was established in 1988.

While you're waiting to board your train at Union Station or if you are looking for a new hobby, The Great Train Store is the store for you. A running model train on the ceiling of the store inspires and delights visitors.

Habitat—National Wildlife Federation

Wildlife & Nature

1400 16th St. NW
Washington, D.C. 20036
202-797-6644
catalog orders: 800-432-6564
FAX 202-797-6646
Hours: Mon.-Fri. 10-5:30

When you leave Habitat, the gift shop sponsored by the National Wildlife Federation, you'll be smiling for two reasons. One, you'll be leaving the store with unique and beautiful books and gifts. Two, a portion of the money you spent goes to support the Federation's conservation education programs.

Fortunately, Habitat has two locations in the Washington area. The shop and the main headquarters of the National Wildlife Federation are located on 16th Street. The other is in Vienna, Virginia, on Leesburg Pike where they also have an educational center. Please also see the write-up for that store.

Some of the most beautiful coffee table books featuring nature and our world are found at Habitat. They also sell books about gardening, nature, birds, animals, and a complete series of children's educational magazines featuring "Ranger Rick."

Audio tapes are for sale and you can purchase cassettes and CD recordings of nature's sounds. Relax with the calm of a flowing stream or of bird and animal sounds.

Through the National Wildlife Federation you can sponsor a wolf or a adopt a whale. When you sponsor a wolf in Montana's Sawtooth pack, you will receive a certificate, a photo of your wolf, and the wolf's name. You'll also get quarterly updates, a full-color poster, and information about wolves. Your sponsorship supports further wolf recovery and educational outreach efforts.

You can choose one of fifty whales from a brochure to adopt. Each whale may have more than one sponsor. You receive a photo, adoption certificate and four quarterly updates on your whale. Your money protects whale breeding and feeding grounds, and supports a coastal network to help stranded whales.

Habitat is wheelchair and stroller accessible. Other items for sale make unique and beautiful gifts. They also have clothing for all ages and sizes.

If you can't visit Habitat, call them for a copy of their full color catalog. You'll be pleased you did.

Hillwood Museum Gift Shop

Museum

4155 Linnean Ave. NW
Washington, D.C. 20008
202-686-8510
FAX 202-966-7846
<u>Hours:</u> Daily 10-5; closed February

Hillwood Museum is tucked away on 25 acres and, according to gift shop manager, Barbara Jacoby, "is the best kept secret in Washington." Books sold include decorative arts from Russia, history, architecture, and Native American art.

To enter the grounds and visit the gift shop, you must make a reservation and pay $2 per person as a donation. The gift shop is wheelchair accessible. A catalog is being published and should be available in the fall of 1993.

Hirshhorn Museum & Sculpture Garden Bookshop

Museum

Independence Ave. at 8th SW
Washington, D.C. 20560
202-357-1429
<u>Hours:</u> Daily 10-5:20 (except Dec. 25)

Filled with treasures of modern art, the Hirshhorn Museum and Sculpture Garden holds the works of Auguste Rodin, Georgia O'Keeffe, Andy Warhol, Henry Moore, and so many more. The sunken garden, reflecting pool, and terraces with works by master sculptors, are places of awe and contemplation.

The museum shop reflects the modern art collection and offers wonderful books about modern art for both adults and children. They also sell jewelry, posters, toys, and assorted gifts.

Like all the Smithsonian Museums and shops, the Hirshhorn Museum and Sculpture Garden is wheelchair accessible.

Home Builder Bookstore

Home Building

1201 15th Street NW
Washington, D.C. 20005
202-861-2149
800-223-2665
FAX 202-822-0391
Hours: Mon.-Fri. 9-5

Naturally, The National Association of Home Builders is located in a beautiful, modern building in the heart of Washington. Fortunately for the home improvement fanatics, the Association has a bookstore open to the public.

Bookstore Manager Stephanie Thomas is dedicated to expanding the volume of books in order to make specialized books available to everyone. She is also dedicated to making sure you purchase just the right book you need.

The people in their mail order department also have this philosophy. For example, I called them, explained that I wanted a book about making my home accessible now that I use a wheelchair. Julie Wilson and I discussed the materials available and I requested one that we both agreed would help me. She later called me to say that after comparing the book I ordered to another, she felt that this other book would suit my needs better. That book was even less expensive than the one I originally ordered. I revised my order and she sent me the book right away. She was right! I appreciated her concern in getting the correct book and so will you.

In the small bookstore, you will be able to scan the 70+ titles that cover everything from remodeling your kitchen to building a treehouse that looks like a mini-castle. Stephanie showed me a book that she found particularly helpful. The title is "Everything Sold in Hardware Stores" which explained what every little gadget and do-dad can be found there and also how you properly use it and why it is important in making your life easier!

If you're a professional home builder or love redoing your living space, you must contact the Home Builder Bookstore. You will definitely be put in touch with just the right book.

Howard University Bookstore

College

2401 Fourth St. NW
Washington, D.C. 20059
202-806-6657
FAX 202-462-9800
Hours: Mon.-Fri. 8:30-6:30; Sat. 10-2; shorter summer hours

Howard University Bookstore is open to the 12-14,000 students and the general public. Books sold include textbooks, general interest, reference, computer, and black history. At the time that this book is being written, they are expanding the children's book department.

The store has 4-5,000 titles including books required for the Law School and the School of Divinity. The bookstore is staffed by Howard University students.

Also for sale in the bookstore are the traditional items featuring the Howard University logo. The store is wheelchair accessible. Please note that they are open longer hours when classes are in session.

Icon & Book Service of the Monastery of the Holy Cross

Religious-Christian

1217 Quincy St. NE
Washington, D.C. 20017
202-526-6061
FAX 202-526-3316
Hours: Tues.-Fri. 10-noon & 1-4;
Sat. 1-4; closed Sun. & Mon.

"The bookshop is the service of an Orthodox Christian monastery offering books, icons, and various other items for devotional use," said manager Father David of Icon & Book Service of the Monastery of the Holy Cross.

Book topics focus on Christian religion and history. Other items sold include icons, icon reproductions, audio books, video tapes, posters, calendars, and greeting cards. They do place special orders.

Customers can reach the bookshop by telephone, mail, and FAX or climbing the five steps to the door. They do publish a catalog. The book service was established in Washington, D.C. in 1988.

Idle Time Books

Used-General

2410 18th St. NW
Washington, D.C. 20009
202-232-4774
Hours: Daily 11-10

After you find Idle Time Books, you'll know just where to spend all of your idle time. They are conveniently open long hours everyday and offer you 30,000 used books with a general interest theme.

Located in a busy area of Washington, Idle Time Books is located on the third floor of an old rail house. Parts of the store are wheelchair accessible. Owner Jacques Morgan is happy to help you find the books you desire, and some you didn't know you couldn't live without!

Indian Craft Shop

Native American Crafts   Department of Interior
1849 C Street
Washington, D.C. 20240
202-208-4743
Hours: Mon.-Fri. 8:30-4:30

Sponsored by the Department of the Interior, the Indian Craft Shop has sold handmade crafts to the public since 1938. Books for sale discuss Native American arts and crafts, how items are made, and how to judge quality of crafts.

The store is wheelchair accessible. Because the Indian Craft Shop has been so popular, a second shop has opened in Georgetown.

The Department of the Interior Museum outlines the history of the National Park Service and includes documents such as original land grants and surveys on display.

Indian Craft Shop

Native American Crafts   Georgetown Park Mall
3222 M Street
Washington, D.C. 20007
202-342-3918
Hours: Mon.-Sat. 10-9; Sun. noon-6

Georgetown's Indian Craft Shop is an expansion of the Native American arts and craft store found in the Department of the Interior. Books sold present the arts and explain how they are crafted and how to judge quality. Located in the Georgetown Park Mall, the store is wheelchair accessible.

As the store manager said, "The store sells one of a kind items."

International Language Center

Foreign Language   1753 Connecticut Ave. NW
Washington, D.C. 20009
202-332-2894
FAX 202-462-6657
Hours: Daily 9-5

On the mezzanine section of one of Washington's popular news stores, the Newsroom, you'll find the equally popular Foreign Language Center. Sold are books including grammar and learning titles, reference books, and audio-visual materials for approximately 130 languages.

Special orders are welcomed and they can even obtain books from abroad. Business is also conducted by telephone and mail order. You can call them and they will send you a customized list of items available to meet your needs. If you use a wheelchair, this may be the easiest way to shop. The language center is located up one flight of stairs.

Once you have mastered a language, you'll be able to maintain your knowledge by reading the many newspapers and magazines of the Newsroom. This combination of foreign language study with news and magazines from around the world makes for a unique store, the only one of its kind in the U.S.

International Monetary Fund Bookstore

Economics

700 19th Street NW
Washington, D.C. 20431
202-623-7430
FAX 202-623-7201
Hours: Mon.-Fri. 10-5

The International Monetary Fund (IMF) is an "organization with over 178 member countries pledged to assist each other with information and financial support so as to create a world economic environment in which all will prosper," states their catalog.

The bookstore offers books that specialize in world economics, statistics, and banking. Books for sale here are certainly unique and not found in mainstream bookstores.

The organization publishes a thorough catalog annually which describes books, pamphlets, statistical publications, video tapes, and software. Twice per month they publish a newsletter called "IMF Survey." Quarterly they publish the magazine "Finance & Development" in conjunction with the World Bank. The shop is not wheelchair accessible so catalog shopping is the way to go for wheelchair users.

Islamic Center Shop

Islamic & Arabic Languages

2551 Massachusetts Ave. NW
Washington, D.C. 20008
202-332-8343
FAX 202-234-5035
Hours: Daily 10-5

Fine craftsmen from the Middle East constructed the majestic white marble with inlaid turquoise and gold building used as a religious center for embassy staffs. The Islamic congregation is one of the most active in the country.

Books written in Arabic can be purchased in the bookstore or by catalog. Topics include history, religion and philosophy of the Arab nations. Many other gift items, such as perfume and audio tapes, are also sold. The bookstore is not wheelchair accessible.

A quarterly magazine named "Al Nur: The Light" is published by the Islamic Center.

Jefferson Memorial Bookshop

Americana

900 Ohio Dr. SW
Washington, D.C. 20042
202-472-3083
Hours: Daily 9-9
(closed 11-noon & 4:30-5)

In life, Thomas Jefferson stood 6 feet 2 1/2 inches tall but at the extremely popular Jefferson Memorial, you'll see his bronzed image a full 19 feet high. The distinguished building is a fitting tribute to one of our finest statesmen as well as a distinguished architect.

Just inside the Jefferson Memorial on the ground floor, you'll find the memorial shop. In addition to biographies about Thomas Jefferson, they sell histories of the Revolutionary War and of our Capital itself. Many books are written for children. Also available are reproductions of the Declaration of Independence and the U.S. Constitution. The shop and memorial are wheelchair accessible.

Joshua Heller Rare Books, Inc.

Antiquarian-General

PO Box 39114
Washington, D.C. 20016
202-966-9411
FAX 202-363-5658
Hours: Appointment only

"A Miscellany of Fine Printing and Illustration by Masters of the Craft" is the title of the catalog published by Joshua Heller Rare Books, Inc.

The catalog includes books about book binding, typographical masterpieces, Holbein woodblocks, early printed music, Japanese pattern books for leather design from the 19th century, photography, new hand-crafted books with original calligraphic drawings, and Shakespearian books. He also has a fine copy of "The Ballad of Reading Goal" which was autographed by the author, Oscar Wilde.

As a general description of the books sold, Joshua said that they are "finely printed and illustrated books through five centuries." The collection offered to you numbers in the thousands.

Established in 1985, Joshua Heller Rare Books is open by appointment or through telephone and mail ordering. If you are a true bibliophile who appreciates the finest of books, you will want to contact Joshua.

Kenilworth Aquatic Gardens Shop

Aquatic Gardening

1900 Anacostia Dr. SE
Washington, D.C. 20020
202-426-6905
Hours: Daily 8:30-4

What began as a man bringing a few water lilies from Maine has turned into the beautiful and seldom visited Kenilworth Aquatic Gardens. An early morning visit is best to see the many blooming flowers. The gardens are also a perfect place to study the native trees and catch glimpses of the raccoons, muskrats, turtles, or frogs that call the garden-area home.

The Kenilworth Aquatic Gardens conducts garden walks and educational programs about the environment that are suited for the entire family. For the pleasure of the public, the Gardens are open daily.

The Nature/Visitor Center has three steps to enter but they also have a ramp making the center accessible to all. A shop sells more than twenty titles all, addressing sights you'll see at the garden. You can pick up a book describing how you can create your own aquatic garden, along with books for children.

When you want some fresh air away from the bustling Capital, visit the peaceful Kenilworth Aquatic Gardens.

Kennedy Center for the Performing Arts Shop

Performing Arts

2700 F Street
Washington, D.C. 20566
202-254-3624
800-444-8744
FAX 202-416-8744
Hours: Daily 10-9

Located on the Potomac River banks, the Kennedy Center for the Performing Arts houses theaters, galleries, and a nice gift shop that includes many books.

Topics include books about performing arts, dance, composition and conducting orchestras, directing, staging, the Kennedy Center itself, "Profiles in Courage," and Washington area guides. Approximately 200 titles are in stock. Also for sale are video tapes and audio tapes.

Mail orders are accepted although no catalog is issued. The center and gift shop are wheelchair accessible. For performances, infrasound headsets are available for hearing-impaired people.

Call the center for information about events, showtimes, and ticket availability. If you don't have time to enjoy one of the many programs, you can enjoy a tour of the center and visit the gift shop.

The Kennedy Center for the Performing Arts has a beautiful 7-foot bronze bust of the slain president. The center hosts excellent programs featuring top national and international artists.

Kramerbooks & Afterwords

Fiction

1517 Connecticut Ave. NW
Washington, D.C. 20036
202-387-1400
FAX 202-232-7481
Hours: Mon.-Thurs. 7:30 am-1:00 am;
Open 24 hours Fri. & Sat.

When asked what special programs that Kramerbooks & Afterwords offer customers, employee Misty Brown says, "We are a special program!"

In addition to conducting normal business as if it were a special program, their stock is also special. They offer approximately 25,000 works of fiction and all are new books. Also sold are magazines, newspapers, and calendars.

But "special" doesn't stop there; a cafe is located in the store. Even the hours that Kramerbooks & Afterwords is open is special. On Friday and Saturday, they're open 24 hours and during the week they operate from 7:30 a.m. until 1:00 the next morning!

Other special features are the meet-the-author luncheons, their 32-page catalog, and desktop-publishing sci-fi newsletters. Children delight in the writing contests held here.

Established in 1976 and located just off Dupont Circle, Kramerbooks & Afterwords is partially wheelchair accessible. Some departments are located on different levels. Employees do ask if they can assist those who cannot climb the few steps.

Kramerbooks & Afterwords is known in the community as a bookstore, bus-station, half-way house; library, fashion centre, hospitality room, and conference center.

A branch of Kramerbooks & Afterwords opened in Arlington, Virginia in September 1993. Please see the Virginia section of this book to read about the store.

Again, what makes this place so special? Owner Bill Kramer says that the store's informal atmosphere is the key to its popularity. The community knows that Kramerbooks & Afterwords is a terrific bookstore where you can lose yourself.

Kulturas Books & Records

Used-General

1741 Connecticut Ave. NW
Washington, D.C. 20009
202-462-2541
Hours: Mon.-Sat. 11-8; Sun. 11-6

Approximately 15,000 books adorn the shelves of the second-hand bookstore, Kulturas Books and Records. Owners Irene Coray and Andrew MacDonald have developed a quality stock of general interest books for scholars, collectors, and the common folk. Books in the humanities are bought and sold. Other strong areas include art, fiction, foreign language, philosophy, and poetry.

Established in 1989, Kulturas Books and Records is open everyday. There is one step at the entrance but the store is wheelchair accessible inside. Seating inside the store is a welcome relief for long-time browsers. A bulletin board in the store is filled with store and community activities.

Lado International Books

Foreign Language

2233 Wisconsin Ave. NW
Washington, D.C. 20007
202-338-3133
800-229-5236
FAX 202-337-1118
<u>Hours:</u> Mon.-Thurs. 9-7:30;
Fri. 9-4:30; Sat. 9-2

"The sum of human wisdom is not contained in any one language, and no single language is capable of expressing all forms and degrees of human comprehension," said Ezra Pound in 1934.

Lado International Books does much more than bring you books and cassette tapes that assist you in learning other languages. Lado's goal is to help you better understand the world through languages.

Dr. Robert Lado, an author and owner of Lado International Books, has written more than 86 books, many of which are used as textbooks in more than fifty countries around the world. For 21 years he was the Dean of the Georgetown University School of Languages and Linguistics.

In 1982 he founded the bookstore which also has an attached school for people learning English as a second language. English courses are offered on many levels of knowledge. Students can enroll in intensive programs, part-time programs, and even Saturday programs. Computer courses are also offered at Lado International Books. Lado International College has eight worldwide locations including Lima, Peru, Tokyo, Japan, and Seoul, Korea.

Lado International Books does sell many books by mail and telephone orders. They welcome special orders. The store is also wheelchair accessible.

Whether you want phrase books to assist you in vacation travelling or you want to imprint a language on your soul, visit Lado International Books.

Lambda Rising Inc.

Gay & Lesbian

1625 Connecticut Ave. NW
Washington, D.C. 20009
202-462-6969
FAX 202-462-7257
<u>Hours:</u> Everyday 10 am-midnight

"Lambda Rising is the world's largest gay and lesbian bookstore stocking virtually every gay and lesbian book in print, as well as thousands of out-of-print titles," said manager L.P. Maccubbin.

Being experts, they publish "The Lambda Book Report," a bimonthly review of contemporary gay and lesbian literature. In the store, you'll find approximately 20,000 titles, most of which are new releases. They do carry a few used and antiquarian quality books. Some audio books are also available. If, by chance, they don't have the book that you are looking for, they will conduct searches and place special orders.

Books aren't the only items for sale at Lambda Rising. All items pertain to lesbian and/or gay themes and include magazines, greeting cards, music, videos, T-shirts, jewelry, and gift items.

"We also offer free copies of local gay newspapers and map guides, tickets for gay concerts and events, and information about Washington's gay community," said L.P. Maccubbin.

With a dedication to the gay community, they also publish a quarterly newsletter and maintain a bulletin board in the store with announcements. Authors visit the store for autographing sessions.

Lambda Rising is accessible to wheelchair users and is open generously long hours—everyday from 10am until midnight. If you can't visit the store, they offer a catalog and happily accept telephone and mail orders.

Established in 1974, Lambda Rising achieves their goal of providing comprehensive book services to the community.

Lammas Books

Feminism

1426 21st St. NW
Washington, D.C. 20036
202-775-8218
FAX 202-775-8218
<u>Hours:</u> Mon.-Sat. 10-10; Sun. 11-8

Lammas Books is Washington's only feminist bookstore. The term Lammas comes from a thanksgiving feast celebrated in England marking the harvest of the first wheat of the season. At Lammas Books, you'll celebrate a feast of a different sort: a feast of approximately 10,000 books.

Featuring new and used books, Lammas Books specializes in women's studies, alternative life styles, and fiction. Also sold are magazines, newspapers, calendars, video tapes, greeting cards, T-shirts, posters, and even games.

Lammas Books publishes a bimonthly newsletter and keeps an information-filled bulletin board in the store. Happy to help you find a special book, employees do conduct searches and place special orders. Telephone and mail orders are no problem. At times, authors visit the store for autograph sessions.

A comfortable, inviting bookstore, Lammas Books is open everyday. Although there are three steps at the front door, Lammas Books also has a ramp for wheelchair users and shoppers with strollers.

When books with a feminist touch are just what you need, visit Lammas Books.

The Lantern Bryn Mawr Bookshop

Used-General

3160 O St. NW
Washington, D.C. 20007
202-333-3222
Hours: Mon.-Fri. 11-4;
Sat. 11-5; Sun. noon-4

The Lantern Bryn Mawr Bookshop, staffed by volunteers, sells donated used and rare books. Proceeds fund scholarships at Bryn Mawr College. It is sponsored by the alumni of Bryn Mawr.

The Lantern is located in Georgetown among busy antique and jewelry shops. Steps at the entrance make it impractical for wheelchairs.

Book lovers are often thrilled with their "finds" at The Lantern. There are several similar stores in operation around the country.

Latin American Books

Latin America

Box 39090
Washington, D.C. 20016
202-244-4173
Hours: Telephone & mail order only

If you're running into brick walls when trying to find extremely hard-to-find titles, contact Latin American Books. They have more than 200,000 titles in all languages and all disciplines. A particularly interesting department is African colonies in the Caribbean and Hispanic United States.

Most books sold are rare and out-of-print. The stock changes constantly. Latin American Books operates by telephone and mail order only. The business started with a small collection and has exploded so that it now has today's massive stock.

Lerner Law Book Co., Inc.

Law   111 Massachusetts Ave. NW
                                   Washington, D.C. 20001
                                   202-842-4334
                                   800-253-1594
                                   FAX 202-842-3963
                                   Hours: Mon.-Fri. 10-6; Sat. noon-5

Associated with a law school, Lerner Law Book Co., Inc., sells textbooks as well as study aids and school supplies. The public is welcomed here. Although it is a small store, they have 3,000 titles in stock. They are wheelchair accessible and have extended hours when classes begin.

Liberty Library

Patriotic books   300 Independence Ave. SE
                                   Washington, D.C. 20003
                                   202-546-5611
                                   FAX 202-544-4101
                                   Hours: Telephone & mail order only

The great thing about Liberty Library is that they sell the books they have on their shelves. Some books have been autographed by the author. Their specialty is new hard-to-find books on patriotic topics. Children's books are also available, as well as books on audio tapes, video tapes, newspapers, T-shirts and calendars.

Liberty Library conducts business solely by telephone and mail order. They publish a catalog and weekly newsletter. Also contact them by FAX. Liberty Library was established in 1955 and continues to fill the gap often left open by other bookstores.

Library of Congress Shop

Law   Jefferson Building
                                   1st St. SE
                                   Washington, D.C. 20540
                                   202-707-5000
                                   Hours: Mon.-Sat. 9-5;
                                   Summer also open Sun. 1-5

Every hour, 400 items are added to the Library of Congress' collection of nearly 90 million items. In 1800 the Library was a one-room reference collection for Congress. After the Library was burned in 1814, Thomas Jefferson offered his private library as a replacement. Researchers, members of Congress, and their staff are the only persons able to use the nation's library but visitors are all welcome to the exhibition halls.

Twice in the last 40 years the Library has been forced to find additional space. They first expanded into the John Adams Building then the James Madison Memorial Building. The giftshop, as well as a cafeteria, is located in the Madison building.

Although the giftshop is small, they carry quality gifts and souvenirs. Approximately one-third of the store is books. Most of the books are beautiful, coffee-table books describing past exhibits at the library that are published by the government and are not available anywhere else. They also stock books addressing history, geography, maps, and children's books.

The tour of the Library of Congress and the gift shop are wheelchair accessible. If you are unable to visit the Library, you can write for a catalog of gift shop items to: Library of Congress, Office Systems Service, Printing & Processing Section, Washington, D.C. 20540.

Lincoln Memorial Bookshop

Americana

23rd & Lincoln Mem. Circle
Washington, D.C. 2004
202-653-9088
Hours: Daily 8am-11pm

The majestic Lincoln Memorial with its Greek-style temple and colonnade of 36 Doric columns is one of Washington's most-visited memorials. Walk behind the columns and you'll see the famous sculpture of Lincoln sitting majestically, staring toward the Reflecting Pool and Washington Memorial. The statue and walls engraved with the Gettysburg Address truly is awesome.

A shop sells biographies of Lincoln and books about the strenuous times in which he lived. Books for children are also available. Look for small signs around the Memorial to guide those using wheelchairs to the shop.

Literal Books

Spanish

7705 Georgia Ave. NW #102
Washington, D.C. 20012
202-723-8688
800-366-8680
FAX 202-882-6592
Hours: Mon.-Fri. 10-5; Sat. 10-1

Literal Books are such experts in handling books written in Spanish, they supply most major university bookstores with their Spanish books. In their store in Washington, D.C., you'll find more than 5,000 titles.

A publisher as well as a bookstore, Literal Books also has a catalog for telephone and mail orders. There are five steps to enter the store so wheelchair users will want to shop-by-catalog.

Topics include fiction, history, philosophy, poetry, psychology, reference, Christian religion, women's studies, and children's books. Naturally they have books to aid you in learning the Spanish language. They also will do searches for books you want and appraisals of books you own. Special orders are no problem.

Dedicated to promoting the Spanish language, Literal Books sponsors reading groups. Authors visit the store to autograph their books.

Whether you habla espanol or want to learn, Literal Books have just the books you need.

Logic & Literature

Antiquarian-General

3075 M St. NW
2nd Floor
Washington, D.C. 20007
202-625-1668
Hours: Wed.-Sat. 1:00 pm - 6:30 pm

If the classical studies inspire you, you'll want to visit Logic & Literature. Selections include the themes of fine art, history, philosophy, and science. Owner Candee Harris has a collection of approximately 5,000 titles.

With twenty stairs to enter Logic & Literature, the store is not wheelchair accessible. But have no fear. Candee publishes a catalog of her books. Call her with titles that you are looking for and Candee will conduct a search. An expert in her field, Candee also does appraisals.

Established in 1989, Logic & Literature is the place to start your quest for the classics.

Mail Order Division—Parks & History Assoc.

Americana

McArthur Blvd & Elliot Pl. NW
PO Box 40060
Washington, D.C. 20016
202-472-3083
Hours: Mail order only

The Parks and History Association operates bookshops in the parks and national monuments in Washington and the surrounding areas. Funds gathered from the sales of items in the bookshops support the educational and interpretive programs.

Through a catalog, you can also purchase approximately 4,000 publications through a mail order service by contacting their offices at the telephone number mentioned above.

The Map Store Inc.

Cartography & Travel

1636 I (Eye) St. NW
Washington, D.C. 20006
202-628-2610
800-544-2659
FAX 202-783-0346
Hours: Mon.-Fri. 9-5:30; Sat. 10-4

With all the changes in our modern world, there is one bustling little store in Washington that is a source to the world. The Map Store, Inc. sells maps, books, guides, travel books, street guides, cartography, weather books, globes, flags, and even satellite photos suitable for framing. Annually, The Map Store sponsors a geography-bee for elementary schools.

Although the store is small, it is wheelchair accessible. The volume and uniqueness of articles sold will certainly lead you to agree that this small spot on the map of Washington is one that you won't want to miss.

Marine Corps Museum Shop

Marine Corps

Washington Navy Yard
Bldg. 58
Washington, D.C. 20374
202-433-6330 (museum shop)
800-336-0291
Hours: Mon.-Sat. 10-3:30;
on weekends & holidays call ahead

The U.S. Marine Corps originated in 1775 when the Continental Congress voted that "two Battalions of Marines be raised." Since then, Marines have participated in all U.S. wars and are often the first to go into battle. Today's Marine is known for his dedication and fighting spirit.

Washington, D.C. honors the Marine Corp with a museum presenting a history of the Corps and displays of uniforms, weapons, equipment, and various art works. The museum is free and wheelchair accessible.

Located inside the museum is a giftshop staffed by volunteers. Books are the main feature of the shop that also sells clothing, office, household items, and souvenirs with the Marine Corps logo. They publish an extensive catalog and do a great deal of sales through it.

To obtain the museum shop catalog or to place an order, call toll free at the above number and ask for the Museum Shop, or write to: Museum Shop, MCHF, P.O. Box 420, Quantico, VA 22134.

Martin Luther King, Jr. Library Giftshop

African Americans   901 G Street NW
                                       Washington, D.C. 20001
                                       202-727-6834
                                       <u>Hours:</u> Mon.-Sat. 11-5; Sun. 1:30-4:30

"The ultimate measure of a man is not where he stands in moments of comfort and convenience, but where he stands at times of challenge and controversy," said Dr. Martin Luther King, Jr.

Many of Dr. King's words are imbedded in the hearts of some people but until they become a part of one's soul, we may never see his dream become reality. Dr. King's dedication to the principle of nonviolent civil disobedience to attain social and political goals was and is inspirational to everyone.

The main branch of the Washington, D.C. public library system is dedicated to Dr. King. The Library is open to everyone but the small giftshop is open much shorter hours. Approximately 100 titles for sale focus on African-Americans, the history, art, culture, and biographies of the African-American past and present. Some books are written for children. There are also some regional Washington guidebooks. In addition to books, the shop sells gifts, posters, T-shirts, and assorted souvenirs. They will mail items to you.

The library and shop are completely wheelchair accessible.

The library sponsors a citywide arts program and has a permanent collection of paintings, sculpture, and photographs on display throughout the building. The Washingtoniana Room holds the largest collection of DC-related information in the world.

After you browse, study, or research the volumes at the Martin Luther King, Jr., Library, take a moment to reflect on Dr. King's dream so that we all can make it to the mountaintop.

Metropolitan Baptist Bookstore

Religious-Christian   1225 R Street NW
                                       Washington, D.C. 20009
                                       202-332-7590
                                       <u>Hours:</u> Tues.-Fri. 11-7; Sat. & Sun 9-3

Enter the Metropolitan Baptist Church and you'll be able to access the bookstore. About 70 percent of the stock of books are Bibles and books written by Christian authors. The other 30 percent of books are general interest topics.

Dedicated to counseling and self-help, the Bookstore has many titles in these areas. They publish a catalog and have a strong mail order service. The bookstore also sells sermons on cassette tapes, family videos, gospel music, sheet music, and gift items.

The Metropolitan Baptist Church Bookstore sells literature for Christian education to other churches. Wheelchair accessible, the bookstore is closed during church services.

Mrs. Duff Gilfond Fugitive Books Intercepted

Search service   1722 19th St. NW
                                     Ste. 811
                                     Washington, D.C. 20009
                                     202-387-1418
                                     Hours: Mail order only

Take the first initial of this book businesses name, Fugitive Books Intercepted and you'll notice the initials "FBI." Just like the FBI hunt for their man, Mrs. Duff Gilfond hunts for her books. A delightful lady, Mrs. Gilfond searches for unusual and hard-to-find books for libraries and individuals. Business is conducted through the mail.

Mrs. Duff Gilfond Fugitive Books Intercepted was established in the 1940's. Mrs. Gilfond took on the business after her husband passed away fifteen years ago. A journalist in her youth, Mrs. Gilfond has written two books herself; one is a biography of Calvin Coolidge and the other titled "I Go Horizontal" which describes her first-hand experience handling a serious illness. Today, Mrs. Gilfond enjoys hunting rare books.

Mystery Books

Mystery   1715 Connecticut Ave.
                                     Washington, D.C. 20016
                                     202-483-1600
                                     800-955-2279
                                     Hours: Mon.-Fri. 11-7;
                                     Sat. 10-6; Sun. noon-5

"Sending the right gift can be murder," claims a Mystery Books brochure. "When you haven't a clue what to give someone, try our Crime and Nourishment Gift Baskets. They'll satisfy anyone's appetite for good reading and gourmet treats."

The gift baskets are just one feature that makes Mystery Books a special place. In addition to selling a complete line of mystery books, they also sell the Maltese Falcon, framed lithographs from the PBS "Mystery" program, mystery games, and even computer games.

Some of the 14,000+ titles have been autographed. Authors frequently visit the store to sign books and do readings. You'll find the store decorated like a little old English parlor complete with paisley wallpaper and a cozy fireplace.

In 1992, in conjunction with Mystery Books, the Smithsonian Institute Campus on the Mall conducted a seven night program of discussions led by mystery writers and titled "Mystery They Wrote."

Located in the busy Dupont Circle area of Washington, Mystery Books is completely accessible to everyone. The store has a delightful little spy character as a logo who appears on many items for sale in the store including coffee mugs, T-shirts, and sweatshirts.

Throughout their lengthy catalog, the little spy shows up carrying a dagger, a revolver, and a bomb. Once you see him, you'll be sure to remember him. Once you visit Mystery Books, you won't forget the store and the marvelous stock and atmosphere. You'll be sure to stop by the store every time you're in Dupont Circle.

National Air & Space Museum Bookshop

Museum   Independence Ave. at 6th, NW
                                  Washington, D.C. 20560
                                  202-357-1387
                                  Hours: Daily 10-6:30 (except Dec. 25)

Rarely do you tour a museum where some of the exhibits are suspended from the ceiling, but that's just what you'll find at the National Air and Space Museum. Look up and see Lucky Lindbergh's Spirit of St. Louis and the little red jet that Chuck Yeager flew when he broke the sound barrier. Here you can also touch a moon rock, walk through Skylab, and feel like you're flying when watching the 50-foot tall movie screen showing "To Fly."

At the museum shop you'll be able to purchase books for readers of all ages, space, flight, and science-related gifts, videos, model airplanes and spacecraft. Don't forget to purchase your supply of astronaut's food while you're there. Speaking of food, the Air and Space Museum has two cafeterias appropriately named "Flight Line" and "The Wright Place."

The museum and shop are wheelchair accessible and they have a limited number of wheelchairs and strollers for visitors to the museum.

Whether you're from the age of Telstar or Star Trek, you're sure to enjoy the National Air and Space Museum.

National Aquarium Giftshop

Aquatics & Water Animals   14th & Constitution Streets
                                  Washington, D.C. 20005
                                  202-482-3679
                                  Hours: Daily 9-5 except Christmas
                                  Day

The National Aquarium, which is the nation's oldest aquarium, has sixty-five tanks which display more than 1,200 fresh- and saltwater marine specimens. A green sea turtle and alligators also call The National Aquarium home. The Touch Tank is a favorite of children.

The aquarium shop sells many marine related gifts and souvenirs plus books for children and adults about water animals and fish. Call or visit them if you are looking for books in this specialty.

National Archives Museum Store

Museum-Archives

Constitution Ave. between 7th & 9th
Washington, D.C. 20408
202-501-5235
Events: 202-501-5000
Hours: April-Labor Day: 10-9;
Labor Day-March 31: 10-5:30

Speaking of our young country's most precious documents, Thomas Jefferson warned, "Time and accident are committing daily havoc on the originals deposited in our public offices."

Imagine the original copy of the Declaration of Independence gathering dust among a pile of papers in Jefferson's office, or the Constitution in George Washington's "To Be Filed" folder, or Ben Franklin grabbing a piece of paper from his desk drawer to fold into a kite and it was the Bill of Rights!

No one heeded Jefferson's warning until just prior to World War I after a number of government buildings had suffered damaging fires. The National Archives wasn't formally established until the Great Depression. Then historians searched every desk and attic in Washington for important documents that were to be preserved.

Today, you can visit The National Archives and Records Administration to see not only the most famous of American documents but also the Japanese surrender document that was signed in 1945, the court record of the Dred Scott Case, and passenger listings from European and slave ships entering the United States. You can also see one of the seven copies of the Magna Carta in existence, on loan to the Archives from H. Ross Perot.

After touring the National Archives and attending one of their many special events, visit the Museum Store and choose from more than 1,000 titles of books focusing on the archive holdings, American history, militaria, genealogy, politics, biographies, foreign relations, humor, and regional Washington, D.C. tourist guide books. Many specialized books for children are also for sale. Some books are available on audio tape.

The Museum Store also carries a full line of gifts and memorabilia which includes some items exclusive to the Archives Museum Store. They publish a catalog for mail orders. In addition to the events held in The Archives, the Museum Shop sponsors a free lecture series and supports children's story-telling time. A free monthly calendar of events is published which describes events including author lectures and book signings, genealogy workshops, films, and an Arts and Culture Series.

People using wheelchairs should note that The National Archives has an alternate wheelchair entrance on Pennsylvania Avenue. The front door has a mountain of stairs but the wheelchair entrance is well marked and Archive guards are happy to direct you. The National Archives is located midway between the Capitol and the White House on the Mall.

National Building Museum Shop

Architecture & Design

401 F Street NW
Washington, D.C. 20001
202-272-7706
FAX 202-272-2564
<u>Hours:</u> Mon.-Sat. 10-4; Sun. noon-4

Can you imagine being asked to build our nation's capitol city? Who gets a memorial and what kind of monument should that be? What kind of buildings will be needed and how do they best reflect the new American democracy?

To see just how Washington grew, visit the National Building Museum to view the permanent display titled "Washington: Symbol and City" and see, according to a flyer, "the struggle between an aesthetic vision for a national capital and the needs of the people who live in the city."

Completely wheelchair accessible, the museum tour has created an exhibit accessible to blind and visually impaired visitors through tactile models, audiotapes, a guide-rail system, and braille labels.

The museum shop sells an extensive collection of books about architecture, design, city planning, home improvement, and guides to Washington. They also have excellent books for children.

All too often, we don't take the time to look at our world from afar or up-close. The National Building Museum brings Washington into clear focus.

National Gallery of Art Bookstore

Museum

Constitution Ave. at 6th, NW
Washington, D.C. 20565
202-842-6466
FAX 202-842-4043
<u>Hours:</u> Mon.-Sat. 10-5; Sun. 11-6; or by appointment

The National Gallery of Art has two museums each with a different focus. Each store sells books relating to the special exhibits that have been displayed in the Gallery and of their permanent collection as well as the history, theory, and criticism of fine art, sculpture, architecture, and photography. They also sell prints and posters adapted from the original artworks of the gallery. Both museum shops are wheelchair accessible.

The museum shop in the West Building features books and gift items through the 18th century whereas the East Building shop sells items for more contemporary art. Each shop holds approximately 5,000 titles and authors do visit the shops to discuss and sign their books.

Fortunately, there is a cafe on the premises and you can make a full day of touring the Gallery.

National Geographic Society Store

Geography

Explorers Hall
17th & M Streets, NW
Washington, D.C. 20036
202-857-7588
Hours: Mon.-Sat. 9-5; Sun. 10-5

Most everyone is familiar with the wondrous photographs and tales that the National Geographic magazine has brought to the public for years. Now you can visit a museum called Explorers Hall at the National Geographic Society headquarters and be amazed at the fascinating interactive exhibits.

No matter what your age, you'll delight in the many interactive exhibits. Other displays bring history and environments of the world to your fingertips.

After visiting Explorers Hall, you won't be able to resist the luscious books, maps, globes, and posters sold at the National Geographic Society Store. They sell beautiful pop-up books to delight and teach children. A fabulous learning tool is a video atlas which presents the world as only the National Geographic Society can. The store is offering more CD-ROM's all the time.

The museum and shop are wheelchair accessible. The main entrance is on 17th Street but there is a wheelchair ramp on M Street. Handicapped parking can be arranged if you call ahead.

National Intelligence Book Center

Espionage Nonfiction

Lock Box Mail Unit 18757
Washington, D.C. 20036
202-785-4334
FAX 202-331-7456
Hours: Mail order only--Magazine subscription

Although National Intelligence Book Center (NIBC) does not sell books (they refer you to Olsson's Books & Records at Dupont Circle), they are a unique business that pertains to books.

They publish a bi-monthly booklet, Surveillant, that presents descriptions of current and out-of-print books, dissertations, and governmental documents that are rarely found in bookstores. Surveillant describes more than 1,400 new titles per year.

The books and papers that NIBC discusses are mainly of interest to intelligence officials, academicians, researchers, corporations, teachers, writers, and journalists. According to NIBC, many congressmen and their aides, U.S. and foreign government officials, and diplomats from around the world subscribe to the booklet. Other subscribers, states the NIBC business card, are "those curious 'spy book' readers in the general public seeking the real thing."

Categories presented in Surveillant include espionage, counter-intelligence, surveillance, cryptography, wire-tapping, military intelligence, propaganda, industrial espionage, terrorism, resistance movements, computer security, aerial and space reconnaissance, and histories of intelligence agencies such as the FBI and CIA.

According to one of their flyers, "Surveillant is produced as a public service." The business was established in 1986. Contact NIBC to subscribe to Surveillant or with any questions.

National Museum of African Art

African Art

950 Independence Ave. SW
Washington, D.C. 20560
202-257-4600
<u>Hours:</u> Daily 10-5:30 (except Dec. 25)

The National Museum of African Art is dedicated to African arts. The collection reflects how the many cultures in Africa interweave art with daily living. Most of the works in the collection were created in the late 19th and early 20th centuries because most items are made of organic materials. In addition to the exhibition galleries, the museum is a mecca for research.

The shop and museum are wheelchair accessible. The shop sells books about Africa, its history and art, as well as African crafts, textiles, musical instruments, jewelry, baskets, and children's toys.

National Museum of American Art

Fine Art

8th & G Streets NW
Washington, D.C. 20560
202-357-1545
<u>Hours:</u> Daily 10-5:30 (except Dec. 25)

The Old U.S. Patent Office now is home to an exquisite collection of American art which is known as the National Museum of American Art. The collection spans the years and artistic styles popular throughout our history. With the largest collection in the country, the museum has more than 33,000 pieces.

The building that houses the American Art collection is also the home of the National Portrait Gallery. The building itself is a replica of the Parthenon. During the Civil War, it served as a hospital and morgue. Both Clara Barton and Walt Whitman cared for the wounded here.

With books reflecting the art collection, the museum shop sells the largest selection of books and videos of all the Smithsonian Museum shops. They also sell Revolutionary reproductions and contemporary American crafts, jewelry, children's toys, and many gift items.

The National Museum of American Art and the museum shop are wheelchair accessible.

National Museum of American History

American History   Constitution Ave. at 14th St. NW
                                      Washington, D.C. 20560
                                      202-357-1527
                                      Hours: Daily 10-5:30 (except Dec. 25)

One of the most popular Smithsonian Museums, The National Museum of American History, documents some of America's most treasured artifacts such as the actual Star-Spangled Banner that inspired Francis Scott Key to write our national anthem, Alexander Graham Bell's original experimental telephones, and gowns worn by the First Ladies. All exhibits are dedicated to capturing America's scientific, technological, and cultural heritage. Many exhibits are interactive videos.

The museum shop for The National Museum of American History sells more books than any of the other museum shops. You'll find books about exhibits, both permanent and temporary, in the shop as well as books about American history and everyday life. Also sold are Revolutionary War reproductions and contemporary American crafts, video tapes, jewelry, toys, and foods. They naturally have many books written for children.

The museum and shop are wheelchair accessible. This museum is one of the favorite tourist attractions in Washington. Once you see the precise Foucault pendulum, you won't soon forget it.

National Museum of Natural History

Natural History   10th St. & Constitution Ave. NW
                                      Washington, D.C. 20560
                                      202-357-1536
                                      Hours: Daily 10-5:30 (except Dec. 25)

When your children want to see dinosaur bones in Washington, take them to The National Museum of Natural History for a real treat. After oooh-ing and awww-ing at the dinosaurs, they'll be intrigued to see other exhibits.

The museum features exhibits depicting humankind's earliest moments on earth through the development of modern countries. You will see thousands of mammals, birds, amphibians, reptiles, insects, sea life, gems, rocks, and even meteorites. You'll want to see the legendary 45.5-carat Hope Diamond.

In the museum shop you can purchase museum books, ethnic crafts, jewelry, textile and ceramic reproductions, dinosaur toys, and many items guaranteed to allow you to enjoy your Washington, D.C. vacation for years to come.

The National Museum of Natural History, also a Smithsonian Museum, and the museum shop are wheelchair accessible. The museums welcome visitors from all over the world.

National Museum of Women in the Arts

Women artists

1250 New York Ave. NW
Washington, D.C. 20005
202-783-5000
800-222-7270
Hours: Mon.-Sat. 10-5; Sun. noon-5

Art created by women has consistently been under-represented in exhibitions and museum collections. The mission of The National Museum of Women in the Arts is to recognize the achievements of women artists from all times and from around the world through exhibitions, research, and preservation of that art.

The museum displays a permanent collection of art as well as special exhibits and extensive educational programs. Art at the museum does not just focus on drawing and painting. Other disciplines featured include composers, musicians, architects, poets, dancers, actors, landscape designers, choreographers, and playwrights. The museum has a state-of-the-art 200-seat auditorium to present the performing arts.

The museum shop abounds in books about women in the arts and the art they create. The titles stocked number 200-300 and continue to grow. About 75 titles on cassette tape are also sold. Other gift and momento items are sold.

Fortunately, the museum is accessible to visitors in wheelchairs and a limited number of wheelchairs are available. A cafe is located in the museum.

If Annie Liebowitz, Mary Cassat, and Hollywood's beauties are the only women artists you recognize, you must visit the museum to fully appreciate the contributions of women artists.

National Portrait Gallery Bookshop

Museum-Fine art

Eighth & G Streets, NW
Washington, D.C. 20560
202-357-1447
Hours: Daily 10-5:15 (except Dec. 25)

When you visit the National Portrait Gallery, you will look into the faces of people who have contributed to the development of our nation. You'll see portraits in the Hall of Presidents, Matthew Brady photographs, a Time magazine cover collection, and many works done by our premier artists including the famous portrait of Mary Cassatt by Edgar Degas. The National Portrait Gallery shares the Old Patent Office building with the National Museum of American Art.

At the museum shop you can purchase reproductions of the President's portraits that are popular decorations for elementary school rooms. You can also take home books about art and of the permanent collection and special exhibits. The museums and shops are wheelchair accessible.

National Shrine of the Immaculate Conception

Religious-Christian

4th & Michigan Ave. NE
Washington, D.C. 20017
202-526-8300
Hours: Daily 8:30-7

Every Catholic parish in America contributed funds to the building of the National Shrine of the Immaculate Conception. The sacraments are celebrated in the beautiful shrine daily.

A gift shop open everyday sells religious books about the Catholic faith, statues, rosaries, and religious plaques. The shop is located in the basement but is wheelchair accessible.

National Woman's Party Gift Shop

Women's Studies

Sewall-Belmont House
144 Constitution Ave. NE
Washington, D.C. 20002
202-546-3989
Hours: Tues.-Fri. 10-3;
Sat. & Sun. noon-4

Another of Washington's beautiful houses, the Sewall-Belmont House was the home of Alice Paul who founded the National Woman's Party in 1913. Alice wrote the original Equal Rights Amendments. The house has become a museum honoring American woman's political achievements and is also the home of the National Woman's Party.

The house, a quilt of many architectural styles, is not wheelchair accessible. Exhibits inside the house commemorate the suffragette movement and includes banners and memorabilia. Also on display are many pieces of artwork about and crafted by women.

The giftshop sells four books: 2 biographies, a history of the suffrage movement, and one about today's Equal Rights Amendment. They also sell a video tape documenting "How We Got the Vote."

National Zoological Park Bookstore

Zoology

3001 Connecticut Ave.
Washington, D.C. 20008
202-673-4967
FAX 202-673-4738
Hours: Daily 9-6 (except Dec. 25)

There are nearly 5,000 animals of 500 different species that live at the National Zoological Park but there are two residents that are the most famous: the two Giant Pandas. The zoo works internationally in an effort to preserve endangered species. It was established in 1889 to save an endangered species of the day: the American bison.

You'll find books about animals, their natural environments, and species preservation. Of course you'll find all sorts of momentos and fine gifts in a wide range of prices. The zoo has four giftshops: The Bookstore/Gallery, the Panda Gift Shop, the Mane Gift Shop, and the Seal Shop.

The zoo and shops are wheelchair accessible.

The Nature Company

Natural History   1323-25 Wisconsin Ave. NW
Washington, D.C. 20007
202-333-4100
Hours: Mon.-Wed. 10-9;
Thurs.-Sat. 10-10; Sun. noon-6

Dedicated to the preservation of the world around us and to the education of people about our environment, The Nature Company has developed an excellent chain of stores. Fortunately, the store has six branches in the Washington area.

The Nature Company proudly brings you top quality books and gifts in a store that is sure to intrigue you and your entire family. With nature sounds softly playing in place of piped-in music, the store offers research and reference books, children's books, and scholarly books discussing nature from minute insects to the vastness of outer space. As supplements to the books, the store sells telescopes, gyroscopes, globes, and charts.

With a special interest in children, The Nature Company sells many interactive toys and books that teach children about this fascinating world while they are having fun. Items for sale that are of interest to everyone include such things as agate bookends, coral reef T-shirts, lifesize inflatable penguins, raindrop earrings made of Brazilian Quartz, a 30-power magnifier that makes a grain of sand look like a Colorado boulder, a 3-D polar bear puzzle, a unisex field jacket, and so much more.

With main headquarters in Berkeley, California, The Nature Company has well over 75 stores across the nation and plan to expand abroad in 1993. You can become a member of The Nature Conservancy which is a non-profit organization dedicated to protecting endangered wildlife areas. In addition to receiving bi-monthly catalogs filled with items sold at The Nature Company stores, as a member of the Conservancy, you'll also receive a monthly magazine and information from your local chapter about preserves and activities in your area. A percentage of the funds from products sold at The Nature Company or through catalogs go directly to the Nature Conservancy.

Visit The Nature Company when you are looking for something different. All five stores in the Washington area are wheelchair accessible. The stores are a delight to visit and employees are extremely helpful and friendly.

The Nature Company

Natural History

Union Station
50 Massachusetts Ave.
Washington, D.C. 20002
202-842-3700
Hours: Mon.-Sat. 10-9; Sun. noon-6

The Nature Company is a wonderful place to catch your breath when the city is just too much to take. Selling books, gifts, clothing, and family projects all focusing on our world, The Nature Company has five locations in the Washington area. This branch is located inside Union Station.

For a more complete description, please refer to the write-up for the Wisconsin Ave branch in Washington, D.C.

Newman Bookstore

Religion-Christian

3329 Eighth St. NE
Washington, D.C. 20017
202-526-1036
FAX 202-526-6725
Hours: Mon., Wed., Fri. 9-5;
Tues., Thurs. 9-6; Sat. 10-4

The Newman Bookstore of Washington, a Paulist Press Book Center, sells over 12,500 titles of books in the areas of theology and religious studies with an emphasis on academic and specialized books. They have large selections of titles in women's studies, African-American studies, Judaica, and ancient Christian writers. They also sell critical editions of biblical texts in Hebrew, Greek, and Latin.

While Roman Catholic in orientation, Newman Bookstore is ecumenical in its selection of titles including studies in non-Christian religions, spirituality, prayer, psychology, reference, and recovery. They also feature a new Spanish-language section, greeting cards, and selected periodicals.

Newman Bookstore is wheelchair accessible through a side entrance. A catalog of select books is available. You may prefer to telephone or FAX orders. The staff orders in-print books which are not stocked in the store. Books can be shipped world-wide. A special discount program is available for those customers paying by cash or personal check.

As one of the largest theological bookstores on the East Coast, Newman Bookstore is ready and able to meet your needs in religious studies.

Newman Gallery & Custom Framing

Political Cartoons

513 11th Street SE
Washington, D.C. 20003
202-544-7577
Hours: Tues.-Sat. 10-6

Newman Gallery and Custom Framing sells only one book but what a terrific book. It's a collection of political cartoons from 1988-1992 titled KalToons by Kevin Kallaugher.

The small shop is up a flight of stairs and not wheelchair accessible.

News World

News & Magazines

1001 Connecticut Ave.
Washington, D.C. 20036
202-872-0190
Hours: Mon.-Fri. 7am-8:30pm;
Sat. & Sun. 7-7

Athough News World primarily sells magazines and newspapers from all over the world, they also sell about 120 titles of paperbacks. Since the store is not large, it can be a tight squeeze for those in wheelchairs or pushing strollers, but employees will retrieve materials you request.

The busy News World is open twelve hours or more everyday.

Newsroom

News & Magazines

1753 Connecticut Ave. NW
Washington, D.C. 20009
202-332-1489
Hours: Mon.-Fri. 7am-10pm;
Sat. 7am-11pm; Sun. 7am-9pm

Open from 12 to 16 hours everyday, Newsroom is one of the busiest newsstands in Washington. In addition to international and domestic newspapers and magazines, Newsroom also sells Washington regional guide books and postcards along with a few bestselling paperbacks.

Located on the second floor of the Newsroom is the International Language Center, which sells books to assist in learning a foreign language. For a description of the center, see the write-up for the International Language Center in this book.

Newsroom is surprisingly wheelchair accessible in spite of the volume of items sold here. When you're looking for the latest word from around the world, get in touch with Newsroom.

The Octagon Museum

Historical Landmark

1799 New York Ave. NW
Washington, D.C. 20006
202-638-3105
Hours: Tues.-Fri. 10-4;
Sat. & Sun. noon-4

In 1970, The Octagon was opened as a museum for architecture and design, under the auspices of The American Architectural Foundation. The Octagon Museum Bookstop features books and exhibition catalogs about the museum, Washington's architectural and social history, and architectural restoration. The shop will be expanded in 1994. For wheelchair access, call ahead to make arrangements.

The Old Forest Bookshop

Used-General

3145 Dumbarton St. NW
Washington, D.C. 20007
202-965-3842
Hours: Tues.-Sat. 11-7;
Mon. & Sun. noon-6

In the heart of historic Georgetown in a quaint townhouse built in the 1830's, The Old Forest Bookshop has settled into their home and welcomes you with open doors.

The used bookstore specializes in literature, history, and art but carries many general interest books. Their stock includes approximately 10,000 titles.

"We are more interested in the intrinsic value (content) of books than collectability," says owner Derrick Hsu.

Open everyday, The Old Forest Bookshop has two steps to enter. Be sure to plan to browse in the area for an afternoon--there are eight other secondhand shops within walking distance.

The Old Print Gallery

Antiquarian-General

1220 31st St. NW
Washington, D.C. 20007
202-965-1818
Hours: Mon.-Sat. 10-5:30

Although The Old Print Gallery doesn't sell books, they present the public with a fascinating collection of antiquarian maps and prints that are sure to delight book lovers. Owners Judith Blakely and James von Ruster are experts in the field and perform appraisals on your treasured prints and maps. They also can work miracles in repairing prints and maps.

The prints in their collection covers architecture, history, militaria, nature, nautical, ornithology, sports, and zoology. Call them with subjects you would like and they may assist in finding the pieces.

A catalog is published four times per year and they accept telephone and mail orders. The shop, modern and well-lit, has one step at the entrance. Open shelving makes browsing a pleasure.

Book lovers certainly won't want to miss The Old Print Gallery.

Olsson's Books & Records

General
                                        Dupont Circle
                                        1307 19th Street NW
                                        Washington, D.C. 20036
                                        202-785-1133
                                        Hours: Mon.-Sat. 10-10; Sun. noon-6

When you say "bookstore" to a Washingtonian, they'll instinctively say "Olsson's."

Each store in the 5-store chain "has its own personality and unique inventory," said Parker Orr, manager of the Olsson's in Dupont Circle. Each store makes its own buying decisions to make them individually oriented to the surrounding community.

Parker also notes that because each store is computerized, they can tap into the stock of the other stores. They usually have the book you are looking for at one of their locations and can quickly get the book for you.

Established in 1972, Olsson's Books & Records may have to change their name to Olsson's Books & CD's or Olsson's Books & Music. Many of the Olsson's stores utilize half their floor space for books and the other half for music. Many branches also sell audio books, greeting cards, and calendars.

Service is important to Olsson's employees. They try their best to help customers in the store or by placing special orders. The store often sponsors author autographing sessions and publishes a newsletter every other month. Olsson's also offers a card that pre-authorizes your personal checks so that you can hurry your purchases through the check-out line.

This book carries brief descriptions of the each Olsson's Books & Records. For specifics about the other stores, please see each branch's write-up.

The Olsson's Books & Records located in Dupont Circle is split half-and-half between books and records. About one-fourth of the store is up two steps which makes it inaccessible to wheelchair clients. Employees are quick to offer assistance.

Olsson's Books & Records

General
1239 Wisconsin Ave. NW
Washington, D.C. 20007
202-338-9544
FAX 202-342-2342
Hours: Mon.-Thurs. 10am-10:45pm;
Fri. & Sat. 10am-midnight;
Sun. noon-7

Another of the Olsson's Books & Records stores, this Georgetown location is the largest of the five stores in the chain. Because Georgetown retains its "Old World" flavor, many businesses are not wheelchair accessible. The Olsson's here has one large step at the entrance. The doors are narrow. The second floor is not accessible to wheelchair and stroller users.

As mentioned in the longer description of Olsson's Books & Records, employees are very helpful. See the main write-up for the Dupont Circle store.

Olsson's Books & Records

General
Metro Center
1200 F Street NW
Washington, D.C. 20041
202-347-3686
Hours: Mon.-Sat. 10-7; Sun. noon-6

This branch of the local 5-chain general interest bookstore is wheelchair accessible. Olsson's Books & Records is a popular bookstore in the Washington area.

For more details see the write-up for the Dupont Circle store.

Oscar Shapiro

Antiquarian-Music
3726 Connecticut Ave. NW
Washington, D.C. 20008
202-244-4446
Hours: Mail order only

"Music exists—not on canvas nor yet on the staff—only in motion. The good listener will hear it as the present prolonged," Ned Rorem said in "Music from Inside Out" in 1967.

Oscar Shapiro brings you music for the violin that will help you to prolong the present. He sells out-of-print, new, and rare books. He also sells lithography and autographed manuscripts.

Business is conducted by correspondence only. A catalog is published yearly. He maintains thousands of books for and about the violin and music for that finest of instruments.

The Phillips Collection Giftshop

Museum-Fine Art   1600 21st St. NW
                                    Washington, D.C. 20009
                                    202-387-2151
                                    FAX 202-387-2436
                                    Hours: Mon.-Sat. 10-5; Sun. noon-7

Maintaining the private home atmosphere which can be traced to its beginning, the Phillips Collection stems from the modern art collection of Duncan and Marjorie Phillips. They opened their 4-story brownstone home to the public in 1921.

Since then, thousands of visitors have enjoyed viewing the collection, the special exhibits, and the weekly concert. Gallery talks, programs for adults and school groups, self-guided tours, and even family workshops are coordinated by the educational office.

The shop at the Phillips Collection is open through a street entrance or from within the museum. There you will find books highlighting the art from the 20th century American and French impressionism, cubism, and art genres of today, along with artist biographies, and art instruction books. Many other gifts are also sold. Mail orders are accepted.

The Phillips Collection is open everyday and completely wheelchair accessible. A cafe serves luncheons and light fare. To receive a copy of the news and events, contact them.

With the many museums to visit in Washington, the Phillips Collection ranks with the best.

Pierce Mill, Rock Creek Park Shop

Americana   5000 Glover Rd. NW
                                    Washington, D.C. 20015
                                    202-426-6908
                                    Hours: Wed.-Sun. 10-4

Step back into the history of the late 1700's and 1800's and take a little piece home with you today. Pierce Mill in Rock Creek Park is one of the oldest working mills in the country. After seeing how gravity and water runs the entire mill process, you can purchase and bring the stone-ground grains home with you.

Before you leave the site, you must visit the quaint tea shop which serves "Harding waffles." Inside the working flour mill, you'll find the bookshop. Although they sell a small number of books, they are likely to be unique to the mill. Topics include the how-to's of flour milling, architecture of mills, and cooking with stone ground flour from the 18th and 19th centuries.

Pierce Mill has operated on and off through the years but since 1890 Congress has directed that Rock Creek's wild valley be set aside to preserve wildlife and the natural scenery. Included in the directive was the Pierce Mill. Today it operates under the auspices of the Parks & History Association.

The mill is in operation Wednesday through Sunday throughout the year but, unfortunately, is not wheelchair accessible.

Pierce Mill offers grinding demonstrations and interpretive programs that will bring a wealth of knowledge about history to students, young and old.

Politics & Prose Bookstore

Fiction & Psychology   5015 Connecticut Ave.
                                  Washington, D.C. 20008
                                  202-364-1919
                                  800-722-0790
                                  FAX 202-966-7532
                                  Hours: Sun.-Thurs. 9-10;
                                  Fri. & Sat. 9-midnight

After visiting Politics & Prose Bookstore, you'll wish they were located in your neighborhood. In addition to being a terrific general interest bookstore that offers many books not found in other stores, Politics & Prose is a true get-away-from-it-all meeting place complete with a coffee/luncheon room.

The comfortable store is located on two floors and has approximately 30,000 titles in stock. The main floor, which faces Connecticut Avenue, stocks books featuring politics, justice, media, law, foreign relations, international business, literature, fiction, poetry, biography, and essay collections. Downstairs you'll find books featuring travel, coffee-table artistic books, and children's books as well as the cafe. Many author autographed books are available.

In addition to the in-store staircase, the downstairs portion of the store is also accessible through the back of the store where there is parking available. Wheelchair users, however, either can shop on one level or the other or go around the block to reach the other entrance. Friendly employees are happy to do the running and retrieving of books for those not able to use the stairs.

The owners of Politics & Prose are committed to bringing quality events to the community. They support authors visiting the store to autograph and celebrate their books which often includes discussions or readings. Many authors, such as Joyce Carol Oates, are world-renowned.

Knowing that readers enjoy discussing books, Politics & Prose sponsors a book group that meets every month. The Coffeehouse Poetry Series has become a successful venture for both the bookstore and it's clients. A newsletter and announcements on a bulletin board inform customers of the events. Employees are happy to assist you with special ordering books and will gift wrap your purchases.

The stock at Politics & Prose includes audio books, books with large type, video tapes, T-shirts, posters, games, stationery, children's toys, and calendars.

While here, you must visit the cafe. A blackboard menu describes the daily gourmet sandwich and soup specials and you won't be able to resist the bakery treats. They also have a refrigerator filled with a variety of juices and waters. With the feel of a writer's haven, the cafe has an assortment of tables and chairs, newspapers, photographs (which are for sale) hanging on the walls, and pots of herbs and flowers.

Clients have been enjoying Politics & Prose Bookstore since 1984. You are a welcomed friend here.

The President's Box Bookshop

Antiquarian-History

PO Box 1255
Washington, D.C. 20013
703-998-7390
Hours: Mail order only

"An effort to preserve the literature of the 'dark side' of American history—the assassination of our nation's Presidents," is how the 40-page catalog from The President's Box Bookshop describes its purpose.

A random sampling of topics include a possible conspiracy between Booth and Bob Lincoln in Lincoln's assassination; the life and trial of the man who assassinated President James Garfield; the attempted assassinations of Teddy Roosevelt and Ronald Reagan; the assassinations of Dr. Martin Luther King, Jr., and Senator Robert F. Kennedy; Secret Service protection of Presidents; and general interest crime events and espionage titles. Perhaps one of the more intriguing titles carries the subtitle "Mad Prophets, Crackpots, Kooks and True Visionaries."

One of the few experts in his field, David Lovett, owner of the bookstore, has been cited by researchers writing books, particularly about President John Kennedy's assassination.

Twice yearly a catalog is published but David notes his stock constantly fluctuates. All books sold are quality out-of-print titles. Also for sale are manuscripts, autographs, and selected ephemera.

Pursell's Church Supply, Inc.

Religion-Christian

401 M Street NW
Washington, D.C. 20024
202-484-9563
Hours: Mon.-Fri. 10-6; Sat. 10-2

Perhaps one of the oldest bookstores in Washington, D.C., Pursell's Church Supply Inc. was established in 1869. A Christian bookstore, they carry approximately 1,500 titles of books some of which are printed in large type. They also sell audio books, magazines, calendars, greeting cards, T-shirts, games and children's toys.

At times, authors visit the store for autographing sessions. Pursell's Church Supply does place special orders for books, book imprinting, and gift wrapping. Charge accounts make shopping here easy. For the community, Pursell's Church Supply does have a bulletin board filled with announcements.

Physically, the store is completely wheelchair and stroller accessible. Everyone is welcome to browse and to find that perfect gift or book.

Pyramid Bookstore

General

2849 Georgia Ave. NW
Washington, D.C. 20001
202-328-0190
202-265-6921
Hours: Daily 11-7

Pyramid Books has three bookstores in the Washington area specializing in books by and about people of African descent. Owner and founder of Pyramid Books, Hodari Abdul-Ali says that there has been a recent surge in the volume of African-American literature. He stocks Pyramid with approximately 2,000 titles which continues to grow.

Children's books have a special place within Pyramid Books. The store also sells audio and video tapes. Special orders are welcomed and mail orders can be placed by telephone using their catalog. Authors visit the store to discuss and autograph their books.

A Howard University graduate, Hodari was the first to open a bookstore near the university in 1981. The other two locations of Pyramid Books are in Hechinger Mall and Hyattsville, MD.

All branches of Pyramid Books are open everyday. This branch, on Georgia Avenue, is not wheelchair accessible and is located on the third floor. The other two locations are wheelchair accessible.

Whichever Pyramid Books you choose to visit, you are sure to find a king's treasure of books to take home.

Pyramid Bookstore

General

Hechinger Mall
1548 Benning Rd. NE
Washington, D.C. 20002
202-396-1100
Hours: Mon.-Sat. 10-9; Sun. noon-5

With its grand opening on the anniversary of the birth of Malcolm X on May, 19, 1990, this third branch of Pyramid Books is located in Hechinger Mall and is wheelchair accessible.

Please refer to the description for the Georgia Street store (above) for a complete description of Pyramid Books.

Rainbow Records and Books

General

401 M St. SW
Washington, D.C. 20042
202-646-1120
Hours: Mon.-Sat. 10-7:30;
Sun. 10-5:30

Rainbow Records and Books sells new and a few out-of-print books of general interest. A majority of the business conducted at Rainbow Records and Books involves records. The store is wheelchair accessible.

The Rampant Lion

Silver reference books

PO Box 5887
Washington, D.C. 20016
202-364-2431
Hours: Telephone & Mail order only

Gwendolyn Kelso is an expert on items made of silver (silverware, coffee and tea pots, trays, etc.) and has a business selling silver. She also sells reference books about silver for appraisers and collectors. Her books are available by mail order.

Rand McNally—The Map & Travel Store

Travel & Cartography

1201 Connecticut Ave. NW
Washington, D.C. 20036
202-223-6751
Hours: Mon.-Fri. 9-6:30;
Thurs. until 7:30; Sat. 10-6

The name Rand McNally is almost synonymous with maps. With all of the changes of the world, it's good to know that Rand McNally cartographers are keeping up with all the changes.

With three locations in Washington and the suburbs, Rand McNally—The Map and Travel Store is keeping everyone up-to-date. In addition to the many different sorts of maps they sell, they also offer globes, educational tools, travel guides and assorted gifts with the earth motif. You can purchase jackets with maps of the world imprinted on the cloth, key chains that are globes, and much more. Children easily learn about this world through games and puzzles. For computer whizzes, Rand McNally sells software.

The store often sponsors author autographing sessions and hosts elementary school children participating in a "Kid's Day" program.

Manager Katrina Wulfekuhler of the Washington store recognizes the value of employees in the store who hale from all over the world when she says, "It's important to have knowledgeable staff who have lived abroad and speak many languages because we are in such an international market."

All three Rand McNally stores are wheelchair accessible. They also publish a catalog that focuses on their many gifts.

You won't believe just how many different sorts of maps that are available. You can buy everything from city street maps to satellite photos of the Earth.

Reiter's Scientific & Professional Books

Science & Professional

2021 K Street NW
Washington, D.C. 20006
202-223-3327
800-537-4314
FAX 202-296-9103
Hours: Mon.-Fri. 9-7:30;
Sat. 9:30-6; Sun. noon-5

Reiter's caters primarily to the book needs of college and university students and professors, medical students, nurses and doctors, computer scientists, engineers, and business professionals. In addition, Reiter's has large sections devoted to philosophy, psychology, the history of science, writing and journalism, chess (and other games), dictionaries (English and foreign language), and both general and specialized reference books covering most scientific, medical, technical, social science, and business fields. Special orders are welcome, even for books falling outside of Reiter's areas of specialization. National and international shipping is available. Internet users can contact Reiter's via e-mail: books@reiters.com.

Reiter's also offers scientific and technical magazines and academic journals, posters, games, calendars, and gift certificates. Reiter's publishes a monthly newsletter and an annual store catalog. Author appearances and special publisher sales occur throughout the year. The store is wheelchair accessible.

Established in 1936, Reiter's Scientific and Professional Books serves book lovers from the neighborhood, the region, the nation, and the world.

Renwick Gallery

American crafts

17th & Pennsylvania Ave. NW
Washington, D.C. 20560
202-357-1445
Hours: Daily 10-5:30 (except Dec. 25)

The building that is home to the Renwick Gallery was completed in 1874 and was the site of Washington's first private art museum. The Renwick Gallery is a department of the National Museum of American Art and displays ever-changing exhibits of American crafts.

The museum shop brings you, naturally, books about art, design, and architecture. They also sell handmade American crafts, jewelry, and gifts.

Like all of the Smithsonian Museums, the Renwick Gallery and shop are wheelchair accessible, open everyday (except Dec. 25), and free.

Reprint Bookstore

General   456 L'Enfant Plaza SW
                                                Washington, D.C. 20024
                                                202-554-5070
                                                <u>Hours:</u> Mon.-Fri. 9-6

In 1791, Pierre L'Enfant described to George Washington a design for "the Capital of a powerful Empire." His plan was followed and a hotel and plaza was named for him. Inside that plaza is one of the busiest and most popular bookstore in Washington.

While L'Enfant Plaza houses shops whose specialties range from take-out lunches to high fashion clothing, you're sure to hear more than one person in the halls call to a friend, "I'll meet you at Reprint Book Shop," or "I'm going to Reprint."

A general interest bookshop, Reprint is small but incredibly well stocked. In additional to the traditional bestsellers, they have large selections of African-American, politics, journalism, travel, computers, and children's books. Their Washington, D.C., books and maps selections are terrific. They have a special group of Native American and Old West titles printed by the University of Oklahoma press.

They also sell books-on-cassette-tape which employee Elizabeth Binkama says "is an integral part of bookselling today." She also reports that the staff of Reprint Book Shop are "a family" although no one is actually related to each other. Employees enjoy their work and the upbeat atmosphere at the bookshop.

One employee of twenty years, Michael Sullivan, bought Reprint in 1989 from Jack Cooper. Born in 1896, Jack still stops by the store "to make sure we're still running it right," said Elizabeth.

Authors often appear at Reprint to sign books during lunch-times. The store also features specific departments and offer books in those categories at a special discount for a month. A monthly newsletter of announcements is published.

Reprint Book Shop is only open weekdays because it does not have a street entrance. Street level signs mark the portal. The plaza is surrounded by government offices and the L'Enfant Hotel and completely wheelchair accessible.

Knowledgeable employees help you locate books and will place special orders on books in print. They also will gift wrap books.

After purchasing the books of your choice, you'll be able to immediately dig into them while relaxing at the espresso bar next door.

Revolution Books

Political Philosophy

P.O. Box 21511
Washington, D.C. 20009
202-265-1969
Hours: Call ahead; not open at time
of printing

When you call Revolution Books, an answering machine tells you that they are a revolution "in exile." Currently closed, Revolution Books then informs you how you can donate funds to re-open the store.

Revolution Books is one of a dozen bookstores of the Revolutionary Communist Party USA. They have bookstores in major cities across the country.

The theme of the store is "Mao more than ever." Books sold include works by Marx, Lenin, Stalin and Mao Tse-tung.

If the store does reopen in the same location, people in wheelchairs won't be able to reach the second floor store but if you call, I'm sure they will find a way to get the books in your hands.

With the break-up of the USSR, one may think that communism is dead. Not so, according to Revolution Books whose newspaper claimed, "Phony Communism is Dead, Long Live Real Communism."

Rock Creek Bookshop

Used-Militaria

1214 Wisconsin Ave. NW
PO Box 25692
Washington, D.C. 20007
202-342-8046
Hours: Most afternoons--call ahead

Peter Scaborg, owner of Rock Creek Bookshop, offers a fine collection of between 12-15,000 volumes of used books. Some books are of antiquarian quality. The specialties of the store include history, militaria, philosophy, and religion.

Some authors who write books about the Civil War, military history, or military theory have visited the store to discuss and sign their books.

Rock Creek Bookshop is located on the second and third floors of a century old building. Peter has attempted to make the building accessible to wheelchairs but all efforts have failed. He is open to suggestions.

Open most afternoons, call Peter before travelling to the bookshop. If your interests lie within Peter's specialties, make it a point to visit Rock Creek Bookshop.

Rock Creek Park Nature Center Bookshop

Nature   5200 Glover Rd. NW
                                      Rock Creek Park
                                      Washington, D.C. 20015
                                      202-472-3083
                                      Hours: Wed.-Sun. 9-5

Given a million-dollar endowment in 1890 for preservation of animal and wildlife, Rock Creek Park is an oasis in the Georgetown area where nature lovers convene. The Park once was home to Algonquin Indians, bear, elk, and bison. Today the park has winding trails of wildflowers perfect for bird and animal watchers to sight wildlife.

Near the trails of Rock Creek Park are the National Zoo and Old Pierce Mill. The hilly terrain is a challenge for runners and walkers. The park has bicycle routes, a public golf course, picnic areas, playgrounds, tennis courts, and even a horse center where you can ride or take riding lessons. They also offer riding lessons for the disabled.

Filled with interesting exhibits including nature films, planetarium shows, a glass enclosed working beehive, and wild animal exhibits, The Rock Creek Nature Center is the place to start when orienting yourself to the park. This is also a place to meet for a guided hike of the area.

Inside the Rock Creek Nature Center, book lovers will find approximately 200 titles of environmental, nature, science, and children's books. Attractive and educational posters are also available. Many trails and the Nature Center are wheelchair accessible. Please note that the bookshop is open Wednesday through Sunday.

Whether you live nearby or must drive for miles to reach the Rock Creek Park, you'll be happy that you visited.

Rock Uniform & Christian Bookstore

Religious-Christian   1104 H Street NE
                                      Washington, D.C. 20002
                                      202-398-3333
                                      Hours: Mon.-Sat. 10-6;
                                      Wed. closed 5pm

Associated with Solid Rock Full Gospel Baptist Church, Rock Uniform & Christian Bookstore supplies the church, as well as other churches and the public, with Christian books, Bibles, personalized placques, music, children's books, and even chairs. They do place special orders and will mail orders.

Nehemiah Rhinehart, Sr., established the store in 1979. Whether you are a member of the church or not, everyone is invited to shop at Rock Uniform & Christian Bookstore.

Rosey Cross

Metaphysical

3061 M St. NW
Washington, D.C. 20007
202-333-7420
Hours: Mon.-Thurs. 11-11;
Fri., Sat. 11-midnight; Sun. noon-9

Upbeat, eclectic, and esoteric is how to describe the bookstore, Rosey Cross.

With hundreds of titles, Rosey Cross specializes in metaphysical books especially Western mystery tradition, hermetic mystery, tarot, meditation, alchemy, magic, herbalism, and related material. Some books are available on audio tape.

Books aren't the only items you can buy at Rosey Cross. Included are: jewelry, minerals, incense, candles, essential oils, gift items, T-shirts, posters, stationery, greeting cards, and calendars.

Rosey Cross is wheelchair and stroller accessible. The hours kept at Rosey Cross are sure to fit into everyone's schedule; most evenings they're open until 11 pm or midnight.

When you're ready to open your mind to ideas different from the main stream, you must visit Rosey Cross.

Samuel Yudkin & Associates

Used-General

Woodner, 3636 16th St. NW
Room A 232
Washington, D.C. 20010
202-232-6249
FAX 202-234-0786
Hours: Mon.-Fri. 10-6

On television, we have all seen the auction where characters scratching their nose or straightening their collars have inadvertently placed bids on outrageous items. At Samuel Yudkin & Associates you can place bids and purchase books and prints by telephone or mail order. Their catalog describes just how to do this. They also sell merchandise by auction and you can call them for auction dates.

Books are new, used, and antiquarian quality in a broad range of topics. Samuel Yudkin & Associates also sell maps, prints, and first editions. They are able to conduct searches and obtain books you want. Of course, they do appraisals.

The store has two floors but those using wheelchairs may prefer to shop by mail. They usually maintain a stock of 20,000 books.

In business since 1970, Samuel Yudkin & Associates have created an interesting book business and one every book lover should contact.

Scavengers of Georgetown

Antiquarian-General   PO Box 3733
Washington, D.C. 20007
202-972-7661
<u>Hours:</u> Telephone & Mail order only

Literature has painted pictures of beachcombers searching the sand with seagulls flying overhead and ragged men sifting through the garbage looking for discarded treasures but when your hunt involves a quest for antiquarian books, what are you called? Why, an educated scavenger, of course.

Your hunt has been made easier with a business named Scavengers of Georgetown. Dana and Garry McConnell do the hunting for antiquarian books about sports and politics. You reap the benefits by a mere telephone call or letter mailed to them. They're happy to part with books in their 300-400 title collection.

The McConnells attend various antique markets in the Mid-Atlantic but also travel to the Southeast and Midwest with their books. Experts in their field, they conduct appraisals on books you have in your collection.

Call Scavengers of Georgetown to discuss the books you are searching for and they're pleased to assist you.

Second Story Books & Antiques

Used-General   Dupont Circle
2000 P Street NW
Washington, D.C. 20036
202-659-8884
FAX 301-770-9544
<u>Hours:</u> Daily 10-10

A smaller branch of Second Story Books & Antiques is located in busy Washington, D.C. proper. This store carries approximately 100,000 titles of used and antiquarian books. It's hard to believe that a store with that many titles is one of the smallest of their three locations. The largest store is located in Rockville and its stock can be easily accessed from the other two stores.

Because the store abounds in books, the shelves can't hold all of the stock and must be piled on the floor. Wheelchair using shoppers find that you can just squeak by the stacks. Off street parking and mass transit are nearby. Special services of searching and placing special orders, conducting appraisals, and repairing books are available here.

Whatever topic you crave, Second Story Books & Antiques is sure to have a book, or many books, in that category.

Ship's Store

Nautical/Maritime

701 Pennsylvania Ave. NW Suite 123
Washington, D.C. 20004
202-737-2300 x731
800-821-8892 x731
FAX 202-737-2308
Hours: Call-hours changed Jan. 1994

Our nation's capitol is the site of many memorials to those who have served our country's armed forces. Flanked by two ship's masts, a bronze relief, and a sculpture wall, the United States Navy Memorial & Visitor Center is found near the National Archives.

The west pool of flowing waters in front of the memorial has been salted by the Seven Seas and the east pool contains water from the Great Lakes. The Memorial includes sculptures, interactive videos, a glass Wave Wall displaying U.S. ships throughout history, and a film in the Memorial's theater. The famous *Lone Sailor* sculpture stands watch on the granite map on the Plaza.

The Navy Memorial and the Ship's Store in The Visitor's Center are all wheelchair accessible. Among the books sold in the store are histories, biographies, children's books, and books about ships and aircraft. You will also be able to purchase clothing with Navy emblems, Navy Memorial souvenirs, and personalized gifts. A catalog is available.

The Ship's Store is the only shop of its kind in Washington and sure to please those associated with the Navy or lovers of the sea.

Sidney Kramer Books, Inc.

History/Economics/Intl.

1825 I (Eye) St. NW
Washington, D.C. 20006
202-293-2685
800-423-2665
FAX 301-881-1930
Hours: Mon.-Fri. 9-6:30; Sun. 10-5

Established in 1946, Sidney Kramer Books, Inc. is now owned by William J. Kramer. The store has approximately 15,000 titles specializing in economics, history, and international affairs. Economics is such a strong department for the store, they print a listing of forthcoming books in International Economics, including the prices, authors, and dates when the books will be available. They also publish a military history mail order catalog. Other popular departments not usually found at other bookstores are Intelligence, Terrorism, and Espionage.

If you are not interested in those titles, have no fear. The store stocks plenty of titles of general interest including children's books and travel guides. Also for sale are the popular audio books and calendars.

Special orders and maintaining institutional charge accounts are two of the fine services of Sidney Kramer Books, Inc. The bookstore also sponsors author autographing sessions, ships worldwide, and prepares custom book lists. The staff is extremely knowledgeable and helpful.

The store is split into two levels. The upper level is wheelchair accessible from I (Eye) Street. The lower level is wheelchair accessible from the back door which opens onto International Square. Many customers place orders by telephone or mail order.

Sidney Kramer Books is three distinct divisions serving the retail, library, and direct mail markets. Taken together, the three divisions offer a comprehensive book-acquisition service for individuals, institutional libraries and governmental agencies here and around the world.

Supplying books that people want for almost the past fifty years, Sidney Kramer Books, Inc. is a fine, respected bookstore.

Sullivan's Toy Store

Children's books

3412 Wisconsin Ave. NW
Washington, D.C. 20015
202-362-1343
Hours: Mon.-Fri. 10-6; Thurs. until 8;
Sat. 10-5:30; Sun. noon-4

Family owned for 40 years, Sullivan's Toy Store also sells both hardback and paperback books for children through high school age. Accessories such as dictionaries and atlases are also available.

Wheelchair users can enter the front door but may not be able to peruse the crowded toy store. Strollers fare much better. However, employees are happy to help clients in wheelchairs by retrieving items.

SuperCrown

General

11 Dupont Circle, N.W.
Washington, D.C. 20036
202-319-1374
Hours: Sun.-Thurs. 10-midnight;
Fri. & Sat. 10 am-2am

Pass the crown because a whole new breed of Crown Books must be coronated. Super Crown in Dupont Circle is a beautiful, calm, comfortable place to shop for books in a chaotic section of Washington.

Soft music plays in the carpeted bookstore where you shop among the attractively marked bookshelves and then relax and read your purchases in their Espresso Bar. In addition to the typical categories found in general interest bookstores, this Super Crown has a good selection of books under the headings African-American and Gay and Lesbian. Their art book department is a particularly outstanding collection.

You may forget you are in a SuperCrown when you shop here but you'll happily remember when you are checking out. The same discounts apply at this store just like all of the other Crown Books in the area. (For details, see the description of the M Street Crown Books.)

The Dupont Circle SuperCrown also recognizes that readers enjoy meeting authors. They have a gorgeous desk in a prominent place in the store and often sponsor authors to visit to autograph their latest works.

People using wheelchairs—rejoice. From the outside, the store does not look accessible because you must descend a few steps to enter the store. But, unlike many stores that have alternate entrances for those people with wheelchairs, signs direct you around the corner where you can enter an office building lobby where a wheelchair lift is available. You then proceed through the small lobby to a marked door where you ring a doorbell. Employees promptly open the door for you.

By far, this is the nicest Crown Books I have yet visited. You will also, no doubt, be impressed.

SuperCrown

General   1275 K Street NW
                                       Washington, D.C. 20005
                                       202-289-7170
                                       Hours: Mon.-Fri. 9-7;
                                       Sat. 10-6; Sun. 11-5

Please refer to the write-up for the M Street Crown Books and the Dupont Circle SuperCrown for a description of the discounts and services offered at Crown Books.

Supreme Court Giftshop

Law & Judicial System   1 First St. NE
                                       Washington, D.C. 20543
                                       202-554-8300
                                       FAX 202-547-7730
                                       Hours: Mon.-Fri. 9:30-4:25

When you're on a book-buying spree, don't pass by The Supreme Court. The gift shop carries a wonderful selection of approximately 70-100 titles focusing on law, the history of the Supreme Court, and biographies about many of the Supreme Court Justices. The gift shop stocks books written by justices and about specific Supreme Court cases. Lawyers will delight in the beautifully bound books appropriate for their offices. Children will learn about this branch of our government through coloring books and workbooks.

Other memorabilia for sale includes framed photographs, colored sketches, jewelry, and desk items. They also sell many Washington, D.C. tour books.

The gift shop at the Supreme Court clearly sells titles you won't be able to find in other bookstores. Be sure to browse here.

Sutton Place Gourmet Inc.

Cooking   3201 New Mexico Ave. NW
                                         Washington, D.C. 20016
                                         202-363-5800
                                         <u>Hours:</u> Mon.-Sat. 9-9; Sun. 9-8

        Sutton Place Gourmet on New Mexico Avenue, NW, is open everyday except Christmas. On that holiday, you'll have to plan ahead to get all the food and cookbooks that you'll need in order to prepare a feast. With more than one hundred titles of cookbooks and reference books, Sutton Place Gourmet has just the right book for you whether you are a supreme chef or a first-time fryer.
        The main focus of the store is selling food and with 20,000 square feet of selling space they carry a vast array of foods. It is a marvelous place for gourmets and plain-old-cooks to shop.
        This branch of the four stores in the area is wheelchair accessible.

Sutton Place Gourmet Inc.

Cooking   4872 Massachusetts Ave.
                                         Washington, D.C. 20016
                                         202-966-1740
                                         <u>Hours:</u> Daily 8-8

        This branch of the four Sutton Place Gourmet stores is more like a little express shop of gourmet foods with just a few cookbooks. The smallest of the four branches in the Washington area, the store is wheelchair accessible.

Taj Book Service

African-American   737 Rock Creek Church Rd. NW
                                         Washington, D.C. 20010
                                         202-722-0701
                                         800-223-8250
                                         <u>Hours:</u> Mail order and appt. only

        Timothy A. Jones won't soon forget the name of his book business; it's an acronym of his name, TAJ. Even his toll free number is easy to remember; it's 800-223-TAJ-0. You won't soon forget shopping for used books with TAJ Book Service.
        Describing the books he sells as "eclectic," Tim specializes in college textbooks published by the Negro College Press and books about gambling. He also sells 78rpm, 45rpm, and 33rpm records and videos featuring black topics. Tim is interested in purchasing books, textbooks, CD's, used CD's and records.

Washington, D.C.

In business since 1982, Taj Book Service is conducted by mail
and telephone order and appointment only. Tim does search for books
requested by clients.

Tempo Bookstore

Language Arts   4105 Wisconsin Ave. NW
                                           Washington, D.C. 20016
                                           202-363-6683
                                           FAX 202-363-6686
                                           Hours: Mon.-Sat. 10-7

As our world becomes "smaller," people need to communicate to
others for business and vacation purposes. Eugene W. Lesmez and
Betulia Sanchez established Tempo Bookstore offering new and used
books for learning foreign languages or learning English as a Second
Language. To accompany the books, they also offer language-learning
audio and video tapes. Another specialty: books about operating small
and home-based businesses.

Betulia describes Tempo Bookstore as being a "supermarket" of
books in the three specialties. If they don't have a book that you need,
Eugene will conduct searches and place special orders.

Tempo Bookstore occupies 600 square feet; it is not wheelchair
accessible. Telephone and mail orders are accepted. The bookstore is on
several Metro buslines and close to a Metro Station. Off-street parking is
nearby.

Whatever language you want to add to your repertoire, contact
Tempo Bookstore to start you on the right path.

Textile Museum Shop

Museum-Art   2320 St. NW
                                           Washington, D.C. 20008
                                           202-667-0441
                                           202-483-0983
                                           FAX 202-483-0994
                                           Hours: Mon.-Sat. 10-5; Sun. 1-5

You don't need to know the difference between a fine brocade
or a coarse burlap to visit the Textile Museum. Don't miss the shop in
the museum where you'll find more than 800 titles to enhance your
knowledge of textiles. More than twenty of the titles have been published
by the museum. They sell the largest selection of books about textiles
and oriental rugs in the country. Many orders they receive are from other
bookstores.

Open daily, the Textile Museum Shop has four steps at the
entrance but if you give them advance notice, employees will assist
visitors who need an extra hand to climb the stairs. Wheelchair-users and
those who can't visit the shop are invited to shop by telephone or mail
from their catalog.

The bookstore was formerly the library of George Hewitt Myers, the founder of the museum. The small but attractive shop has wooden floors, high ceilings, and shelving to match, which holds books, textiles, scarves, ties, and related items. The museum sponsors special activities that you will enjoy attending.

Whether you are a student of textile manufacturing, an interior decorator, or decorating your home, you'll enjoy a visit to the Textile Museum. Don't forget to make time to stop into the shop.

Tower Bookshop (Old Post Office Tower)

Historical Washington Tower

Pavillion at the Old Post Office

12th St. & Pennsylvania Ave. NW
Washington, D.C. 20004
202-472-3083
Hours: Sept.-March Daily 10-6;
April-Sept. Daily 8am-9:30pm

"We are an interpretive bookshop associated with the National Park Service," said manager Carl J. Spier. "We exist to make the tourists' experience pleasant and educational."

The 300-500 titles focus on the history of Washington, D.C., its recent redevelopment, along with histories of Pennsylvania Avenue and the Old Post Office. They also have supplemental material for visitors which include maps, audio books, greeting cards, video tapes, calendars, games, and posters.

The store is wheelchair accessible and has a cafe on the premises. A catalog is available for telephone and mail orders. They also publish a monthly newsletter.

Note that the bookstore is open different hours during the seasons. You won't want to miss a visit here.

Travel Merchandise Mart

Travel

1425 K Street NW
Washington, D.C. 20005
202-371-6656
FAX 202-371-0255
Hours: Mon.-Fri. 9-5:30

If you're the kind of person who browses through travel books and just can't wait to escape to a destination, you can set the wheels turning at Travel Merchandise Mart. Inside the same store is a full-service travel agency, Omega World Travel.

The Travel Merchandise Mart sells approximately 100 titles of travel books, along with maps, foreign language books, and video tapes and assorted items to make life on the road easier.

The store and travel agency are completely wheelchair accessible. As if operating a bookstore and travel agency weren't enough to keep them busy, they also operate a publishing business.

No matter where your favorite vacation spot is located or if you're a busy business traveller, you're sure to be satisfied at Travel Merchandise Mart.

Tree Top Toys Inc.

Children's books

3301 New Mexico Ave. NW
Fox Hall Square
Washington, D.C. 20016
202-244-3500
Hours: Mon.-Sat. 9:30-5:30

Just as a tree grows and adds leaves, Tree Top Toys & Books continues to grow and add new selections to their terrific stock of books. The store has dedicated 1,200 square feet for books that appeal to children from birth through eighth grade.

Responsive to the needs of children, Tree Top makes sure they have all the books on local schools' summer reading lists. In addition to story-telling times on Monday and Wednesday, Tree Top brings a wide range of activities to children. The store held a birthday party for Peter Rabbit on his recent 100th anniversary. Craft Day includes demonstrations of how rubber stamps can be used to make stationery and bookmarks. While activities keep the children interested, parents can browse the parenting books that the store sells.

Tree Top Toys & Books was founded in the early 1980's and is wheelchair and stroller accessible. When book shopping, you'll be able to take advantage of the experiences of a librarian.

Decorated in green and white, Tree Top Toys & Books has a delightful atmosphere.

Trinity College Bookstore

College

125 Michigan Ave. NE
Washington, D.C. 20017
202-939-5117
Hours: Mon.-Thurs. 9-4;
Fri. 9-6; Sat. 9-1

The bookstore of Trinity College is open to the public and sells general interest books along with textbooks. Clothing and gifts bearing the college logo are also sold. The store is wheelchair accessible.

Trover Shop

General

800 15th Street NW
Washington, D.C. 20056
202-347-2177
Hours: Mon.-Fri. 8-6

Owner of the three Trover Shops in Washington, Joe Shuman says that the stores have "the largest collection of magazines in the city." They also have impressive collections of general interest titles.

Special orders and mail orders are welcomed by the store. They also sell greeting cards. This branch, on H Street at 15th Street, has one step at the entrance. The youngest of the three, it was founded in late 1970's.

Trover Shop

General

1031 Connecticut Ave. NW
Washington, D.C. 20032
202-659-8138
Hours: Mon.-Fri. 8-6:30; Sat. 9-6

Founded in the 1960's, this branch of the Trover Shop is the second oldest of the three and sells many general interest books. Although a catalog is not published, the store does accept telephone and mail orders and will search for titles. Greeting cards are also sold.

The Trover Shop on Connecticut Street is wheelchair accessible. The other branches are on H & 15th Streets and Pennsylvania SE.

Trover Shop

General

221 Pennsylvania Ave. SE
Washington, D.C. 20003
202-543-8006
FAX 202-547-5584
Hours: Mon.-Fri. 7-9;
Sat. 7-7; Sun. 7-3

Founded by Joe Shuman, the Trover Shop is known as a convenient bookshop where a person can find a wealth of magazines and general interest books. They do accept special and mail orders as well as greeting cards.

This site of the Trover Shop, established in the late 1950's is the oldest of the three shops and is wheelchair accessible. The two other locations are on Connecticut NW and 15th & H Streets.

U.S. Government Printing Office Bookstore

General/Government pubs.   1510 H Street NW
                               Washington, D.C. 20065
                               202-653-5675
                               FAX 202-375-5055
                               Hours: Mon.-Fri. 8-4:30

"We sell only government publications," said William L. Ticknor, Chief of the U.S. Government Printing Office Bookstores said.

Dull, you say? Then you haven't been to one of their two stores in Washington. You may envision books filled with bureaucratic garbled jargon, but this store is unique. Government publications range from National Park Service guides and posters to nutrition, business, the environment, history, gardening, outer space, hobbies, and so much more. They also offer government magazines and the calendar, "We, The People." The best news is that many of the items sold are free or sold for very reasonable prices.

This location on H Street NW is at street level and wheelchair accessible. Telephone and mail orders are accepted from their catalogs.

When you are in the area, don't pass the U.S. Government Printing Office by; you'll be surprised by the books, pamphlets, and booklets you'll find here.

U.S. Government Printing Office Bookstore

General/Government pubs.   710 N. Capitol St. NW
                               Washington, D.C. 20401
                               202-512-0132
                               FAX 202-512-1355
                               Hours: Mon.-Fri. 8-4

For a complete description of this branch of the U.S. Government Printing Office Bookstore, see the write-up of the H Street store.

This location has six steps at the entrance but there is a wheelchair ramp available. First you need to go to the front entrance and inform the guard and he will guide you to the side entrance where the ramp is located.

U.S. Holocaust Memorial Museum Shop

Holocaust History   100 Raul Wallberg Place SW
                        Washington, D.C. 20024
                        202-488-0400
                        Hours: Daily 10-5:20

One of the most heart-wrenching museums in Washington is the United States Holocaust Memorial Museum. The museum is dedicated to informing Americans about the unprecedented crime of the murder of six million Jews and other victims of Nazi tyranny.

Located on the ground level and basement levels of the museum, the shop sells the most complete collection of books about the Holocaust. Included are biographies and autobiographies, history, and photographic essays. There are books available for everyone from serious scholars to children. They also sell documentaries on audio and video tapes.

Although admission is free, you must obtain tickets for the exhibit itself. The entire memorial and shop are wheelchair accessible. The Visitor Services staff wear maroon jackets and are available to answer questions and provide special assistance.

U.S. National Arboretum

Nature   900 Anacostia Dr. SE
                                          Washington, D.C. 20020
                                          202-426-6905
                                          Hours: Daily 7am-4:15pm

Overlooking the Anacostia River is a 440-acre garden and woodland known as the U.S. National Arboretum. Established in 1927 as a research site, the arboretum now boasts the National Bonsai Collection. The park grounds display the blooming azaleas and flowering dogwood and crab apples for which Washington is known.

The Administration Building has a shop which sells books about nature, guidebooks, how-to develop bonsai trees, medicinal plants, specific flowers, and books about the Arboretum itself. Please note that the shop closes two hours before the grounds close. The shop is wheelchair accessible.

University of District of Columbia Bookstore

College   4200 Connecticut Ave.
                                          Washington, D.C. 20008
                                          202-282-7447
                                          Hours: Mon., Thurs. & Fri. 9-4;
                                          Tues. & Wed. 9-6

Open to the public, the University of the District of Columbia Bookstore is open to the public. Most books sold are textbooks for the four-year college but they also sell some general interest titles. The store is wheelchair accessible.

Vertigo Books

Academic

1337 Connecticut Ave. NW
Washington, D.C. 20036
202-429-9272
Hours: Mon.-Fri. 10-7; Sat. 11-7;
Sun. noon-5

The world is at your fingertips when you visit Vertigo Books. Organized by geographic region, you can easily access all books regarding world regions. For example, under "African" the following would all be found: history, politics, biographies, and travel. Even fiction is available by region.

Vertigo has a vast selection of books regarding African-American studies. They specialize in international politics and world literature. Many of the books sold at Vertigo are academic and small press publications. They are often the only store that carries specific titles.

Opened in November, 1991, Vertigo Books is owned by Bridget Warren and husband Todd Stewart. They coordinate activities that are a step ahead of many bookstores. Authors discuss their books with question and answer periods and autograph books at the store. Vertigo also sponsors discussion groups highlighting specific issues.

Vertigo sells some books at a discount but they also sponsor a "book club" type of program in which when the client purchases ten books during one year, they receive their next book free. Customers hold a "Vertigo Reader Card."

"We have the best selection of remainders," said Todd. They also will place special orders for books.

If fascinated with world literature and activities, Vertigo Books is a store you will enjoy.

Vihara Book Service

Religious-Buddhist

5017 16th St. NW
Washington, D.C. 20037
202-723-7001
FAX 202-882-6042
Hours: Daily 9-9

The experts on Buddhism and meditation are found right here in Washington at Vihara Book Service. With approximately 500 book titles, they also sell audio tapes about meditation. Video tapes are also available.

Open long hours, Vihara Book Service has been in business for more than twenty years. The store does have four steps at the entrance but you can call them or fax them your book requests.

The next time you need a break but your vacation isn't scheduled until next month, try meditation. If you are a beginner or skilled at meditation, Vihara Book Service will guide you to the books to meet your needs.

WETA Learningsmith

General   Georgetown Park Mall
                        3222 M Street NW
                        Washington, D.C. 20007
                        202-337-0800
                        Hours: Mon.-Sat. 10-9; Sun. noon-6

Once you visit WETA Learningsmith, you may not want to leave. This location in Georgetown Park Mall opened in 1993 and is wheelchair accessible. The mall has two entrances and people using wheelchairs or pushing strollers will want to use the M Street entrance where you'll find an elevator to reach the second floor Learningsmith.
For a more complete write-up about WETA Learningsmith, please refer to the write-up for store at the Tysons Corner Center in McLean, VA.

Waldenbooks

General   Spring Valley Shopping Center
                        4845 Massachusetts Ave., NW
                        Washington, D.C. 20016
                        202-362-6329
                        Hours: Mon.-Fri. 9:30-7;
                        Sat. 9:30-6; Sun. 10-5

Waldenbooks in the Spring Valley Shopping Center carries a fine collection of literary fiction and classics. The small store reflects the needs and wants of the neighborhood. The store is open everyday and is wheelchair accessible.
You won't want to miss reading about the many special services offered to Waldenbooks and Brentano's (which are owned by the same company) customers. Refer to the write-up for the Brentano's store on Wisconsin Avenue.

Waldenbooks

General   1700 Pennsylvania Ave. NW
                        Washington, D.C. 20007
                        202-393-1490
                        Hours: Mon.-Fri. 9-6; Sat. 10-6;
                        closed Sunday

After touring the White House, stroll just one block away on Pennsylvania Avenue and stop by Waldenbooks. This branch has particularly large selections of current events, political science, and foreign language books. The store is wheelchair accessible.

For more details about their special services, please refer to the write-up for the Brentano's (owned by the same company that owns Waldenbooks) store on Wisconsin Avenue.

Waldenbooks

General   Georgetown Park Mall
                                       3222 M Street NW
                                       Washington, D.C. 20007
                                       202-333-8033
                                       <u>Hours:</u> Mon.-Sat. 10-9; Sun. noon-6

In the heart of Georgetown at the corner of M Street and Wisconsin, is a large mall almost hidden from the street. Georgetown Park is wheelchair accessible and a relief from the busy sidewalks.

For a more detailed description of Waldenbooks special services, please refer to the write-up for the Wisconsin Avenue Brentano's (owned by the same company that owns Waldenbooks) store in this chapter of the book.

Washington Cathedral Bookshop

Religious-Christian   Mount Saint Alban
                                       Washington, D.C. 20016
                                       202-537-6267
                                       FAX 202-537-5766
                                       <u>Hours:</u> Daily 9:30-5

Located in the crypt of the 14th century style gothic cathedral, the Washington Cathedral Bookshop sells titles relating to the life, work, and art of the Cathedral. Some books are for children.

Although most books are new titles, some antiquarian books are available. Topics offered include religious, architectural, inspirational, theological, Bible and prayer books. Some books are printed in large type and some on audio cassettes.

Books aren't the only items offered in the giftshop. They sell video tapes, T-shirts, greeting cards, children's toys, games, posters, stationery, and calendars.

As a service to customers, employees will gift wrap your purchases. They also place special orders for books they do not have in stock. A newsletter is published regularly. Telephone and mail orders are accepted.

As noted, the bookshop is located in the crypt which is down a flight of steps and not wheelchair accessible. The rest of the Cathedral is accessible. A ramp entrance is near the north entrance and elevators are available for exploring the building.

The Washington Cathedral is an inspiring, architectural wonder that is open everyday. From the cathedral you'll see some of the most glorious views of Washington, D.C. After enjoying your tour and visit to the bookshop, you can enjoy the cafe on the premises.

Washington Law Book Co., Inc.

Law

1900 G Street NW
Washington, D.C. 20006
202-371-6667
FAX 202-289-6203
Hours: Mon.-Fri. 9:30-6; Sat. 10-5

Technically oriented, Washington Law Book Company has one of the largest collections of law books in the country, according to owner Leonard Cohn.

Topics of the books include legal systems, legal biographies, and government and private law. Some banking, economics, and accounting books are available. Most books sold are new but they sell some used books.

They do place special orders and will search for out-of-print books. More than half of sales result from their catalog. Washington Law Book Company receives orders and ships books abroad.

Students and lawyers alike find books of interest here.

Washington Monument Bookshop

Americana

490 Foot Level Wash. Monument
15th & Constitution Ave. NW
Washington, D.C. 20042
202-426-6841
Hours: Daily 8am-midnight

You can see the Washington Monument from highways miles away and to see the Washington area for miles, take a look from inside the top of the monument.

While you're there, stroll into the small shop which sells gorgeous photography books, guidebooks, and history books all about the Capital. Also for sale are biographies of George Washington, a few books about the Revolutionary War, and many books written especially for children. Although the shop is small, it is wheelchair accessible.

Way of the Cross Ministry Book & Bible Store

Religious-Christian

3466 14th St. NW
Washington, D.C. 20250
202-265-0908
Hours: Mon.-Sat. 10-6

Affiliated with the Baptist Church, Way of the Cross Ministry Book & Bible Store sells more than 200 titles of Christian Books and, according to manager Ora Dugar, "everything else" related. They sell choir robes, Christian jewelry, music on cassette tapes, greeting cards, and much more. They make customized banners and order personalized wedding invitations and such.

A wonderful program sponsored by the church and bookstore involves helping the needy with food and clothing. Contact them for more details.

The bookstore is located in the basement of the church and, unfortunately, is not wheelchair accessible. If you tap on the window, an employee will happily help you with your purchases.

The White House Historical Assoc.

National History   740 Jackson Place, NW
                                     Washington, D.C. 20503
                                     202-737-8292
                                     Hours: Mon.-Fri. 9-4:30; mail order
                                     catalog available

When our second president, John Adams, moved into the yet unfinished White House, he wrote to his wife, Abigail, "I pray Heaven to bestow the best of blessings on this house and all that shall hereafter inhabit it."

One would think he had moved into a beautiful palace. Not so. When he moved into the White House none of the walls were yet plastered and the wood to be used for the central staircase was in a pile on the floor. When Abigail joined her husband in the White House, she used the unfinished reception room to hang her laundry.

Unfortunately, the British, during the War of 1812, gutted the interior of the house but the walls still stood. The interior was rebuilt. The wings of the White House were added in 1902 but by the time Harry Truman was working in them, they were determined to be structurally unsound. President Truman agreed to interior renovations but insisted that the four walls not be touched. Renovations took three years. Jacqueline Kennedy is credited with decorating the interior House with historically accurate furniture and artwork and, at times, was able to use original furnishings. The White House has been home to all of our Presidents but one: George Washington.

Today, Americans are invited on a guided tour of the White House. For information about the tours, please call (202) 755-7798. Tours are conducted Tuesdays through Saturdays.

The White House Historical Association is a non-profit organization dedicated to bringing information about the White House to the public. To enhance your visit, the Association maintains a sales desk at the White House during the hours that tours are conducted. Books they sell include histories and architectural design books about the house. They also have information about the Presidents and First Ladies while they lived in the House. The Association is located in a townhouse near the White House and they sell prints of selected paintings hanging in the White House, a video tape, slides, postcards, and Christmas Tree ornaments. A catalog is also available.

If you are unable to visit the White House yourself or if you have an interest in the architecture of our country's most famous house, contact the White House Historical Association.

William F. Hale Books

Antiquarian-Fine Art

1222 31st. St. NW
Washington, D.C. 20007
202-338-8272
FAX 202-338-8420
Hours: Approx. 1-6:30; call to confirm

An antiquarian selling general interest books, William F. Hale Books has special selections of fine art, books about music, and travel books. A member of the Antiquarian Booksellers Association of America (ABAA), William has a booth at the ABAA book fairs.

Many people call William to discuss books and place mail orders. He publishes catalogs infrequently. His collection can be seen during the afternoon but it is recommended to call ahead to make sure William is available when you want to visit. There are three steps to enter the showroom.

William has been an antiquarian book dealer since 1978.

Woodrow Wilson House Gift Shop

National Historic Site

2340 S Street NW
Washington, D.C. 20008
202-387-4062
FAX 202-483-1466
Hours: Tues.-Sun. 10-4; closed Mon.

Here's a trivia question that not many Americans can answer: who is the only U.S. president to retire in Washington, D.C.? In 1921, Woodrow Wilson made his home in the Embassy Row section of Washington. His home is a time capsule of the times when he lived and an honor to the man.

The President who led us through World War I is also known for creating the Federal Reserve Board and participated in creating the League of Nations thus expanding America's role in international affairs. In his lifetime, Wilson was a scholar, educator, author, governor, university president, and statesman.

The home and shop are wheelchair accessible. The shop sells more than 50 titles about the times and life of Woodrow Wilson including books about the two World Wars and the League of Nations. A few other gift items are also for sale.

Special events often occur at the house. Each Christmas when you visit the house, you'll step into a holiday house decorated just like it would have been in 1920. Tours are enhanced by the changing special exhibits. For further events, contact the staff at the house.

World Bank Bookstore

Finance

701 18th Street NW
Washington, D.C. 20433
202-473-2941
FAX 202-477-0604
FAX for orders 202-676-0581
Hours: Mon.-Fri. 10-4

The World Bank sells more than 1,000 titles, all relating to finance and debt, finance development environment, economics and social data, industry, trade, country studies, and more. Students and professionals will find their collection superb. The bookstore is wheelchair accessible. A complete catalog is available from the Order Processing and Customer Service Unit at (202) 473-1155.

Yes! Bookshop

Self-Development

1035 31st St. NW
Washington, D.C. 20007
202-338-7874
800-YES-1516
FAX 202-338-8150
Hours: Mon.-Thurs. 10-7:30;
Fri. & Sat. 10-10; Sun. noon-7

Are you looking for a bookstore whose theme is self-improvement? Yes? Then you must visit Yes!

Yes! Bookshop is one of the nation's largest New Age bookshop that stocks such topics as metaphysics, health, self-help, philosophy, psychology, and alternative healing. They offer a full line of music on cassettes and CD's which feature meditative music, African jungle sounds, nature sounds, and even medieval hymns. Among the video tapes sold are proper methods of massage. They publish a free catalog twice per year.

"We are constantly improving," said owner Rajesh Kale. Partner Mahest Naithani handles the other duties of owning a bookstore.

Yes! Bookshop sells worldwide and places special orders for clients. Those fortunate enough to live near Yes! can partake of the many classes about yoga and meditation that they conduct. Authors do visit the store to discuss their writings.

You'll also find the store to be a truly unique place. When someone asks which bookstore you want to visit, say "Yes!"

Yesterday's Books

Antiquarian-General

4702 Wisconsin Ave. NW
Washington, D.C. 20016
202-363-0581
Hours: Mon.-Thurs. 11-9;
Fri., Sat. 11-10; Sun. 1-7

Established in 1974, Yesterday's Books is a fixture in it's neighborhood. In addition to the 21,000 titles in house, the bookstore maintains a top rate book search service. They also are able to appraise your book treasures.

Although most new, used, and antiquarian books are of general interest, Yesterday's Books specialize in fiction, Christian literature, and science fiction. They also sell books with large type print, video tapes, book bags, and posters.

Although there are two steps at the front door, Yesterday's Books is wheelchair accessible inside. If you can't manage the steps, they are happy to accept telephone and mail orders. Call them to discuss the books you would like to purchase.

Owner Katina Stockbridge has comfortably designed the store with easy chairs. Customers are welcome to help themselves to fruit, bread, and coffee especially chosen for their delight.

Katina reports that, "We are the one store Michael Jackson stops in when visiting D.C."

When you visit Yesterday's Books, you'll be give the same royal treatment as Michael gets. Every customer is important here.

Maryland Suburbs

A-Z Used Books

Used-General   Festival Shopping Center
                                   373 Muddy Branch Road
                                   Gaithersburg, MD 20878
                                   301-590-0022
                                   Hours: Mon.-Fri. 10:30-8;
                                   Sat. 10:30-7; Sun. 11-5

From A to Z you'll find it all at A-Z Used Books. Although they are only one year old, co-owner Barbara Fagan reports that they are growing rapidly.

The stock is of a general nature, all used books. The books are well displayed in wide aisles and organized for easy access. The quaint store has seating inside which makes for comfortable browsing.

A-Z Used Books is located in the Festival Shopping Center. There are two steps at the entrance, but do not fear. There is also a ramp for wheelchairs and strollers. Inside, the store is completely accessible to all. Employees are happy to assist all bookstore patrons.

"You will always be greeted by a friendly someone who cares," Barbara promises.

All Books Considered

Antiquarian   3776 Howard Ave.
                                   Kensington, MD 20795
                                   301-929-8419
                                   Hours: Mon., Wed.-Sat. 10-5:30;
                                   Sun. noon-5:30

Do you want to brush up on Sufism? Wouldn't you like to impress your dinner guests by dropping little tidbits of info about Rosicrucianism? Has that serious talk between your kids and you about theosophy been long overdue and you want some supplemental material? Does your make-up expert at the local department store think she knows all there is to know about cosmology but you want to prove her wrong?

At All Books Considered you'll find used, antiquarian, rare, and out-of-print books about those topics and many more including: yoga, graphology, health and healing, anthroposophy, Buddhism, Hinduism, reincarnation, astrology, hypnosis, parapsychology, spiritism, tarot, reincarnation, and, as their advertisement says, "other spooky stuff."

For those whose interests lie in other fields, All Books Considered is still the place to check. They maintain a large collection of books for children, about antiques, literature, books about books, militaria, and those of a general interest. They have a stock of approximately 5,000 books.

Located in Kensington, Maryland, Antique Village, All Books Considered shares a space with Time Frames, an antique frame shop. Don't miss the beautiful antique bookends for sale at All Books Considered.

Established in 1991, All Books Considered is a delight to visit not only to investigate the unique books but also because they have a tea room in the center and a piano in the store. Sadly, the location has five steps.

Monthly, a door prize is awarded to a lucky shopper. The store gives customers a 10% discount on purchases and orders that total more than $50.00. With any purchase, customers are given a free book from a selected group in the store.

In the first paragraph, I tossed around some words that I didn't know and curiosity sent me to check my American Heritage dictionary. Here's what I found: Sufism--Islamic mysticism; Rosicrucianism--a member of the Order devoted to the study of ancient mystical, philosophical and religious doctrines as they relate to modern life; Theosophy--religious philosophy or speculation about the nature of the soul based on mystical insight into the nature of God. Make-up artists know cosmetology. Cosmology is the study of the history, structure, and dynamics of the universe.

All Books Considered also has a room at Paul Feng Emporium which is just a few doors away. Located in a busy antique district, All Books Considered sells antique reference books in the Emporium.

In closing, a quote from their advertisement: "Religions are like many colors of glass on a lantern. The light is always the same."

Alphaville Bookshop

Used-General

5612-B Connecticut Ave.
Chevy Chase, MD 20782
301-363-2775
Hours: Mon.-Thurs. 11-8;
Fri. 11-9; Sat. 10-9; Sun. 10-5

"This is a serious bookstore for serious people," said Carlo Parcelli, owner of Alphaville Bookshop.

Whether you are a serious philosopher or a serious cook, you'll find used and some antiquarian books at Alphaville to meet your book wants. The store also covers a wide variety of interests including Americana, fine art, fiction, history, law, militaria, nature, photography, poetry, psychology, science, and technology. Don't leave the kids at home; Alphaville also has children's books.

You'll find approximately 12,000 volumes here. All books are quality hardbacks and paperbacks. Of special interest, Alphaville sells jazz records and original Russian art.

Established on May 1, 1993, Alphaville Bookshop is wheelchair accessible. Stop by Alphaville and enjoy the many fine selections.

Antiquarian Bookworm

Antiquarian-Americana   1307 Templeton Pl.
Rockville, MD 20852
301-309-8888
<u>Hours:</u> Appointment only

Since 1990, Billie Weetall has offered her fine collection of antiquarian books for sale under the name of Antiquarian Bookworm. The books focus on the themes of Americana, architecture, and history.

Call Billie to discuss her collection or to make an appointment to view her collection.

Arawak Books

Caribbean, African, & Third World 1401 University Blvd.
Langley Park, MD 20783
301-434-2373
<u>Hours:</u> Sun.-Fri. noon-6; Sat. noon-9

Here's a bookstore you can't miss. Arawak Books specializes in Caribbean and African literature, Africamerican, and Third World Issues. The 3,000 titles feature fiction, ethnic studies, foreign language, cookery, history, poetry, and politics with a strong emphasis on Caribbean perspectives.

Arawak Books also sells items other than books. Included are audio books, video tapes, magazines, greeting cards, and calendars.

Established in 1991, Arawak Books is open everyday except Monday. The store is completely accessible to everyone both inside and out. Mass transit and off-street parking are available nearby. Arawak Books is a delight to visit. Employees special order books for customers and they coordinate author autographing sessions. The reading group sponsored by the store is especially appreciated by participants. Check the in-store bulletin for information about the reading group as well as other events.

Arawak Books is THE place to find a wonderful selection of books regarding their specialties.

Ashe & Deane Fine Books

Antiquarian-18th & 19th Centuries PO Box 15601
Chevy Chase, MD 20825
301-588-9590
Hours: Mail order only

The delightful owner of Ashe & Deane Fine Books, Anita Macy has developed a grand collection of books featuring 18th and 19th century English literature. She travels to England to bring her clients the treasures she finds.

Ashe & Deane Fine Books also sells unusual fine art and history books as well as many modern first editions.

"It's so much fun to help people build their book collections," Anita said. She conducts searches and appraisals.

How did she become enthralled with the book business? It began when, as a student at Georgetown University, she persuaded her father to purchase a bookstore. Her love for books continues today.

Most business is conducted by telephone and mail order but Anita does make some appointments. She issues catalogs regularly.

Attic Books

Used-General   100 Washington Blvd.
Laurel, MD 20707
301-725-3725
Hours: Mon.-Sat. 10-7; Sun. 1-5
(Closed Tuesdays)

Have you ever visited your grandmother's attic and found a cache of aged books? You'll experience the same elated feeling when you visit Attic Books in Laurel, Maryland. With approximately 25,000 books available, you'll reap the bounty. The books you find cover general interests: something for everyone.

Like Grandma's attic, Attic Books is not wheelchair accessible due to the three steps to enter the store. Established in 1973, Attic Books is closed on Tuesdays.

When asked to describe Attic Books, owner Richard Cook stated, "Retailer recollects rapacious reading. Reflectively reveals relative recalcitrance, reticence, rumination. Regrets response, request reprieve. Regards, Rick."

Audubon Naturalist Bookshop

Natural history

8940 Jones Mill Rd.
Chevy Chase, MD 20815
301-652-3606
FAX 301-951-7179
Hours: Tues.-Fri. 10-6; Sat. 9-5

During difficult times of his life, John James Audubon turned to his extraordinary skill of bird drawing and painting to escape from pressures. As a boy, he was taken to France from Haiti and was adopted and given his name. As a youngster, he studied art with the famous painter Jacques Louis David.

When age 18, he was sent to live on his father's farm near Philadelphia where he spent a great deal of time in the woods sketching the birds he saw. After marrying, he went to New Orleans and was unsuccessful in many businesses and also unsuccessful in finding a publisher for his book of drawings.

It wasn't until he went to London that he found a publisher and found success. He returned to New York City and became the idealized and successful artist that we know him to be today. He was acclaimed as a naturalist.

The Audubon Naturalist Society is located on 40 acres of a wildlife sanctuary, known as Woodend, inside a Georgian mansion that was designed by the architect of the Jefferson Memorial. The society publishes a monthly newspaper featuring conservation news, book reviews, activity calendars, and society news.

A small bookshop features natural history, the environment, botany, bird watching guides, and associated topics including works of fiction. Of course, Audubon's work dominates the collection. The store also sells audio books and nature sounds, binoculars, telescopes, video tapes, T-shirts, games, nature jewelry, children's toys, stationery and beautiful art made by local craftsmen. Many programs suitable for the family are conducted at the trails of Woodend.

The shop at Woodend is not wheelchair accessible due to the three steps at the entrance. However, the store in Washington is wheelchair accessible.

When you're looking for a space to contemplate the world or escape the fast-pace of Washington life, visit Woodend. If you only have a few spare moments, visit the shop in Washington. You'll be surprised at how refreshing it is to spend a few moments in the calm atmosphere of the store.

B. Dalton Bookseller

General
Montgomery Mall
7101 Democracy Blvd.
Bethesda, MD 20817
301-365-6209
Hours: Mon.-Sat. 10-9:30; Sun. 11-6

"This store presents a new concept of stores for us," said Joe Ewing, the Washington area district manager of B. Dalton. "The front one-fourth of the store is a complete children's store within a store."

As you stroll through this section, you'll see some of your old favorites from your childhood. No doubt, you'll want to introduce the children in your life to your past pals such as Clifford, Curious George, and the Cat in the Hat. The store has a birthday club for little ones under the age of 13. Be sure to ask them about details.

The other departments that are particularly strong are fiction, computers, business, and cookbooks. They also sell books with large print type, audio books, magazines, and calendars. Authors visit for autographing sessions and the store will special order books not in stock.

Located in Montgomery Mall, B. Dalton was moved to the new wing of the mall in late 1991. The store is wheelchair accessible and comfortable for all shoppers.

B. Dalton Bookseller

General
Lake Forest Mall
701 Russell Ave.
Gaithersburg, MD 20877
301-926-6443
Hours: Mon.-Sat. 10-9:30; Sun. noon-6

Located on a spur off the beltway at I-270, B. Dalton located in Lake Forest Mall is also near the "technology corridor" and serves many of the computer and scientific companies located in the area.

In addition to a huge computer department, B. Dalton's 4,500 square feet of selling space also carries a complete collection of general interest books.

B. Dalton is on the lower level of Lake Forest Mall and is completely wheelchair accessible. If you park near Sears, you will be close to the bookstore once you enter the mall.

B. Dalton Bookseller

General

Prince Georges Plaza
3500 East West Hwy.
Hyattsville, MD 20782
301-559-9779
Hours: Mon.-Sat. 10-9:30; Sun. noon-6

Located in Prince Georges Plaza within two miles from the University of Maryland, B. Dalton pays attention to the needs and wants of the local community.

They have a particularly large African-American interest section as well as fiction, children's books, non-fiction, and magazines. They also have a collection of quality bargain books. The store has 3,000 square feet of selling space which is wheelchair accessible.

The managers of the store coordinate author autographing sessions, publish a bi-monthly newsletter, and attend bookfairs. In the store you can also purchase audio books, books printed with large type, magazines, calendars, and greeting cards.

After browsing at B. Dalton, you must pick up a treat from the mall's food court.

Bay Books, Inc.

General

Wildewood Center
2021 State Hwy. 235
California, MD 20619
301-862-1424
FAX 301-862-1472
Hours: Mon.-Sat. 9:30-9; Sun. noon-6

The artwork of local artists decorate the walls and, along with general interest books, are for sale at Bay Books, Inc. They sell approximately 30,000 titles and have a large children's selection. Individuals and big businesses tap into their special ordering system. Also sold are some musical CD's and cassettes as well as books on cassette tape.

Not only does Bay Books conduct story-telling time, but they often are visited by a local lady who brings animals and talks about wildlife.

The store is open everyday and is wheelchair accessible.

Beall-Dawson House Giftshop

History

103 W. Montgomery Ave.
Rockville, MD 20850
301-762-1492
<u>Hours:</u> Daily noon-4

Another of the Washington area's famous houses, the Beall-Dawson House is a museum featuring the furnishings from 1815 through the Victorian area. On the grounds, you'll also find the office and small medical museum from the late 1800's.

Along with gift items, the shop sells books about Montgomery County, Maryland history, the Civil War, gardening and herbs. They also have guides to a walking tour of the area.

Beautiful Day Bookstore

Health & Healing

5010 Berwyn Rd.
College Park, MD 20740
301-345-2121
<u>Hours:</u> Mon.-Sat. 9-7:30; Sun. 10-4

Beautiful Day Bookstore wants to make everyday a beautiful one for you. Specializing in health, healing, homeopathy, alternative medicine, and vegetarian cooking, they also special order and conduct searches for specific titles.

In addition to books, Beautiful Day sells artistic crafts made of clay, cosmetics, organic fruit and vegetables, soy and dairy products, making it a grocery store as well as a bookstore. Patrons using wheelchairs may use a back door entrance to partake in the bounty of Beautiful Day Bookstore.

Betz Publishing Co., Inc.

Health & Science

932 Hungerford Dr. #33
Rockville, MD 20850
301-340-0030
<u>Hours:</u> Mon.-Fri. 9-5

Health and science are the specialties of Betz Publishing Company. Among their publications are books for preparation of the following professional health science exams: MCAT, OAT, DAT, VCAT, PCAT, and AHPAT. In addition to selling books at their store, they also offer books through telephone and mail orders.

Blue Beetle Comics & Baseball Cards

Comics
5814 Allentown Way
Camp Springs, MD 20748
301-449-3307
<u>Hours:</u> Mon.-Fri. noon-8

Not many people can blame their wives for getting them into a crazy business but Sid Pennington sure can. Because his wife, Liz, knew he loved comic books as a child, she bought him a Spiderman comic book that had Spiderman in a black and white outfit. Now, everyone knows that Spiderman wore red and blue.

That black and white Spiderman comic book renewed Sid's interest and comic books and now, the Pennington's own two popular and lively comic book stores called Blue Beetle Comics and Baseball Cards.

One store, their largest, is located near Andrews Air Force Base in Camp Springs and the other is in Festival Way Shopping Center in Waldorf. Both stores are wheelchair accessible and open everyday.

Liz said that they receive shipments of comic books every Monday and Wednesday and they always have clients waiting for the truck to pull in. It seems that comic book lovers are just as addicted to story lines as the soap opera fan.

Blue Beetle caters to all the needs of the serious collector by selling book sleeves, stiff backings to deter bent books, special poster holders that maintain their quality, and other supplies. They take the same consideration of card collectors by selling baseball, football, Star Trek, etc. cards and supplies.

Liz reported that Blue Beetle sells comic books for everyone. The super heros are popular as well as Barbie and Archie comic books. The little tykes still like Teenage Mutant Ninja Turtles. Comic books of classical literature tried to make a come-back a few years ago but have gone out of business. Blue Beetle maintains an extensive back issue collection.

Whether you have a special place in your heart for comic books or baseball cards, Blue Beetle is the place for you.

Blue Beetle Comics & Baseball Cards

Comics
4815 C Festival Way
Waldorf, MD 20601
301-843-1434
<u>Hours:</u> Mon.-Thurs. 11-8; Fri. noon-8;
Sat. 10-8; Sun. noon-5

Blue Beetle Comics & Baseball Cards in Waldorf is one of two stores that are owned by Sid & Liz Pennington and located in the Washington area. The larger is in Camp Springs, Maryland. Please refer to that write-up for a full description of Blue Beetle.

Bonifant Books

Antiquarian-General

11240 Georgia Ave.
Wheaton, MD 20902
301-946-1526
Hours: Mon.-Fri. 10-8;
Sat. 10-6; Sun. 11-6

With 50,000 titles, Bonifant Books brings you top quality used books with topics of interest for everyone. Particularly strong departments include history, militaria, science fiction, mystery, and children's books. Many of the excellent selections include recent review books. They even have used LP records and posters of such renowned people as Einstein and Virginia Wolfe for sale.

Located in the Wheaton Triangle strip mall, Bonifant Books is completely wheelchair accessible. Customers needing assistance reaching for books near the top of the tall cases are helped by employees. The aisles are comfortably wide and books are nicely organized.

In addition to buying books and records, Bonifant Books has a stock that is constantly evolving, making each visit here seem like you are in a whole new store.

Book Alcove

Used-General

15976 Shady Grove Rd.
Gaithersburg, MD 20877
301-977-9166
Hours: Mon.-Fri. 10-9;
Sat. 9:30-9; Sun. noon-6

Carl Sickles is proud to tell you about Book Alcove, a used bookstore, which he established with his lovely wife, Elinor, that has now expanded to three locations, managed by sons Ray and John.

The stores are each special because of the quality books, records, CD's, cassettes and books on cassette tape at terrific prices, but also because they make the custom bookcases that you need to organize your personal book collection. Craftsmanship is unparalleled and prices are extremely reasonable.

The bookcases are "not made of particle board because we love our customers," Carl emphatically said. They only use quality pine, oak, and birch to make beautiful bookcases or practically any other wooden custom product you may want. They also make computer tables, corner cabinets, entertainment centers, desk organizers, stero/tv units and cases for books, videos, records, toys, workshops, and curio collections. They have made many bookcases for bookstores in the area.

When it comes to customization, they have a philosophy posted in the store which reads: "We don't tell you what to take, YOU tell us what to make."

The Gaithersburg Book Alcove is located on the lower level of the Shady Grove Center behind the Maryland National Bank. The bookcase showroom is located in their Gaithersburg store. All Book Alcoves, located in Gaithersburg, Rockville, and Reston, are wheelchair accessible.

Visit all three of the Book Alcoves and you're sure to find books you must have in your library. Because they are always purchasing books, their stock turns over rapidly. You'll also find people at Book Alcove who are proud of their work and stock, which is refreshing these days.

Book Alcove

Used-General

5210 Randolph Rd.
Rockville, MD 20852
301-770-5590
Hours: Mon.-Fri. 10-9;
Sat. 9:30-9; Sun. noon-6

Owned by the Sickles family, Book Alcove of Rockville maintains a quality stock of used books at excellent prices. Also for sale are records, cassettes, CD's, and books on cassette tape. Located in Loehmann's Plaza, Book Alcove also has stores in Gaithersburg and Reston. All three are wheelchair accessible.

A special feature of Book Alcove is the custom-made beautiful bookcases that they make. The showroom is in Gaithersburg, Maryland, and for a detailed description of their woodworking, see the write-up for the Gaithersburg store.

Whether you are buying or selling books, you must visit all three of the Book Alcoves.

The Book Cellar

Antiquarian-General

8227 Woodmont Ave.
Bethesda, MD 20814
301-654-1898
Hours: Mon.-Fri. 11-6;
Sat. 10-5; Sun. 11-5

The Book Cellar is truly a bookstore that lives up to its name. The Book Cellar is located in a cellar with fourteen steps to get down to the book treasures you are sure to find here.

The more than 40,000 used books for sale range from inexpensive paperbacks to expensive and rare first editions. However, most books are hardcover reading copies at terrific prices.

Everyone is sure to find a category of books here to suit their needs. Most books offered are on the scholarly side. People wanting books written in foreign languages will be delightfully pleased to find the high proportion of titles written in other languages. If you have a specific title in mind and The Book Cellar doesn't have the book, they do conduct searches.

Open everyday, the store was established in 1976 and purchased by Don and Linda Bloomfield in 1988. Although wheelchair-using shoppers won't be able to browse the bookcases, The Book Cellar does accept telephone and mail orders. Give them a call and they will be happy to talk about their books.

Described by the owner as "crowded but organized," The Book Cellar lives up to its motto "multum in parvo," which means "much in little."

The Book Fair

Religious-Jewish   6125 Montrose Rd.
                                      Rockville, MD 20852
                                      301-881-0100
                                      <u>Hours:</u> Call for book fair dates

The Annual Jewish Book Fair provides a large selection of approximately 3,000 Jewish interest books. Topics include Jewish holidays, fiction, Holocaust, poetry, art and humor books, cookbooks, sociology, philosophy, and children's books.

The Fair is held for one week per year at the Jewish Community Center of Greater Washington. During the Fair, authors attend to autograph their books, nightly lectures are conducted, and programs is targeted for children.

You can call the Director of Literary Arts for the date that the next Book Fair will be held.

Book Nook

Used-General   9933 Rhode Island Ave.
                                      College Park, MD 20740
                                      301-474-4060
                                      <u>Hours:</u> Mon.-Tues., Thurs.-Sat. 10-5;
                                      Wed. 10-7:30

Established in 1975, the Book Nook is "a family-oriented used bookstore," said owner Mary Monteith. The completely accessible store for all has a children's play area equipped with coloring books and toys to amuse the little ones while you can browse at your leisure.

The friendly clerks guide customers through their selection of approximately 60,000 books specializing in cooking, romance, science fiction, religion, and children's books. In addition to selling books on audio tape, they also have some books printed with large type. Some magazines are available.

When you're looking for books at a good price, stop at the Book Nook. Be sure to say "hi" to the delightful owner, Mary.

Bookland

General

Beltway Plaza Regional Center
6064 Greenbelt Road
Greenbelt, MD 20770
301-474-0033
Hours: Mon.-Sat. 10-9:30; Sun. noon-6

"We have the best customer service in the land," said Henry Gershman, manager of Bookland. Open everyday, the bookstore is popular among the community for stocking a large stock of general fiction and non-fiction books. They also have a large children's section. If you want a book that isn't in stock, Bookland employees order and obtain the books in a short time.

Bookland is big on special events also. Approximately every month authors sign their books in the store. Bookland also conducts story telling time for little children when the older children are in school.

In addition, they sell a variety of gifts including coffee mugs, children's toys, assorted office supplies, and calendars. Bookland is wheelchair accessible so everyone can enjoy all they offer.

Bookland is affiliated with the chain Books-A-Million. Both stores have locations in the Potomac Mills Outlet Mall.

Books & Comic Outlet

Comics, Discount hardbacks

7736 Riverdale Rd.
New Carrollton, MD 20784
301-731-5851
Hours: Mon.-Thurs. 10-9;
Fri. & Sat. 10-10; Sun. noon-6

Owners Ernie and Janet Beckner opened Books & Comic Outlet in 1982 and understand the needs of the comic book and used book collector.

For the comic book enthusiast, they let their customers know when comic books will be delivered at the store. They sell all the collecting supplies necessary to maintain the quality of the books.

For the bibliophile, they sell discounted hardback books and offer never-read publisher over-stocks in a wide variety of topics. For the browser and collector of other items, they sell trading cards (such as baseball, football, etc.), T-shirts, posters, and magazines.

Ernie and Janet are also happy to search for paperback books that customers want. They "creatively buy" items for the store by using the good old bartering system.

Books & Comic Outlet is a great place to browse and to discover some great finds.

The Bookstall

General

10144 River Rd.
Potomac, MD 20854
301-469-7800
<u>Hours:</u> Mon.-Fri. 10-7;
Sat. 10-6; Sun. 11-4

A fine general interest bookstore, The Bookstall supports the community and entertains clients with evening readings and children's storytelling. Owners are planning more events in the future.

Special orders placed at The Bookstall are quickly filled. Also sold are selected music tapes and books on cassette tape, greeting cards, and some unique gifts.

The Bookstall, established more than fifteen years ago, is wheelchair accessible.

Borders Book Shop

General

11500 Rockville Pike
Rockville, MD 20852
301-816-1067
<u>Hours:</u> Mon.-Sat. 9am-11pm;
Sun. 11-8

What do you do when your bookshelves are so tight that you have a hard time pulling one out? Or when you have books piled in stacks on the floor because the cases are filled? When we get to that state, we move. Usually we get cracks from the moving crew like, "What did you do, rob all the books from the Public Library?" Moving was also the solution for Borders Book Shop in Rockville. First, they moved the children's department to an adjacent store but it didn't take long until their walls were filled to double the capacity again. Yep, they moved again.

This time they moved to a location in the White Flint Mall just down the street which tripled their floor space. The children's section reconnected with the other beloved departments. They were so delighted with the new store, they added an espresso bar and departments for musical CD's and video tapes. The big move took place in the fall of 1993.

Borders Book Shop is a dream store for every bibliophile. For a history and a more complete description of Borders Book Shop, see the write-up of the Vienna, Virginia, store.

Bowes Books

General   718 Great Mills Rd.
                                   Lexington Park, MD 20653
                                   301-863-6200
                                   <u>Hours:</u> Mon.-Fri. 9-5; Sat. 9-4

In 1960 Joe Bowes established Bowes Books as a general family bookstore. Since then the store has expanded to include Dungeon & Dragon games and accessories, custom framing, office, art, and drafting supplies, and Wilton cake decorating instruments.
        The store is not wheelchair accessible but you can call to discuss items you're looking for and other arrangements so they fulfill your needs.

C&O Canal National Historic Park

19th Century History   11710 MacArthur Blvd.
                                   Potomac, MD 20854
                                   301-469-7800
                                   <u>Hours:</u> Daily 8-4:30 with extended
                                   summer hours

George Washington had a hand in overseeing the construction of Potomac Canal built to bypass the falls and other unnavigable parts of the river. The area later was developed by the Chesapeake and Ohio Canal System.
        Today, the C & O Canal is affiliated with the Parks & History Association. The 184 mile park preserves the towpath, locks, aqueducts, and a tunnel from the 19th century. Seasonally, visitors to the park can ride a mule-drawn boat.
        Located in Maryland, the C & O Visitor's Center has a small bookstore that is wheelchair accessible. The store carries books that informs readers about both canals in general and specific canals. Other books feature nature, hiking, touring, and books for children. Children will delight in fun filled activity books that teach about nature and the seasons in a fun manner.

Calvert Marine Museum Shop

Museum-Nautical   14200 Solomons Island Rd.
                                   PO Box 97
                                   Solomons, MD 20688
                                   410-326-2750
                                   <u>Hours:</u> Daily 10:15-4:45

If you have ever wondered what the inside of a lighthouse looks like, you'll want to walk through the 1883 Drum Point Lighthouse which is a part of the Calvert Marine Museum. The museum features exhibits of naval battles, marine biology, slave ships, boat building, and the fishing and shellfish trade.

The museum shop sells approximately 75 titles of books to further explain the exhibits. Authors sometimes visit the shop to discuss and autograph their books. Books for children are available and the shop does sponsor a children's story telling time. You can also purchase magazines, stationery, posters, T-shirts, and a variety of souvenirs.

Established in 1970, the Calvert Marine Museum is open daily and is wheelchair accessible. A tour of the museum gives you another perspective of the Chesapeake Bay.

Capitol College Bookstores

College   11301 Springfield Rd.
                           Laurel, MD 20708
                           301-953-7561
                           <u>Hours:</u> Mon. & Tues. 9-5:30;
                           Wed.-Fri. 9-4:30; Fri. 9-2

Carrying all the essentials for students of Capitol College, the Bookstore is also open to the public. The college and bookstore specialize in engineering, electronics, and computers. Both new and used textbooks are for sale. The store also carries a variety of computer software and text aids.

The store is wheelchair accessible.

Children's Book Adoption Agency

Antiquarian-Children's books   PO Box 643
                                    Kensington, MD 20895
                                    301-565-2834
                                    FAX 301-585-3091
                                    <u>Hours:</u> Appointment only

Adoption agencies work diligently when finding a loving family for a child and Barbara B. Yoffee does the same when matching a book for a child. An expert in child development, Barbara says she "believes in getting the right book for the right child at the right time."

Children's Book Adoption Agency is the name of Barbara's antiquarian and used bookstore. Open by appointment, much work is done by telephone or mail orders from a catalog. If you want a copy of your favorite book from your childhood, call Barbara and she'll search and special order books just for you. She also conducts appraisals and can repair your books.

With a strong belief in uniting children with books, Barbara visits schools and conferences to present books of special interest. She publishes a newsletter once or twice per year.

Along with children's and illustrated books, Children's Book Adoption Agency has a special collection of African American books you won't want to miss.

Chuck & Dave's

General   7001 Carroll Ave.
Takoma Park, MD 20912
301-891-2665
Hours: Mon.-Fri. 11-8;
Sat. 10-7; Sun. 10-5

Chuck and Dave's is a full service bookstore filled with a terrific selection of books and excellent customer service. The small store is wheelchair accessible and is a much better bookstore than one might imagine from the outside of the store.

Most of Chuck and Dave's collection is of general interest but they have a particularly strong African-American department. They also have one of the city's best New Age and children's selections. Chuck reports that they believe that they are the best source in Washington for museum quality greeting cards. Their sale books are sold at very reasonable rates.

What's in their future? A coffee bar which is scheduled to open in early 1994. No doubt, it will be terrific.

Clara Barton National Historic Site Bookshop

History   5801 Oxford Rd.
Glen Echo, MD 20812
301-492-6245
FAX 301-492-5384
Hours: Daily 10-5

Television brings the horror and pain of war into our homes but imagine that suffering if it were happening right in front of you. Clara Barton saw that suffering of Union soldiers after the first Battle of Bull Run. An ex-schoolteacher and governmental clerk, she immediately organized a food and clothing drive and offered aid to the wounded soldiers. Overcoming opposition, she secured permission to visit the battlefields to tend to the wounded. Eventually, she received a personal commendation by President Lincoln.

After the Civil War, she aided the soldiers in France during the Franco-Prussian War through the International Red Cross. Upon her return to the United States, she founded the Red Cross which, fortunately, has chapters that still flourish and aid people suffering from natural disasters.

Clara Barton's house, located in Maryland, also contains a giftshop that carries souvenirs, video tapes, and approximately 80 titles of books about Clara's life, the Civil War, women in history, and Victorian America. Some books are available for children. Unfortunately, Clara's home is not wheelchair accessible but telephone and mail orders are accepted.

143

Luckily, Clara Barton's spirit still lives through the many people who donate time and resources to the Red Cross.

Closet of Comics

Comics
7319 Baltimore Ave.
College Park, MD 20740
301-699-0498
Hours: Daily 11-6; Fri. 12-7

You won't find Norm from Cheers here, but you will usually find a collection of friends who love to burst into spontaneous deep discussions about the future of the comic book industry or the twisted turn taken by a specific Super Hero in the latest issue.

Where is this magical store? Closet of Comics. The owner and employees enjoy the informal atmosphere created in the store. They also keep the shelves filled with the latest in comic books and collector's supplies. In addition, the store sells trading cards—no sports cards though.

Your new pals at Closet of Comics also sell a selection of video tapes featuring Japanese animation, which every adult cartoon fan knows are the best in the world.

Closet of Comics is wheelchair accessible. So why wait? You have friends waiting for you at Closet of Comics.

Collectors World

Comics
612 Quince Orchard Rd.
Gaithersburg, MD 20878
301-699-0498
Hours: Mon.-Fri. 11-8;
Sat. 11-6:30; Sun. 11-4

"We have the largest selection of comics and more back issues than any other stores in the area," said Jon Cohen, Manager of Collectors World.

Due to the high quality of writing and innovative artwork, comic book authors and artists have won awards and received critical acclaim usually reserved for mainstream writers and artists.

Collectors World stocks every kind of comic book imaginable from children's comics to SuperHero comics to underground comic books. The staff are incredibly knowledgeable even about the most obscure books. Collectors World also sells everything that pertains to comics. They offer clients an in-house subscription service which includes discounts.

Established in 1981, Collectors World has a second branch on Muddy Branch Road of Gaithersburg. Both stores are wheelchair accessible.

If you haven't read a comic book since you were a kid, Jon says that you will be surprised with the changes and quality of the books.

Collectors World

Comics

235 Muddy Branch Road
Gaithersburg, MD 20878
301-840-9729
Hours: Mon.-Fri. 11-7:30;
Sat. 11-6:30; Sun. 11-4

The second location of Collectors World in Gaithersburg, Maryland is found on Muddy Branch Road. In addition to comic books and related media, this branch stocks many more trading cards than the Quince Orchard store. Please refer to the above write-up of Collectors World for a complete description of the store.

Comic Classics

Comics

365 Main St.
Laurel, MD 20707
301-490-9811
Hours: Mon.-Fri. noon-8;
Sat. noon-6; Sun. noon-5

Open everyday and wheelchair accessible, Comic Classics offers you an excellent selection of comic books, collectible cards, and all the supplies that you need to maintain the quality of the books and cards.

Continental Divide Trail Society

Antiquarian-American West

PO Box 30002
Bethesda, MD 20824
301-493-4080
Hours: Telephone & Mail order only

It could have been Coronado, Lewis and Clark, or "Pathfinder" John C. Fremont whose travels first sparked your interest in the American West. If your lust for dreams of the West didn't die there, you'll find a peer group with the Continental Divide Trail Society.

The Society sells about 1,000 titles by telephone and mail order with specialties in Western Americana, the Southwest, and natural history of the West. However, their primary focus is the Continental Divide and those who explored and studied the Continental Divide. They sell new, used, and antiquarian books with an emphasis on scholarly works and government reports. If they don't stock the book you're looking for, they'll search to find it for you.

Contact the Continental Divide Trail Society for the true picture of how our Western United States developed. You might find yourself drawn into the Society yourself.

Cricket Bookshop

General
17800 New Hampshire Ave.
Ashton, MD 20861
301-774-4242
Hours: Mon.-Fri. 10-7; Thurs. 10-8;
Sat. 10-6; Sun. noon-5

"We are a small community bookstore," said co-owner Mary Jo Wilson of Cricket Bookshop. Mary Jo and Mary Miller have developed a general interest bookstore with approximately 20,000 titles with especially large selections of cookbooks and books for children.

To answer the needs of the community, Cricket Bookshop also sells gifts, jewelry, greeting cards, stationery and baby and wedding presents.

Unfortunately the store is not wheelchair accessible but employees will do everything they can to help customers to get items they want. Cricket Bookshop was established in 1969 and purchased by the partners in 1976.

Crown Books

General
3232 Superior Lane
Bowie, MD 20715
301-262-4101
Hours: Mon.-Sat. 10-9; Sun. 11-5

On Superior Lane in Bowie, Maryland you'll find a superior bookstore: Crown Books. The store is wheelchair accessible and has "no jungle clutter to trip you up," according to the Crown Books management.

For a description of their superior discounts and services, read the write-up for the Potomac, Maryland store.

Crown Books

General
13826 Outlet Drive
Silver Spring, MD 20905
301-890-6177
Hours: Mon.-Sat. 10-9; Sun. 11-5

All SuperCrown and Crown Books extend the same discounts and services to customers. For details, see the write-up for the Potomac, Maryland Crown Books.

Crown Books

General   11231 New Hampshire Ave.
                                             Silver Spring, MD 20904
                                             301-593-2599
                                             <u>Hours:</u> Mon.-Sat. 10-9; Sun. 11-5

All SuperCrown and Crown Books extend the same discounts and services to customers. For details, see the write-up for the Potomac, Maryland Crown Books.

Crown Books

General   13663 Georgia Avenue
                                             Silver Spring, MD 20906
                                             301-949-6636
                                             <u>Hours:</u> Mon.-Sat. 10-9; Sun. 11-5

No doubt you are aware that Crown Books gives you terrific discounts. See the write-up for the Potomac, Maryland Crown Books for a complete description.

Crown Books

General   3235 Plaza Way
                                             Waldorf, MD 20602
                                             301-843-2594
                                             <u>Hours:</u> Mon.-Sat. 10-9; Sun. 10-6

You've heard about the terrific discounts offered by Crown Books and you can discover the details in the write-up of the Potomac, Maryland Crown Books.

Crown Books

General   11181 Veirs Mill Road
                                             Wheaton, MD 20902
                                             301-942-7995
                                             <u>Hours:</u> Mon.-Sat. 10-9; Sun. 10-6

To learn about the terrific discounts and services that Crown Books offers you, see the write-up of the Potomac Crown Books in Maryland.

Crown Books

General
632 Quince Orchard Rd.
Gaithersburg, MD 20878
301-258-9330
<u>Hours:</u> Mon.-Sat. 10-9; Sun. 11-5

Read about the discounts and services that Crown Books gives to customers by referring to the write-up for the Potomac, Maryland branch below.

Crown Books

General
7727 Tuckerman Lane
Potomac, MD 20844
301-299-4104
<u>Hours:</u> Mon.-Sat. 10-9; Sun. 11-5

Crown Books maintains 55 very busy branches in the Washington, D.C. area. All stores stock the same fine general interest books. The difference between Crown Books and SuperCrown is merely a matter of numbers. SuperCrown stocks more than 100,000 titles. Most stores are open the same hours and all are wheelchair accessible. If they don't have a particular title in stock, employees are happy to place special orders which are quickly filled. Gift certificates are available at all branches.

When you shop at Crown Books, you know that you will be getting terrific discounts regardless of which store you visit. Crown Books shook the bookstore world in the 1970's by starting to offer discounts everyday. They are as follows: New York Times best-selling hardbacks: 40% off; all other hardbacks: 20% off; New York Times best-selling paperbacks: 25% off; all other paperbacks: 10% off; Best-selling computer books: 25% off; Audio books-on-cassette-tape: 20% off; video tapes, magazines, and CD-Rom: 10% off. Crown Books also have tables with stacks of hardback books that are greatly discounted and are sold for $1.00-$5.00.

With headquarters in Landover, Maryland, Crown Books and SuperCrown can be found nationwide. Everyone knows of the fine reputation of Crown Books. Find the branch closest to you.

Crown Books

General
College Plaza Mall
15130 Frederick Rd.
Rockville, MD 20850
301-424-1676
<u>Hours:</u> Mon.-Sat. 10-9; Sun. 11-5

Please refer to the write-up above for the Crown Books store in Potomac, Maryland for a complete description of the discounts that they offer.

Crown Books

General   1677 Rockville Pike
Rockville, MD 20850
301-468-2912
Hours: Mon.-Sat. 10-9; Sun. 11-5

Crown Books gives you great discounts. For a full description of those discounts, please see the write-up of the Potomac, Maryland Crown Books store.

Crown Books

General   13004 Middlebrook Rd.
Germantown, MD 20874
301-540-8799
Hours: Mon.-Sat. 10-9; Sun. 11-5

All SuperCrown and Crown Books extend the same discounts and services to customers. For details, see the write-up of the Potomac, Maryland Crown Books.

Crown Books

General   5775-A Crain Highway
Upper Marlboro, MD 20772
301-627-8500
Hours: Mon.-Sat. 10-8; Sun. 11-5

Please refer to the write-up of the Potomac store for a description of the discounts and services offered at Crown Books.

Crown Books

General   4601-A East West Hwy.
Bethesda, MD 20814
301-656-5775
Hours: Mon.-Sat. 10-9:30; Sun. 10-6

Do the kids drag you out of Crown Books before you have browsed through all the categories of books? Crown Books in Bethesda has solved the problem. They have a special area called "Crown Kids" where they can read or play while you shop.

For a complete description of discounts and services, see the description of the Potomac Crown Books store in Maryland.

Crown Books

General   18153-5 Village Mart Dr.
                                   Olney, MD 20832
                                   301-774-3917
                                   Hours: Mon.-Sat. 10-9; Sun. 11-5

To read about the discounts and services that all Crown Books and SuperCrown offers, please refer to the description of the Crown Books store in Potomac, Maryland.

Crown Books

General   18302 Contour Rd.
                                   Gaithersburg, MD 20879
                                   301-869-1636
                                   Hours: Mon.-Sat. 10-9; Sun. 11-5

For a complete description of the discounts and services offered by Crown Books, please see the write-up of the Potomac Crown Books store.

Crown Books

General   352 Domer Ave.
                                   Laurel, MD 20707
                                   301-953-9663
                                   Hours: Mon.-Sat. 10-9; Sun. 11-5

Unique to this Crown Books is their Western book section. They have approximately 200 titles written by 50 different authors. If your heros have always been cowboys, this is the store to point your pony to. Don't think other departments have been slighted. Crown Books has more than 30 categories.
Opened in 1978, this Crown Books had 3,000 square feet filled with books. At the end of 1993, they will grow to 10,000 square feet and be renamed to SuperCrown.
This store, like other Crown Books, is wheelchair accessible. To read about their discount and special services, see the write-up for the Crown Books store in Potomac, Maryland.

Crown Books

General   5265 River Road
                                   Bethesda, MD 20814
                                   301-986-0091
                                   Hours: Mon.-Sat. 10-10; Sun. 10-6

    Located in the Kenwood neighborhood of Bethesda, Crown Books is a pleasant store where clients often run into friends. The store is wheelchair accessible.
    For information about Crown's discount system, see the description of the Crown Books in Potomac, Maryland.

Doris Frohnsdorff

Antiquarian-Children's books   PO Box 2306
                                   Gaithersburg, MD 20886
                                   301-869-1256
                                   Hours: Mail order & appt. only

    Beatrix Potter was no dumb bunny. One hundred years ago she illustrated and wrote the Peter Rabbit stories and patented them. She supervised all products, such as dishes and cuddly soft toy animals. Her own watercolor illustrations were said to have the emotional feeling of Constable's landscapes.
    At their farm home in the Lake District of England, Miss Potter and her husband, William Heelis, kept rabbits, ducks, squirrels, hedgehogs, and cats. The 23 books she wrote and illustrated were based upon her observations of the animals.
    A true entrepreneur of her day, Beatrix privately printed "The Tale of Peter Rabbit" in 1900 and it was professionally published in 1902. Peter has celebrated his 100th birthday but still remains a young rabbit to Doris Frohnsdorff who sells first editions of children's books and specializes in Beatrix Potter's ageless tales. The books she sells have fine bindings and most are illustrated.
    Doris conducts business through telephone and mail order and by appointment. She publishes catalogs to make ordering easier and has been selling the antiquarian children's books for the past quarter of a century. Contact her. She's sure to have your favorite story from childhood. Call her also if you would like to tuck away one of the Peter Rabbit stories for Peter's 200th birthday.

Doubleday Book Shop

General   Lake Forest Mall
                                       701 Russell Ave.
                                       Gaithersburg, MD 20877
                                       301-258-9398
                                       Hours: Mon.-Sat. 10-9:30; Sun. noon-6

Both adults and children are thrilled with Doubleday Bookshop in Lake Forest Mall. The store has 70% of merchandise for children while 30% is geared toward adults.

The books written for adults are located in the back of the store which contains many categories including childcare, cookbooks, fiction, humor, travel, diet, and psychology.

Even adults visiting the store will have a hard time pulling themselves away from the children's section of books. The delightfully bright area over-flows with books and related items that children usually only see in their dreams. Along with the "Oldies-but-Goodies" books that we adults remember, such as the Grinch and Curious George, are a full complement of books that children love today. Books are available for infants to teens.

In addition to books, they have many favorite plush animals and dolls whose stories are told in books. You'll also find video tapes, book-ends, puppets, and assorted little items that no child can live without.

Children and adults find it a treat to shop at Doubleday Bookshop.

Dream Wizards

New Age   104G Halpine Rd.
                                       PO Box 2246
                                       Rockville, MD 20852
                                       301-881-3530
                                       Hours: Mon. & Tues. 11-6; Wed.-Fri. 11-8; Sat. 10-6; Sun. noon-5

If you dream of wizards and unnatural occurrences, you'll adore spending time at Dream Wizards bookshop where you'll find books and magazines about New Age, occult, magic, folklore, science fiction and a category that owner Mark Chorvinsky describes as "strange phenomena."

Open everyday and accessible to all, Dream Wizards also publishes a catalog for telephone and mail orders. In addition to books, Dream Wizards carries a full line of games, posters, children's toys, T-shirts, and greeting cards. Mark does place special orders for clients.

Dream Wizards was established in 1978 and is sure to be in existence as long as wizards dream.

Eastern Mountain Sports Inc.

Outdoor Sports

Lake Forest Mall
701 Russell Ave.
Gaithersburg, MD 20877
301-948-8541
Hours: Mon.-Sat. 10-9:30; Sun. noon-6

If you like camping, hiking, fishing, canoeing, mountain climbing, bicycling, bird watching, or just plain enjoy the great outdoors, Eastern Mountain Sports is a store you definitely must check out. They sell books and equipment relating to all of the above plus all the clothes you'll want in order to relax and enjoy your time out-of-doors. They sell many maps and guidebooks for local and national sites.

With three branches in the Washington area, this branch of Eastern Mountain Sports is located in Lake Forest Mall of Gaithersburg. The other two are in McLean and Alexandria, VA.

Sportsmen in wheelchairs may also find guide books especially filled with information for them. One book features accessibility and special information to all of the state parks across our country. Eastern Mountain Sports stores are wheelchair accessible.

The Elegant Needle

Needlecrafts

7945 MacArthur
Cabin John, MD 20818
301-320-0066
Hours: Mon.-Fri. 10-5; Sat. 10-4

When you elegantly cast your needle to fabric, The Elegant Needle is a store that you should first visit. They sell needlework books, including needlepoint and cross-stitch, all the supplies you need and even conduct classes to get you on the right path. Many books and supplies are sold by mail order. The store is wheelchair accessible.

Whether you are a novice or skilled stitcher, you are sure to be inspired at The Elegant Needle.

Ellie's Paperback Shack

Used paperbacks

Acton Square
Box 31 D on Rte. 301
Waldorf, MD 20601
301-934-3140
Hours: Mon.-Fri. 10-6; Sat. 10-5;
Weekday evenings by appointment

Elinore Fortney brings personal service with a small town atmosphere to Ellie's Paperback Shack. She has collected approximately 20,000 titles of previously read books, with especially large collections of romance, mystery, science fiction, fiction, children's books, Christian religion, westerns, and thrillers. She is eager to conduct searches for specific titles.

Ellie's Paperback Shack is open during daytime hours but she is happy to open for evening hours by appointment. The store is wheelchair accessible but Ellie points out that there is a curb outside. Off-street parking nearby is available.

Visit Ellie's Paperback Shack and you'll come back.

Encore Books

General

Burtonsville Crossing
15771 Columbia Pike
Burtonsville, MD 20730
301-421-0292
Hours: Mon.-Sat. 9-9; Sun. 11-6

Let's hear an encore for Encore Books. Their selection of approximately 15,000 titles of general interest books is available seven days per week. Also for sale are books on cassette tape and books printed with large type. They have a large magazine section filled with many hard-to-find magazines.

As a part of a chain of bookstores, Encore Books has a well-trained, friendly staff who enjoy their work and stay with the bookstore for many years. According to manager Charles Billups, employees share a commitment to excellent customer service which includes placing special orders, searching for titles requested, gift wrapping, and maintaining an in-store bulletin board of announcements.

At Encore Books, you'll be able to join a reading group to discuss specific books. Authors visit the store for signing sessions.

Located in a 3,000 square foot strip-mall store, Encore Books plays classical and new age music to ensure a comfortable atmosphere for browsing. The store is completely wheelchair accessible. For your convenience, off-street parking and mass transit is available nearby.

After visiting Encore Books, you will be back for an encore yourself.

Evangel Temple Bookstore

Religious-Christian

13901 Central Ave.
(Bookstore inside church)
Upper Marlboro, MD 20772
301-390-1490
Hours: Mon.-Fri. 10:30-6; Sat. 10:30-4

The Evangel Temple Bookstore is located inside the temple. Most items sold are Bibles and Christian books but they also sell a small selection of greeting cards, musical tapes, and video tapes. The shop is wheelchair accessible. Employees are happy to assist patrons.

Family Bookstores

Religious-Christian   Lake Forest Mall
                                         701 Russell Ave.
                                         Gaithersburg, MD 20877
                                         301-990-6611
                                         <u>Hours:</u> Mon.-Sat. 10-9:30

      Located in Lakeforest Mall, Family Bookstores sells books and gifts intended for Christians. The store is wheelchair accessible. For the background of Family Bookstores, please see the write-up for the Fredericksburg, VA store.

Family Bookstores

Religious-Christian   Laurel Shopping Center
                                         323 Montrose Ave.
                                         Laurel, MD 20707
                                         301-604-2602
                                         <u>Hours:</u> Mon.-Sat. 10-9

      Laurel Shopping Center is home to one of the seven Family Bookstores in the Washington area. The store is wheelchair accessible. To read about Family Bookstores, please refer to the description for the Fredericksburg, VA store.

Family Bookstores

Religious-Christian   St. Charles Towne Center
                                         5000 Rte. 301S
                                         Waldorf, MD 20603
                                         301-705-8199
                                         <u>Hours:</u> Mon.-Sat. 10-9:30

      Located in St. Charles Towne Center, Family Bookstores brings a fine collection of Christian books and items to the Waldorf community. Please refer to the description of the Family Bookstores chain for the Fredricksburg, VA store.

Foundation Bookstore

Medicine

9000 Rockville Pike, Bldg. 10
Room B1-L-101
Bethesda, MD 20892
301-496-5274
FAX 301-480-5319
Hours: Mon.-Fri. 8:30-4

Researchers for the National Institute of Health know just where to find the scientific and medical books they need: Foundation Bookstore.

With more than 5,000 titles in stock, they also will place special orders to supply information to the public as well as the preeminent researchers. Foundation Bookstore also sells books written by scientists and medical professionals at NIH.

Located in the Clinical Center of NIH, the bookstore is wheelchair accessible. They fill orders for people around the world.

To be on the edge of research, contact Foundation Bookstore.

Frazier's Americana

New & Used Americana

10509 Water Point Way
Mitchellville, MD 20721
301-336-3616
Hours: Telephone & mail order only

Johnny came marching home and he left his Civil War books, prints, and engravings at Frazier's Americana in Mitchellville, Maryland. W.D. Frazier will part with new and used books if you call or write to him.

A catalog of the approximately 1,000 books is available upon request. The catalog also contains a listing of newspapers and posters available. Because W.D. Frazier knows Civil War books so well he conducts appraisals and searches for specific books.

Whether you stand behind Johnny Yank or Johnny Reb, you'll find books just for you through Frazier's Americana.

G Street Fabrics Book Dept.

Needlecrafts

11854 Rockville Pike
Rockville, MD 20852
301-231-8998
800-333-9191
FAX 301-770-7522
Hours: Mon.-Fri. 10-9;
Sat. 10-6; Sun. noon-5

You don't often think of book shopping at a fabric store, but don't miss the wonderful selection of books at G Street Fabrics. Topics include home decorating, high fashion clothing, costumes, sewing instructions, and crafts.

Today, you can stop at one store, G Street Fabrics, and purchase books and all the supplies you need to create customized clothing. G Street Fabrics sells more than 1500 titles of instructional books which show you how to make your own fashions, design your wedding gown, or learn the dainty smocking style of needlework included on many little girl's dresses. They also offer evening classes for personal one-on-one instructions.

Don't forget about crafts. G Street Fabrics sells a variety of craft books teaching you how to quilt, make children's toys, and every needlework project you can imagine.

A Washington tradition since 1942, G Street Fabrics is located on two floors and is completely wheelchair accessible. They do have ramps and an elevator inside the store. They also have a strong mail order department.

You ask about notions? You bet they have them. You'll be amazed at extent of the buttons and trims sold. Thimble collectors will be thrilled at the variety of collectable thimbles they offer.

It's known in the community of stitchers, "If G Street doesn't have it, no one does."

Georgetown Book Shop

Antiquarian-General

7770 Woodmont Ave.
Bethesda, MD 20814
301-907-6923
Hours: Daily 10-6

If you wonder where used bookstores find their stock, look to Georgetown Book Shop in Bethesda. Andy Moursund has created a fantastic used book business that specializes in history, military history, fine art, photography, and baseball. The book shop does offer selections in most categories.

Andy doesn't issue catalogs. Why? He says, "The reason we don't issue catalogs or set up at book fairs is that this inevitably dilutes the quality of the stock exposed to the walk-in customer."

Customers are important people at Georgetown Book Shop. Andy has a large nationwide group of fans who stop here every time they're in the area. Andy closely watches what customers buy as well as what they don't buy. He carefully weeds out the "garbage," as he calls it, and brings customers a top-quality selection.

"Our customers seem to agree that we've done a pretty good job in this respect," said Andy.

Fortunately, Georgetown Book Shop is accessible to everyone. Aisles can be a tight squeeze for wheelchairs when books are stacked on the floor. The best news is that they are open seven days per week and only close on Thanksgiving, Christmas, and New Year's Day.

The large display windows at the front of the store tantalize book lovers into the store. Once inside, you won't be disappointed. The store has floor-to-ceiling bookcases as well as free-standing cases. You'll also find boxes of magazines, mostly about sports, and bound volumes of the New York Times. You won't want to miss the bargain table.

You'll note that Georgetown Book Shop isn't in Georgetown at all but is located in Bethesda. Originally, Andy opened a book shop at Georgetown in 1984. By 1989 it was clear that he needed more space and moved to a larger and more convenient location in Bethesda. The new location has better parking and is near the subway. Andy notes that he will be at this location until at least 1998, but after that, who knows, he may need a book shop the size of the Library of Congress!

Currently, Andy reports 15-20,000 titles offered at Georgetown Book Shop. Ninety percent of the books are hardcovers and almost all have dust jackets.

A journalist before opening the book shop, Andy says his background includes reading a lot of books, shooting a lot of pool, and buying books for a local shop for six-and-a-half years.

Although I've tried to describe Georgetown Book Shop here, the only way to fully experience the book shop is to visit.

Geppi's Comic World of Silver Spring

Comic books

8317 Fenton Street
Silver Spring, MD 20910
301-588-2546
Hours: Mon. & Wed. 10-7; Tues, Thurs, Fri. & Sat. 10-6; Sun. noon-5

Geppi's knows comics and they have opened a branch in Silver Spring known as, what else, Geppi's Comic World of Silver Spring. To read more details about this store, see the write-up for the Crystal City store in Arlington.

Geppi's in Silver Spring is wheelchair accessible. They are open later hours on Monday and Wednesdays because those are the days they receive new arrivals of comic books and they tend to be busier then.

Glen Echo Park

National Park

7300 MacArthur Blvd.
Glen Echo, MD 20812
301-492-6245
Hours: Daily 8am-dark

Known best for its 1921 Dentzel carousel, Glen Echo Park was originally an amusement park and entertained people for 70 years. Now a National Park, Glen Echo is almost as busy as it was years ago.

The carousel still operates and you can hop a ride for 50-cents. The Park is home to galleries, studios, and classrooms for artists, a children's theatre where stageplays and puppet shows abound, and a

Spanish ballroom where couples can join in dancing and participate in classes for a variety of styles of dancing. Call (301) 492-6282 for a description of events.

A small shop can be found inside the stone tower in the park. In addition to gift items, they sell 25-30 titles of books which relate to the Carousel, the canal area, the Potomac, and the art exhibits held in the park. Many books are available for children.

Unfortunately, the shop is not wheelchair accessible. However, you can call them and purchase books through the mail. The most popular book sold continues to be about the fantastic Carousel.

Gospel Notes Records & Books

Religious-Christian

6107 Oxon Hill Rd.
Oxon Hill, MD 20745
301-839-2636
<u>Hours:</u> Mon.-Thurs. 10-8;
Fri. & Sat. 10-9; Sun. 1-5

When you want to read Christian literature, Gospel Notes Records & Books has the books for you and your children. When you want to sing out, Gospel Notes sells CD's, cassettes, and sheet music. They also sell Bibles, greeting cards, and gifts.

The store is wheelchair accessible and open everyday. Special orders are welcomed.

Ground Zero Books Ltd.

Military History

P.O. Box 1046 Blair Station
Silver Spring, MD 20910
301-585-1471
<u>Hours:</u> Telephone and Mail order only

Books about "war, peace, and politics," is how Lynne Haims, Vice-President of Ground Zero Books Ltd., described the collection of books, pamphlets, manuscripts, autographs, maps, and ephemera.

Specifically, Ground Zero Books Ltd. sells used and rare books about the Revolutionary War, the Civil War, World Wars I and II, the VietNam War, the British Empire, and a unique category titled military medicine. Most business is conducted by mail order but they do have a showroom at Imagination Books (see their write-up).

Ground Zero Books Ltd. offers a free search service, appraisals, and issues a fully annotated catalog. They maintain a stock of more than 40,000 books.

Alan Lewis, a book lover and collector since childhood, owns Ground Zero Books Ltd. with his wife, Lynne. Both Alan and Lynne are trained historians and have done graduate work in their special fields of history. Customers of Ground Zero Books Ltd. include collectors, scholars, military specialists, research organizations, and colleges and universities.

Hammett's Learning World

Education
Weis Festival at Muddy Branch
241 Muddy Branch Rd.
Gaithersburg, MD 20878
301-330-7680
Hours: Mon.-Fri. 10-9; Sat. 10-6

Have you noticed that children are reading at much younger ages than you did? That's because there are stores like J.L. Hammett Co. conducting business.

Specializing in selling learning materials to parents and teachers, the business today has stores across the country. In addition to establishing the business in 1863, schoolteacher John L. Hammett is also credited with publishing the first booklet of penmanship known as the Palmer Method, inventing the chalkboard eraser, and bringing the first kindergarten materials to America from Germany.

Upon his retirement in 1895, John sold the business and name to a group of men who brought the store into the 20th century. Today the store sells books, arts and crafts supplies, posters, blackboards, learning games, maps and many more items to facilitate learning.

Today's president, Rick Holden, is the great grandson of one of the men who bought the business from John. Rick's brother, Jeffrey, is vice-president of sales.

Founded in Massachusetts, the J.L. Hammett Company maintains headquarters near Boston and sells materials worldwide. All stores are staffed with learning experts such as teachers, librarians, and child development specialists.

The store located in Gaithersburg has been in existence since 1988. Other J.L. Hammett Company stores in the Washington area are located in Springfield and Oakton, both in Virginia.

Heaven Christian Gift Store

Religious-Christian
1160-B Smallwood Dr.
Waldorf, MD 20603
301-645-2828
Hours: Mon.-Thurs. 10-8;
Fri. & Sat. 10-9

A non-denominational Christian bookstore, Heaven Christian Gift Store offers you approximately 400 titles of books all with a general theme. Some of the books are available in large type print and on audio cassettes.

Heaven has more to offer. They also sell magazines, calendars, stationery, greeting cards, video tapes, T-shirts, posters, games, and children's toys, not to mention the many items perfect for gifts.

To assist customers, they do place special orders and accept charge accounts. Announcements are posted on a store bulletin board.

Although there is one step at the door, owner Tony Di Giovanni says that customers using wheelchairs do not need assistance to enter the store. If you can't visit Heaven Christian Gift Store, a catalog is available for telephone and mail orders.

Historic Saint Mary's City Museum Shop

Museum   PO Box 395
                            Saint Mary's City, MD 20686
                            301-862-3785
                            Hours: Wed.-Sun. 10-5

With approximately 700 titles, Historic Saint Mary's City Museum Shop focuses on books about 17th century life in Maryland, archaeology, gardening, and nature. Many of the books highlight both town life and plantation life. They do place special orders for books not in stock.

Also for sale in the shop are T-shirts, children's toys, posters, games, and stationery. The shop is wheelchair accessible.

After visiting the stately and refreshing grounds of Historic Saint Mary's City, be sure to visit the shop where you'll find interesting items as well as friendly employees.

Imagination Books

Used-General   946 Sligo Ave.
                            Silver Spring, MD 20910
                            301-589-2223
                            Hours: Mon.-Thurs. 10-7;
                            Fri. & Sat. 10-8; Sun. 10-5

Imagination Books has the books to spark all sorts of imaginative thinking. They sell used books to please interests of all sorts. They also buy and trade books.

The store has a unique lay-out in that books are sold in ten separate rooms. Two of the rooms are allocated to Ground Zero Books (see their write-up). Because Imagination Books does have two floors, those using wheelchairs will not be able to reach part of the stock but employees are ready to assist with retrieving books or answering questions.

Iranbooks Inc.

Iran & Persian Language   8014 Old Georgetown Rd.
Bethesda, MD 20814
301-986-0079
FAX 301-907-8707
Hours: Mon.-Sat. 10-6

Iranbooks Inc. sells between 10-20,000 titles of books about Iran and in the Persian language. Both new and used books are found here. But if they don't have the book you want, they do conduct search services and place special orders. At Iranbooks Inc. you'll find some books on audio tape. Also for sale are greeting cards.

Established in 1979, the bookstore also is a publishing house. There are four steps to enter Iranbooks Inc., making it impossible for wheelchair users. Inside the small store, aisles are tight. However, a catalog and telephone/mail orders make their stock is available to everyone.

Jacob's Well Christian Books

Religious-Christian   170 Great Mills Rd.
Lexington Park, MD 20653
301-863-6388
Hours: Mon.-Fri. 10-8; Sat. 10-6

Jacob's Well Christian Books brings inspirational books from Christian authors featuring fiction, biography, and study guides. Imprinting on Bibles is a special service offered.

Also available are Sunday School supplies, gifts, video and audio tapes, greeting cards, Christian jewelry, wall hangings, Precious Moments, and much more. Special orders pose no problems to employees.

The store is wheelchair accessible. Existing for years as a small store, Jacob's Well Christian Books was purchased by Pam and David Laur and Larry and Ann Reggan in January, 1993. They have expanded the stock and continue to develop it as a place that meets the needs of the Christian community.

Jesus' Bookstore Inc.

Religious-Christian   4823 Allentown Rd.
Camp Springs, MD 20746
301-735-1100
FAX 301-420-7920
Hours: Mon. & Tues. 9-8;
Wed.-Sat. 9-5

A Christian bookstore, Jesus' Bookstore, Inc., carries a full line of religious gifts, church items, study guides, children's books, and songbooks, in addition to beautiful Bibles which can be imprinted with names or initials. The store carries approximately 20,000 titles. It is wheelchair accessible.

During the summer, Jesus' Bookstore conducts vacation Bible study workshops. The store is owned by Mike Rice and his wife and was established in 1972.

The Jewish Bookstore of Greater Washington

Religious-Jewish

11252 Georgia Ave.
Wheaton, MD 20902
301-942-2237
Hours: Mon.-Thurs. 10-7;
Fri. 10-3; Sun. 10-5

In the summer of 1993, The Jewish Bookstore of Greater Washington was bursting at the seams. The answer: they moved to a larger store just a door away from where they had been located.

"If it's Jewish, we have it," states the business card of bookstore owner Joshua Youlus.

He is a man who tells the truth. You will find a multitude of Jewish items in addition to the many books written in Hebrew and English. Joshua said that there are Jewish scholars and people from all over the country who have stopped at The Jewish Bookstore once and continue to shop through the mail. Many people point to the completeness of the stock and the personal assistance as two reasons to shop here.

The store is huge and completely wheelchair accessible. Located in the Wheaton Triangle strip mall, The Jewish Bookstore of Greater Washington is a store not to be missed.

John C. Rather: Old & Rare Books

Chess, Magic, Mountaineering

PO Box 273
Kensington, MD 20895
301-942-0515
Hours: Mail order only

John Rather began selling books in 1976. He specializes in chess, backgammon, magic, and mountaineering. His primary focus is on chess with which he has been involved for 58 years. In this field his stock comprises more than 7,000 volumes in many languages.

All business is conducted by telephone and mail order with the aid of catalogs published during the year. He also makes it a point to check customers' want lists against his stock and keeps an eye out for desired titles.

Leonard S. Blondes Used Law Books

Used-Law

7100 Crail Dr.
Bethesda, MD 20817
301-229-7102
FAX 301-229-7102
Hours: 24 hours daily

Since 1952, Mr. Leonard S. Blondes has been collecting used law books. Whether you're involved with law in some respect or not, you're sure to find his collection interesting. All business is conducted by mail order. Since Mr. Blondes works from his home, he notes that his business is conducted 24 hours per day!

Maryland Book Exchange

College

4500 College Ave.
College Park, MD 20740
301-927-2501
Hours: Fall: Mon.-Fri. 9-6; Sat. 10-5;
Sun. noon-5; Summer: Mon-Fri. 9-5;
Sat. 10-5

With a whopping 125,000 titles, Maryland Book Exchange is a haven for all book lovers. Most books are of general interest. Selected titles and bestsellers are discounted; some are 25-50% off the cover price. Computer books, business, reference, and technical books for professionals are all large departments at the Book Exchange.

Established in 1936, the Maryland Book Exchange also supplies books for the University of Maryland. New and used textbooks are located downstairs. You'll also be able to purchase school clothing with the insignia, art and school supplies, and gifts. Since the University has a strong engineering school, many items sold in the bookstore relate to engineering.

Employees place special orders to get the books you need into your hands. The main floor of the store is wheelchair accessible.

After visiting the Maryland Book Exchange, take a stroll on the University campus or pop into the deli across the street. The Maryland Book Exchange is a store you'll return to often.

Mystery Bookshop: Bethesda

Mystery
7700 Old Georgetown Rd.
Bethesda, MD 20814
301-657-2665
800-572-8533
Hours: Mon.-Sat. 10-7; Sun. noon-5

Every month you'll notice a group of people disappearing into a quaint shop inside the Chevy Chase Garden Plaza. They are on a mission—a mission they crave—a mission they can't live without.

Who are these people and where are they going? They're members of the Chesapeake-Potomac Chapter of Mystery Readers International and they're entering Mystery Bookshop: Bethesda for their monthly meeting which is sponsored by the store.

Owners Jean and Ron McMillen have created a wonderful specialty bookshop filled with 20,000 titles of new books specialized in crime and detective fiction, suspense, espionage, thrillers, chillers, true crime, and books for writers of mystery genre. Some books sold are first editions autographed by the authors. They also have a little room stacked with used mystery books. In total, the store is 1,000 square feet and "a cozy book boutique," says Jean.

The experts working at the bookshop are well-read lovers of mystery books. You can ask for a topic and they immediately can retrieve a wealth of books to suit your interest. When I visited them, I asked for a mystery book taking place in Alaska and they immediately found me four books!

When the store was envisioned by Jean, she wanted to create an atmosphere suitable for both readers and writers. The store opened March 1, 1989 and, wow, has she succeeded. "A Question of Murder" is a seminar series which features author readings and signings. You can also purchase tickets to mystery events happening in the area. Check the weekly "Mystery on the Menu" events which may include a mystery cruise, a mystery train ride, mystery dinners in the country and a mystery afternoon tea.

The "extras" abound at Mystery Bookshop: Bethesda. They sell T-shirts with the store's logo and shirts with their slogan: "So Many Mysteries...So Little Time!" You'll also find mystery games, puzzles, tote bags, mugs, children's mystery books, video tapes, magazines, audio books, notecards, special orders, gift wrapping, shipping, a bulletin board of announcements, a newsletter, and more. Their annual catalog is an incredibly complete list of title available as well as excerpts from and descriptions for many.

Perhaps one of the most exciting items they sell are custom-made gift baskets that are created for all price ranges. You can request a multitude of items to be included in your basket including hardback and paperback mystery books, Maltese Falcons, Sherlock Holmes teapots and playing cards, jellies, jams and chocolates. They ship the baskets anywhere in the world.

Everywhere you look inside the store you see Jean's decorating expertise in creating a perfect setting for book browsing. The two wingbacked green chairs have doilies just like Grandma used to crochet. Between the chairs is a little table with a teapot just waiting to be used. With flowing ribbons, dolls and bunnies and baskets of potpourri sit appropriately in corners of the store. In gold brass letters on a deep green background a sign exclaims Sherlock Holmes favorite phrase, "The Game is Afoot."

Park your car underground and enter Mystery Bookshop: Bethesda through the marble lobby of Chevy Chase Garden Plaza. Fortunately, shoppers with wheelchairs or strollers will have no problem here.

Jean and Ron have kept a promise to their customers that was made when the store was first opened. That promise was to continue to evolve and grow to meet the changing needs and wants of their clients. Jean says that she feels that the store belongs to the customers and she is always happy to receive questions.

While many bookstores have cats on their logos or roaming the store, Mystery Bookshop: Bethesda has a dog on its logo. It happens to be a member of Jean and Ron's family, it's "Windsor," their English Cocker Spaniel.

It's no mystery when you step into Mystery Bookshop: Bethesda that you have stepped into a delightful world where you will want to return often.

Natural Wonders Inc.

General

Montgomery Mall
7101 Democracy Blvd.
Bethesda, MD 20817
301-365-8620
Hours: Mon.-Sat. 10-9:30; Sun. 11-6

A store that is a hit with nature lovers, Natural Wonders has a branch in the Montgomery Mall in Bethesda. The store is wheelchair accessible.

Please see the descriptive write-up about Natural Wonders' Springfield, VA, store.

Natural Wonders Inc.

General

Lake Forest Mall
Gaithersburg, MD 20877
301-926-7633
Hours: Mon.-Sat. 10-9:30; Sun. noon-6

An environmental educational store, Natural Wonders is also a fun store to visit. The branch in Gaithersburg, MD, is in the Lakeforest Mall and is wheelchair accessible.

For a more detailed description of Natural Wonders, see the write-up for the Springfield, Virginia store.

Old Hickory Bookshop

Antiquarian-Medicine

20225 New Hampshire Ave.
Brinklow, MD 20862
301-924-2225
Hours: Mail order or appt. only

Old Hickory Bookshop specializes in antiquarian medical books, the oldest one for sale is dated 1498. Owner Johanna Grines conducts business by mail and telephone orders and by appointment. An expert in the field, she also conducts appraisals of medical books.

Old World Mail Auctions

Antiquarian-Maps, Newspapers

5614 Northfield Rd.
Bethesda, MD 20817
301-657-9074
FAX 301-652-0418
Hours: Telephone and mail order only

Check out this unique way to buy antique maps, prints, and historical newspapers; you make your purchases by bidding through mail auction. A catalog is published five times per year.

Contact Tim and Jeannie Coss, owners of Old World Mail Auctions, to discuss just how you can purchase the treasures they offer.

Olde Soldier Books, Inc.

Civil War

18779 B N Frederick Ave.
Gaithersburg, MD 20879
301-963-2929
FAX 301-963-9556
Hours: Mon.-Sat. 9-4

Dave Zullo and wife, Chris, are responsible for keeping old soldiers alive through books. The owners of Olde Soldier Books, they sell rare, out-of-print, and antiquarian books all of which strictly relate to the Civil War. The Zullos have kept some books from drifting into obscurity by persuading publishers to reprint more than 100 titles.

"We have the largest Civil War bookshop in the country," said Dave. He added that they conduct business internationally.

They also sell autographs, photographs, letters, currency, maps, documents, and even medals from that war. Because of the many historical objects in the store, schoolchildren and interested clubs and groups have toured the store for educational purposes.

Olde Soldier Books is located in an industrial park warehouse, but don't let that fool you. The store is carpeted, has couches, and is comfortable for long-time browsing or talking with the knowledgeable Zullos. It is wheelchair accessible.

It can be tricky to find Olde Soldier Books but not if you follow Dave's directions: 270 North; Exit 11 take Route 124 East; turn left on 355; drive 1.2 miles and turn right on Gane Preserve Rd. The building's number is 18779 B. They are one block off of 355.

The Zullos publish a catalog 11 times per year and have a strong mail order business. The store maintains approximately 12,000 titles.

What began as a hobby in 1975, has developed into the fine bookstore Olde Soldier Books. You don't need to be a Civil War buff to enjoy this specialty bookstore.

The Olive Branch

Religious-Christian   765 Rockville Pike
Rockville, MD 20852
301-340-1129
Hours: Mon. & Wed. 9:30-6; Tues.,
Thurs., & Fri. 9:30-9; Sat. 0-4:30

A nondenominational Christian bookstore, The Olive Branch sells Bibles, church supplies, choir robes, educational materials, printed music, and assorted cards and gifts. Occasionally authors visit the store. The store is wheelchair accessible.

Established in May, 1977, The Olive Branch is owned by Leonard Bertsch and his wife.

Olsson's Books & Records

General   7647 Old Georgetown Rd.
Bethesda, MD 20814
301-652-3336
Hours: Mon.-Sat. 10-10; Sun. 11-7

Olsson's Books & Records in Bethesda sells general interest books which includes a fine collection of scholarly books not usually found in other bookstores.

The store is wheelchair accessible from the outside; however inside the store some displays can hamper maneuverability. The displays are moveable and employees are happy to assist.

See the write-up of the Dupont Circle store in Washington for a more detailed description of Olsson's.

Pyramid Bookstore

General

Prince Georges Plaza
3500 East-West Highway
Hyattsville, MD 20782
301-559-5200
FAX 301-559-5202
Hours: Daily 10-9:30

Opened on the anniversary of Martin Luther King's birth, January 15 in 1990, this branch of Pyramid Books is located in Prince George's Plaza and is wheelchair accessible.

Please refer to the description in the northwest Washington section of this book for a complete description of Pyramid Books.

Q. M. Dabney & Co.

Antiquarian-History

11910 Park Lawn Dr., #P
Rockville, MD 20852
301-881-1470
FAX 301-881-0843
Hours: Mail order or appt. only

You'll snap to attention when you browse the catalog of books sold by Q.M. Dabney & Company because they specialize in military books. Most are used but a few are recently published books.

Q.M. Dabney has a number of sub-specialties: military history, American history, European history, legal history, music history and ancient history. They usually have a total of 25,000 books in stock.

In business since 1963, Q.M. Dabney & Company also conduct searches and repair tattered books. They keep lists of client's interests and watch for books they may find interesting.

Owner Michael Schnitter reports that most business is conducted by telephone and mail order. Catalogs are regularly published. The showroom in Rockville is wheelchair accessible with assistance through a back door.

When you dust off your spectacles and want to replace cobwebs on your bookshelves with historical books, you'll find quality books with Q.M. Dabney & Company.

Quill & Brush Bookstore

Antiquarian-20th cent. 1st edition

14717 Janice Dr.
Rockville, MD 20848
301-460-3700
FAX 301-871-5425
Hours: Appointment only

In addition to selling books, Patricia and Allen Ahearn are busy writing books. They collaborated on "Collected Books: The Guide to Values" and Allen penned "Book Collecting: A Comprehensive Guide." Whether you are new to the hobby of book collecting or want to brush-up your skills, both books prove to be valuable.

You can meet the Ahearns and purchase books from their collection of 20th century first editions. The business, conducted by appointment only, is known as Quill & Brush.

When you contact them, you will be able to tap into a unique service called Author Price Guides (APG). When you purchase a specific APG for a nominal charge, you receive a facsimile of the author's signature; a brief biographical sketch; an up-to-date list of the author's first editions (American and British) with entries for limited and trade editions; numbers of copies (if available); how to identify the first edition; and estimated prices. As you develop your book collection, APG information will prove to be valuable.

When you seek professionals who are willing to share their knowledge of the antiquarian book collecting, contact Patricia and Allen at Quill & Brush.

R. Quick, Bookseller

Used & Scarce-General

7155 Wisconsin Ave.
Bethesda, MD 20814
301-654-5030
Hours: Appointment only and at the Market Wed. & Sat. 8-4

In 1985, Robert Quick retired and looked around his home to find a massive collection of books. He decided to sell half of his own library and liked doing it so much, he kept at it.

Specializing in used and scarce books about the classics, fiction, cooking, and books for children, Robert sees client by appointment. He maintains a section in the Montgomery Farmer Women's Cooperative Market. He also does some business by mail.

Give him a call now. You'll enjoy discussing a passion you share: books.

Rand McNally—The Map & Travel Store

Travel & Cartography

Montgomery Mall
7101 Democracy Blvd.
Bethesda, MD 20817
301-365-6277
Hours: Mon.-Sat. 10-9:30; Sun. 11-6

Rand McNally—The Map and Travel Store has three fine locations in the Washington area. One of the newer locations of Rand McNally, this branch is located in Montgomery Mall, and is wheelchair accessible.

Manager Mario A. Ramon notes that this branch focuses on families and the travelling businessman's needs.

For a complete description of this store, please refer to the description of the Washington, D.C. branch.

Recreational Equipment Inc.

Recreation

9801 Rhode Island Ave.
College Park, MD 20740
301-982-9681
FAX 301-982-0335
<u>Hours:</u> Mon.-Fri. 10-9;
Sat. 10-6; Sun. noon-5

When you step into Recreational Equipment Inc. (REI), you're stepping into more than just a store that sells outdoor clothing, equipment, and adventure guides. You're experiencing a unique business.

Established in 1938 by a group of climbers in Seattle, Washington, the business was formed so that they could obtain quality climbing equipment from Europe at good prices. Their high standards, focus on quality, and dedication to personal service remains today.

REI is the nation's largest consumer cooperative dedicated to supporting conservation of our environment through educational and recreational programs. Although the stores are open to everyone, REI members receive announcements of special discounts on purchases and rental equipment, free catalogs, labor discounts on repairs, and more. Members also receive yearly dividends!

The two REI stores in the Washington area are located here in College Park and in Baileys Crossroads in Virginia. Each store carries 500-1,000 titles of books relating to camping, climbing, hiking, cooking, backpacking, running, first aid, and other topics of interest to the outdoor enthusiast. Some books are outdoor guidebooks, fictional accounts of other's outdoor experiences, and books for children. A multitude of related maps and magazines are available. The two Washington area stores can tap into 36 REI stores country-wide for items they may not have in stock. A catalog is published for telephone and mail orders. The catalog includes clothing, shoes, and equipment.

Both store locations here are wheelchair accessible. In parts of the store that may not be accessible, friendly employees are happy to retrieve the items you need.

Contact the stores to discover the programs they conduct such as REI adventures that range from bicycling in Russia to hiking in Hawaii. Activities are arranged for enthusiasts for abilities ranging from strenuous to leisurely.

Rejoice Christian Store

Religious-Christian

5682 Silver Hill Rd.
District Heights, MD 20747
301-420-2471
FAX 301-735-2747
Hours: Mon.-Wed. 10-7;
Thurs.-Sat. 10-8

Bibles, study guides, Christian literature, and children's books are the main focus of Rejoice Christian Store. They also sell many gifts including videos (which are also rented), Christian jewelry, T-shirts, sweatshirts, greeting cards, and music on cassettes and CD's. They carry some sheet music.

The store is wheelchair accessible. According to the manager, Betty Harris, Rejoice Christian Store has enjoyed serving the public since 1984.

Robert A. Madle Science Fiction-Fantasy Books

Science Fiction-Fantasy

4406 Bestor Drive
Rockville, MD 20853
301-460-4712
Hours: Appt. or mail order only

If you think you have the best collection of science fiction, fantasy, or horror books, call Robert A. Madle. He has books and magazines that you didn't know existed. He has thousands of sci-fi and horror magazines, some dating back to 1900.

A 64-page catalog featuring approximately 25,000 titles, which is available on request, describes the many new, used, and antiquarian books he sells. Some books have been autographed by the authors. With a show place open by appointment only, a majority of his sales are conducted by telephone and mail order.

An expert in the field, Robert Madle does appraisals of your book gems. If, by some far out chance he doesn't have the book you're looking for, he does conduct searches and place special orders.

No matter what world is your destination, call Robert A. Madle for a guidebook before you blast off.

Sakura Books & Food

Japanese books

15809 S. Frederick Rd.
Rockville, MD 20855
301-948-5112
FAX 301-926-9844
Hours: Tues.-Sun. 10-7

When you browse through the Japanese cookbooks at Sakura Books and Foods, you won't have to wait very long before you can satisfy those active taste buds. You can buy both cookbooks and food all in the same store. No matter what Japanese book you want, you'll find it at Sakura. They also sell Japanese magazines and assorted gifts. The store is wheelchair accessible.

Schweitzer Japanese Prints Inc.

Orientalia

6313 Lenox Rd.
Bethesda, MD 20817
301-229-6574
FAX 301-229-0345
Hours: Appointment only

An expert in Japanese books and woodblock books, Paul R. Schweitzer sells and buys these as well as reference books on these and Japanese art in general. He also has a good inventory of other art, fiction, and mystery fiction books.

John has approximately 1,500-2,000 titles. Those he does not have in stock, he can conduct searches for. Also contact him for appraisals of your books.

Second Story Books & Antiques

Used-General

12160 Parklawn Dr.
Rockville, MD 20852
301-770-0477
FAX 301-770-9544
Hours: Sun.-Thurs. 10-7;
Fri. & Sat. 10-9

The largest used and out-of-print store in the Washington area according to Allan Stypeck, is Second Story Books & Antiques. Allan, the owner, has been developing an excellent selection of used and antiquarian books since 1973.

One of three stores, this Rockville location boasts approximately 400,000 titles. Both the Washington and Bethesda locations each have 100,000 titles. If, by some wild chance, they don't have just the book you want, they do conduct searches and place special orders. A catalog is available for at-home book shopping. Of special note is that Second Story Books & Antiques conducts appraisals and also skillfully repairs books.

The three Second Story Books & Antiques are open everyday. Unfortunately, the Rockville store is not wheelchair accessible due to four steps at the entrance.

No matter which of the three stores that you visit, you're sure to enjoy browsing.

Second Story Books & Antiques

Used-General   4836 Bethesda Ave.
                                              Bethesda, MD 20814
                                              301-656-0170
                                              FAX 301-770-9544
                                              Hours: Daily 10-10

With approximately 100,000 titles in stock, Second Story Books & Antiques is one of three fine antiquarian and used bookstores that owner Allan Stypeck oversees. This Bethesda location can tap into the other stores collective 500,000 titles.

Open everyday, Second Story Books & Antiques in Bethesda is wheelchair accessible, near to off-street parking and mass transit. Check with Second Story Books & Antiques for books and also enjoy the antiques they sell.

Silver Spring Books

Used-General   938 Bonifant St.
                                              Silver Spring, MD 20910
                                              301-587-7484
                                              Hours: Thurs.-Mon. 10:30-6:30;
                                              Sun. 10:30-5; closed Tues. & Wed.

A group of dealers have gathered a wonderful collection of used books that are sold through Silver Spring Books. Particularly strong departments are literature, history, science fiction, and romance. Silver Spring Books also sells a few comic books and sports cards.

If you let one of the dealers know where your interests lie, they will be sure to keep an eye out for titles you will be sure to enjoy.

The store is wheelchair accessible. Please note that they are closed on Tuesdays and Wednesdays.

Smile Herb Shop

Health & Nutrition   4908 Berwyn Rd.
                                              College Park, MD 20740
                                              301-474-8791
                                              Hours: Mon.-Sat. 10-6

"We are the largest herb shop in the mid-Atlantic region with an extensive selection of books on alternative health care and personal growth issues," said Linda Wolfe, co-owner of Smile Herb & Book Shop.

Located near the University of Maryland, Smile Herb & Book Shop sells approximately 2,500 titles which also feature philosophy, alternative life styles, ethnic studies, cookery, medicine, metaphysics, nature, parenting, new age, psychology, recovery, science, and self-help.

They do sell some audio books and magazines. If they don't have the book you're looking for, they will place special orders.

In addition to books, the store sells more than 14,000 different products including herbal teas, gourmet coffees, natural and gourmet food items, vitamins, natural cosmetics, educational children's books and toys, to name only a few.

Interested in education, co-owners of Smile Herb & Book Shop bring experts and authors into the store for seminars.

Because the Smile Herb & Book Shop is located in an attractive Victorian house with four steps at the front porch, it is not accessible to wheelchair users without assistance. Off-street parking and mass transit are both nearby.

To experience a truly unique bookstore, visit Smile Herb & Book Shop.

Steven C. Bernard First Editions

Antiquarian-General

15011 Plainfield Lane
Darnestown, MD 20874
301-948-8423
<u>Hours:</u> Mail order or appt. only

If you are a book collector, you know the value of a first edition book. When you're ready to add to your personal collection of first editions, Steven C. Bernard is the man for you. He has conducted business under the name Steven C. Bernard First Editions since 1974.

Steven has a collection of approximately 5,000 used books first published between 1920-1990. The quality are of fine or "as new" condition. His specialty is mainstream literature, mystery/detective fiction, and science fiction/fantasy and horror tales.

While Steven was a credit reporter and later a National Institutes of Health administrator, he kept his love for books. He started his book business as a part-time venture in 1974 but by 1987, he was involved full-time in the book business.

Today, together with his wife, Sharon, Steven conducts business mainly by mail and telephone orders or by appointment. They issue catalogs five to six times per year. They are also happy to search for books not in their current collection.

Located in a Cape Cod style home twenty miles from Washington, D.C., be sure to contact Steven C. Bernard First Editions when you are looking for those special first edition books.

Stewart's Used Bookstore

Used-General

6504 Old Branch Ave.
Camp Springs, MD 20748
301-449-6766
<u>Hours:</u> Tues.-Fri. 111-5; Sat. 10-5

Since 1975 Mrs. Frances M. Stewart sells just a little bit of everything in her used bookstore. Whatever topic interests you, she's sure to have a used book on the topic.

She has a stock of 20,000 titles in "three rooms small," as she says. The store is tight and wheelchairs will find it impossible to maneuver. There are two steps at the front door.

In addition to books, she sells old post cards, stamps and supplies for collectors, and old games. Visit Mrs. Stewart and you're sure not to go home with empty hands.

SuperCrown

General   7495 Greenbelt Road
                                Greenbelt, MD 20770
                                301-441-8220
                                <u>Hours:</u> Mon.-Sat. 10-10; Sun. 10-6

Located near NASA, SuperCrown has one of the largest computer book sections in the area. At the intersection of the Baltimore/Washington Parkway and the Beltway, SuperCrown has approximately 30,000 titles of general interest books.

For a description of services and discounts, see the write-up of the Potomac, Maryland Crown Books. This store in Greenbelt is wheelchair accessible.

SuperCrown

General   5108 Nicholson Lane
                                Kensington, MD 20895
                                301-770-6729
                                <u>Hours:</u> Mon.-Sat. 10-10; Sun. 10-7

If a super-bookstore doesn't impress you, try SuperCrown at White Flint Mall in Kensington, Maryland. It's a MEGA SuperCrown. In November, 1993, the store expanded to 35,000 square feet of absolute heaven for the book lover.

With such a huge stock of well over 80,000 titles, they are able to bring clients in touch with books from small publishers and a tremendous selection of book-related materials that are often not stocked in other stores. Items include audio tapes, video tapes, Dungeons & Dragons role-playing games, children's novelty items, and more.

For a description of Crown Books discounts and special services, please refer to the write-up of the Potomac, Maryland Crown Books.

Sutton Place Gourmet Inc.

Cooking   Wildwood Shopping Center
                                   10323 Old Georgetown Road
                                   Bethesda, MD 20814
                                   301-564-3100
                                   <u>Hours:</u> Mon.-Sat. 9-9; Sun. 9-8

The largest of the four Sutton Place Gourmet stores in the Washington area, this branch in Bethesda is intriguing even to non-cooks. Mainly the store sells food that make even ordinary everyday meals special, but they also sell approximately one hundred books that aren't found in most bookstores.

Manager Shaun Hunt said that they carry at least one book from each specialty cooking region, such as french, chinese, cajun, etc. Many of the books make beautiful gifts which become treasures. However, they also sell reference books for cooks.

Sutton Place Gourmet in Bethesda is wheelchair accessible. Have no fear if you're not a chef, employees happily lead you to the books and food you will need to create delicious delicacies that no one could pass up.

Swann's Religious Gifts

Religious-Christian   9400 Livingston Rd., Ste. 135A
                                   Fort Washington, MD 20744
                                   301-248-1526
                                   <u>Hours:</u> Mon.-Thurs. 10-5;
                                   Fri. 10-6:30; Sat. 10-4

Swann's Religious Gifts sells Christian items, primarily Catholic, sells books as well as religious items for adults and children alike. Among items for sale are statues, rosaries, medals, and greeting cards.

The store, owned by Joan and John Staken, is wheelchair accessible.

T.A. Borden

Antiquarian-General   17119 Old Baltimore Rd.
                                   Olney, MD 20832
                                   301-774-4669
                                   <u>Hours:</u> Appointment only

As well as selling quality antiquarian books, the co-owners of T.A. Borden consult on collection development, especially for scholarly books.

Available by appointment only, T.A. Borden describes their stock in six categories: 1. the arts including architecture, photography, music, and practical arts; 2. letters--19th and 20th century first editions, some science fiction and children's material, books about books, and illustrated works; 3. Americana-both regional and topical including Western Americana and military; 4. travel-worldwide including anthropology and ancient studies; 5. science and nature, both technical and historical; and 6. scholarly history, humanities, social sciences, religion, and foreign area studies.

Their growing collection, 3,500 to 4,000 titles in mid-1993, is arranged by topics. During Fall, 1993, the stock will be computerized. Occasionally catalogs are issued. A catalog on the arts is scheduled for the Fall of 1993. Call for specific wants or appointments.

The antiquarian and used book business known as T.A. Borden has been operating since 1987.

Takoma Kids

Children's books

7040 Carroll Ave.
Takoma Park, MD 20912
301-853-3237
Hours: Mon.-Fri. 11-6:30;
Sat. 10-5; Sun. 10-2

From the street, Takoma Kids looks like a children's clothing store. But don't pass them by. They also sell children's books that will interest kids until approximately the age 10. The store is wheelchair accessible and a favorite of the community.

This 'N' That Antiques

Used-General

16650 Georgia Ave.
Olney, MD 20832
301-774-6991
Hours: Wed.-Fri. 11-5;
Sat. & Sun. 11-6

Along with 500 used books specializing in Americana, nature, and biographies, This 'N' That Antiques also sells interesting advertising from early magazines. For example, they sell copies of House and Garden magazine dated from the 1920's and 30's.

Owner Michael Plant has also collected pens (the oldest dated 1898), paper, old postcards, steroviews, china and glassware. Michael often conducts searches for items you want.

This 'N' That Antiques sells items at antique fairs and finds many of their treasures by attending estate sales. Visit This 'N' That and you'll go home with a bit of this and a whole lot of that.

This is the Place

Religious-Christian   10405 Montgomery Ave.
Kensington, MD 20895
301-933-5499
Hours: Mon. 10-4; Tues. & Fri. 10-9;
Wed., Thurs. & Sat. 10-6

This Is The Place really is the place to find one of the largest collections of Mormon literature in the area. Ninety-five percent of the books are written by Mormon authors.

Washington, D.C., has some of the most magnificent architecture in the country and one of the most spectacular is the Mormon Temple. When driving on the highway by the Temple, it almost looks as if it is a vision floating on the tree tops and not real at all.

Located in the Mormon Temple, the shop sells Bibles, prints of the Temple, children's books, genealogy supplies, dehydrated fruit, some self-help books, and, of course, The Book of Mormon. This Is The Place is wheelchair accessible. Once you see the Temple, you're sure to be drawn to its doors.

Toys...Etc. Book Dept.

Children's books   11325 Seven Locks Rd.
Potomac, MD 20854
301-299-8300
Hours: Mon.-Fri. 10-8;
Sat. 10-6; Sun. noon-5

Mention taking your little one to Toys...Etc. and you're sure to hear a rousing cheer. In addition to selling toys in more than 5,000 square feet of goodies, Toys...Etc. has a fantastic selection of books for children of all ages.

Toys...Etc. boasts a staff who are experienced with children's books and how to make books appealing to little ones. Nancy Landon, the head of the book department, has bought books for almost fourteen years and owns her own bookstore on Cape Cod, Brewster Books. Staff member Lucy Ronan comes to Toys...Etc. after years of working in school libraries.

Open everyday, Toys...Etc. is completely accessible to every buggy from wheelchairs to strollers. They also sell audio books, video tapes, greeting cards, and stationery. Once you have made your selections, the staff will gift wrap your items. At times, authors visit the store to autograph books as a special event.

Stop at Toys...Etc. and you'll find books and toys as well as staff members who are happy to help and are genuinely excited about the books they sell.

Travel Books & Language Center Inc.

Travel & Languages

4931 Cordell Ave.
Bethesda, MD 20814
301-951-8533
800-220-2665
FAX 301-951-8546
Hours: Mon.-Sat. 10-9; Sun. noon-5

"Our books cover the world and we search the world for new and interesting titles," said manager Rochelle Jaffe.

Called "The Library of Congress of Travel Bookstores" by Outdoor Magazine, the store offers approximately 35,000 titles specializing in travel as well as foreign language studies. Categories include travel guides, maps, atlases, travel narratives, histories, language phrase books, cassette courses, dictionaries, and self-teaching manuals. Language phrase books feature more than 140 languages and growing. The store has recently added a foreign language literature section which includes fiction, poetry, and essays in French, Spanish, Italian, German, and Russian.

If it sounds like the store is packed with selections, it was until they recently expanded to 2,400 square feet allowing aisles to be wider. "The store is also brighter," said Rochelle, "and roomier. Our expanded staff is eager to answer any inquiry."

Open everyday, Travel Books & Language Center Inc. is comfortably accessible to everyone and has chairs in the store for browsers to be comfortable as they compare their many choices. Off-street parking and mass transit are both nearby. If you can't visit the store, call and ask for their catalog. They welcome telephone and mail orders.

As a special event, the store sponsors author autographing sessions and publishes a newsletter twice per year. You are also able to purchase audio books and video tapes here. Special orders are no problem and employees will gift wrap your selections and place the purchase on special customer charge accounts making for easy gift giving.

When it's time to plan your next vacation, be sure to visit Travel Books & Language Center Inc. to enrich your travel experience.

U.S. Government Printing Office Bookstore

General/Government pubs

8660 Cherry Lane
Laurel, MD 20707
301-953-7974
FAX 301-498-9109
Hours: Mon.-Fri. 8-3:45

The government publishes terrific books and pamphlets in a broad range of categories. If you prefer to flip through books rather than shopping through the mail, you'll be pleased that a branch of the U.S. Government Printing Office Bookstore has opened in Laurel.

For a more complete description of the books sold here, please refer to the write-up for the branch located on K Street in Washington, D.C.

University of Maryland Book Center

College

University of Maryland
College Park, MD 20742
301-314-7525
FAX 301-403-8326
Hours: Mon.-Fri. 8:30-5; Sat. noon-5

With both graduate and undergraduate programs, the University of Maryland is a respected university and has a bookstore that is open to the public. The Book Center sells technical, text, and general interest books.

The Center at times sponsors authors for autographing sessions. Also for sale are school supplies, software, computer supplies, and clothing bearing the U of MD logo.

The Book Center is wheelchair accessible and open weekdays and Saturdays.

Victor Kamkin Inc.

Foreign Language

4956 Boiling Brook Pkwy
Rockville, MD 20852
301-881-5973
FAX 301-881-1637
Hours: Mon.-Sat. 9-5

Many of the world's beloved authors hale from Russia. When you are looking for nonfiction Russian literature, contact Victor Kamkin, Inc. They sell only Russian publications and gift items. A catalog is published monthly and most business is conducted by mail.

The showroom of Victor Kamkin Inc. is wheelchair accessible. Everyone is invited to browse at this very specialized book business.

Waldenbooks

General

Laurel Centre
Laurel, MD 20707
301-953-3807
Hours: Mon.-Sat. 10-9:30; Sun. noon-6

The branch of Waldenbooks located in Laurel Centre, offers an extensive selection of books about the military and history. Have no fear, romance and science fiction fans, they also have large collections for you. In addition to a wealth of general interest books, Waldenbooks and

Brentano's (which are owned by the same company) sell magazines, audio and video tapes, calendars, and posters.

Special services abound at both Waldenbooks and Brentano's. Each store has the capability to track down and quickly place in the hands of customers those books in print that are not stocked in the store.

Top selling hardcover books are sold at a discount. A great way to receive an extra ten percent discount is to join the Preferred Reader Program. As a member, you are entitled to receive an extra ten percent off the price of everything in the store except magazines. So just think, for an annual fee of $10, you can purchase all the books you want at a discount including the bestsellers and even bargain books. But, Waldenbooks doesn't stop there. For every $100 worth of merchandise that a Preferred Reader customer buys, he or she receives a $5.00 store coupon.

If you're in the market for a Bible, Waldenbooks and Brentano's can have the family keepsake imprinted. Ask staff members about the details of this service.

The store is wheelchair accessible and one you won't want to miss while in Laurel.

Waldenbooks

General

Forest Village Park Mall
3325 Donnell Drive
Forestville, MD 20747
301-568-6911
<u>Hours:</u> Mon.-Sat. 10-9:30; Sun. noon-6

Located in Forest Village Park Mall, Waldenbooks offers the community a fine selection of Bibles and Christian literature. They also have an excellent collection of African-American studies. The store and mall are wheelchair accessible.

For a complete description of the special services that Waldenbooks offers you, please see the write-up of Waldenbooks in Laurel.

Waldenbooks

General

Lake Forest Mall
701 Russell Ave.
Gaithersburg, MD 20877
301-921-9248
<u>Hours:</u> Mon.-Sat. 10-9:30; Sun. noon-6

Science fiction fans and readers swept away by romances will enjoy shopping at Waldenbooks located in Lake Forest Mall. The store has large departments in both of those popular categories and is wheelchair accessible.

Please refer to the write-up of the Laurel Waldenbooks for information about the many special services at Waldenbooks.

Waldenbooks

General

St. Charles Towne Center
5000 Hwy 301 South
Waldorf, MD 20603
301-645-0770
Hours: Mon.-Sat. 10-9:30; Sun. noon-6

The Waldenbooks located in St. Charles Towne Center is two stores in one. They combined their traditional Waldenbooks with a new store called Waldenkids. In addition to the general interest books you know you always can find at Waldenbooks, now your little one can enjoy an expanded selection of books and videos. The store is both stroller and wheelchair accessible.

The write-up of the Laurel store will give you the details of the special services and discounts that Waldenbooks offers to customers.

Waldenbooks

General

Montgomery Mall
7101 Democracy Blvd.
Bethesda, MD 20817
301-469-8810
Hours: Mon.-Sat. 10-9:30; Sun. 11-6

A large romance section is the defining mark of the Waldenbooks located in Montgomery Mall. The store is open everyday and is wheelchair accessible.

Don't miss out on the advantages of shopping at Waldenbooks. See the description of the Laurel Waldenbooks store to discover just what they offer you.

Waldenbooks

General

Landover Mall
2223 Brightseat Road
Landover, MD 20785
301-322-9220
Hours: Mon.-Sat. 10-9:30; Sun. noon-6

A large collection of books addressing all aspects of the African-American experience can be found in Landover Mall's Waldenbooks. The store is wheelchair accessible.

Read about the discounts and special services offered by Waldenbooks by referring to the Waldenbooks in Laurel.

Waldenbooks

General

Wheaton Plaza
Wheaton, MD 20902
301-946-0202
Hours: Mon.-Sat. 10-9:30; Sun. noon-6

Waldenbooks in Wheaton Plaza has a showcase African-American studies section and a large children's book department. The store is wheelchair accessible and open for shoppers everyday.

Many special services are offered to you when you shop at Waldenbooks. For a description of these services, please refer to the write-up of the store in Laurel.

Waverly Auctions Inc.

Antiquarian-General

4931 Cordell Ave., Ste. AA
Bethesda, MD 20814
301-951-8883
FAX 301-718-8375
Hours: Call for auction dates & times

Waverly Auctions, Inc. collects books from estate sales, personal libraries, institutions, dealers, and collectors and conducts an auction that you won't want to miss. You'll be delighted with the surprises you find.

If attending auctions aren't your favorite events, you can place bids on catalog items. Waverly Auctions receives bids this way from all over the world.

A former higher education literature and writing instructor, Dale Sorenson answered an advertisement in the New York Times and purchased the book business. That was more than 15 years ago and Dale is still thrilled with the business.

Dale keeps lists of people's interests and when he's collecting his books, he keeps an eye out for the specific titles. He also conducts informal appraisals for clients.

Call Waverly Auctions for the dates of upcoming auctions. As a book lover, you are sure to enjoy attending an auction.

Well Read Books

Used

7050 Carroll Avenue
Takoma Park, MD 20912
301-270-4748
Hours: Mon.-Fri. noon-7;
Sat., Sun. & holidays 11-6

Well Read Books brings you quality used books for the well read family. They have excellent prices and have a variety of books in all topics. Paperbacks are sold for anywhere from a quarter to half of the cover price. Kids enjoy the new comic books and sports cards that arrive each week.

A community bookstore, the three owners are familiar with their customers, their wants, and even their children. Although a sign posted in the store says, "Stray children will be sold to gypsies," you know they aren't serious.

The small store is wheelchair, stroller, and sometimes bicycle accessible. The good feeling you get in Well Read Books will remain with you long after you leave the store.

Wild Bird Center

Ornithology   7687 MacArthur Blvd.
                             Cabin John, MD 20818
                             301-229-3141
                             <u>Hours:</u> Sun.-Fri. 10-6; Sat. 9-6

The U.S. Fish & Wildlife Service reports that bird watching is the second most popular hobby among Americans. The entire family can join together for bird watching on nature hikes. Everyone can enjoy watching local birds as the birds eat at the bird feeder in your backyard.

Wild Bird Centers are stores that you should visit whether you are a beginning bird watcher or an old pro who is looking for new seed. Wild Bird Centers are independently owned franchises and are growing throughout the country.

Typically, the stores sell bird feeders, bird houses, bird boxes for nesting, squirrel feeders, special hummingbird feeders, bird seed, and assorted items, such as binoculars and clothing, to make for an enjoyable bird watching experience. They also sell items decorated with birds such as chimes, flags, clocks, and more.

The books they sell include instructional books about bird feeding, bird identification books, trail guide books, gardening, landscaping, and an entire section of children's books.

But that's not all. Wild Bird Centers offer educational and fun programs promoting the sport of bird watching. Employees at each branch come from a variety of backgrounds thus bringing a different insight to each store's programs. A newsletter and flyers are independently published by each store.

Unfortunately, the Cabin John store is located in an old house and not wheelchair accessible.

This branch of The Wild Bird Center is the national franchise headquarters and the store is owned by the founder, George Petrides. At the time this book was written, there were six Wild Bird Centers in the Washington area with more franchises in the works.

Wild Bird Center

Ornithology   420 E. Diamond Ave.
                                                 Gaithersburg, MD 20877
                                                 301-330-9453
                                                 <u>Hours:</u> Mon.-Sat. 10-6; Sun. 10-5

For a complete description of the Wild Bird Center franchise, see the write-up under the national headquarter's store in Cabin John, MD. At the time that this book went into publication, the above address was correct but the store may be moving to a different location in Gaithersburg. To be safe, call them before you visit.

Located in a quaint Victorian house, this store is not wheelchair accessible. Owner Bill Rogers says he will lend a hand if you really want to come to the store. Call him first.

Wild Bird Center

Ornithology   10831 Lanham-Sevrn Rd.
                                                 Glenndale, MD 20769
                                                 301-805-4858
                                                 <u>Hours:</u> Mon.-Sat. 10-6; Sun. noon-5

The Wild Bird Center has a franchise located in Glenndale that is wheelchair accessible.

For a full description of the Wild Bird Centers, see the write-up for the Cabin John, MD, location.

Wild Bird Center

Ornithology   13444 New Hampshire Ave.
                                                 Silver Spring, MD 20904
                                                 301-989-9453
                                                 <u>Hours:</u> Mon.-Sat. 10-6; Sun. noon-5

A store loved by bird lovers, The Wild Bird Center located in Silver Spring is wheelchair accessible.

Please refer to the description of the Cabin John, MD, store.

Wild Bird Center

Ornithology   Shoppers World Shopping Center
                                                 3320 Crain Highway
                                                 Waldorf, MD 20602
                                                 301-843-2994
                                                 <u>Hours:</u> Mon.-Sat. 10-7;
                                                 Fri. 10-9; Sun. 11-5

A number of franchises of The Wild Bird Center are popular stores and, no doubt, appreciated by local birds. This store in Waldorf is wheelchair accessible.

Please refer to the complete description of the store written for the Cabin John, MD, store.

Wild Bird Company & Absolutely Bats!

Ornithology   591 Hungerford Dr.
                                             Rockville, MD 20850
                                             301-279-0079
                                             FAX 301-424-3938
                                             <u>Hours:</u> Mon.-Fri. 10-6; Wed. 10-8;
                                             Sat. 9-4; Sun. 11-4

Heidi Hughes has a mission in life: to change people's attitudes about those adorable little creatures, bats. Her love for bats began when someone, knowing that Heidi had a big heart when it came to animals, brought her an abandoned baby bat that needed nurturing. Heidi's husband, Tom Valega, insisted that the little bat remain in a covered box overnight. All night long they heard the sad little squeaks of the bat. But in the morning, the squeaks sounded much closer and more pacified than the night before. It should. The bat was sleeping on Heidi's pillow!

An expert extraordinaire about birds and owner of the Wild Bird Company since 1988, Heidi threw herself into studying bats and by 1990, a corner of the store featured bat related books, video tapes, night vision glasses, houses, stuffed animals, backpacks, and a terrific little bat that squeaks when you clap your hands. In the fall of 1993, she will sell chocolate bats made from specially designed molds. She sub-titled the treats "Take a bite out of a bat."

Heidi discovered her love for antiquarian books about bird watching when she was 21 years old. She went on to write the bestselling book titled, "The Expert's Guide to Backyard Bird Feeding." She continues to conduct programs for the Smithsonian Institute about bald eagles, hawk watching, hummingbirds, and, of course, bats.

During her life, Heidi has been a curator for the Los Angeles Zoo, was an outdoor recreation planner for the U.S. Fish and Wildlife Service, and was a broadcast journalist for NBC. Today she does what she enjoys: teaching people to love birds and bats through writing, editing the Wild Bird Observer newsletter, conducting educational and fun programs, and being the owner of two branches of the popular stores.

At The Wild Bird Company and Absolutely Bats! she presents many programs and sponsors visits by authors to discuss their newest books. You can have a "close encounter" with a sweet little bat at the store. Call before you visit to make sure that Heidi has brought one of her pals to the store. At home she keeps a dozen pet bats that she calls her "ball of bats" because they like snuggling together.

Every animal should have a spokesperson who is as dedicated to their care as Heidi. In the store she sells every kind of bird feeder, bird house, bird bath, and bird seed imaginable. But she doesn't limit the store to selling only bird items. As mentioned, she's batty about bats but also gives equal time to squirrels. Because so many squirrels steal food set out for birds, Heidi sells a squirrel proof bird feeder. Not to neglect squirrels, she also sells squirrel feeders and food and "squirrel toys" such as a "squirrel-a-twirl" and "squirrel seesaw."

Inside The Wild Bird Company & Absolutely Bats!, Heidi has created her own little world. The store has a pond and waterfall spotted by aquatic flowers and plants. The area even has an artificial sun. Best of all, there are chairs for customers to browse through books and enjoy the environment. Video and audio tapes run continuously. The store is wheelchair accessible.

The store is open everyday and a catalog is available for shop-at-home orders. Searches and special orders of new and antiquarian books are conducted by Heidi and the staff. Books sold in the store feature nature, natural history, ornithology, and, Heidi's beloved bats. Many books are written for children. Non-book items include those mentioned above and T-shirts, children's toys, greeting cards, stationery, calendars, and more.

Heidi opened a second branch of Wild Bird Company & Absolutely Bats! in Fredrick, MD. You can call them at (301) 698-2545.

One of Heidi's latest projects is creating color posters featuring bird feeding and nesting with New Jersey artist Carol Decker.

Where can Heidi go from here? She cringes and says with trepidation, "insects?"

Willis Van Devanter Books

Antiquarian-Cookery & Culinary   PO Box 277
                                     Poolesville, MD 20837
                                     301-972-7298
                                     or 202-955-5758
                                     <u>Hours:</u> Appointment only

Remember that apple pie that Grandma brought to every picnic or the meatballs that Aunt Josephine's great-aunt made? When you really have a taste for memories or if you love cooking without using today's modern mixes, contact Willis Van Devanter immediately.

Willis specializes in cookbooks and culinary arts of days gone by. Don your Martha Washington dress and use the 1760's cookbook he has for sale. Willis sells hard-to-find, out of print, and rare cookbooks such as a first edition "The Joy of Cooking." He also has titles from 18th century England and conducts searches for specific items.

Grand chefs and homemakers of history all had cooking equipment that they couldn't do without. Some of these treasures have been discovered by Willis and are available to you. He sells old and rare pots and pans, fish poachers, and early toasters, to name a few.

Prices of items sold are extremely reasonable so that you can even decorate your kitchen with the antique cookery. Willis also sells ephemeral paper paraphernalia such as restaurant menus and postcards suitable for framing.

Willis, a one-time librarian, began selling books in 1973. A connoisseur of books, he conducts appraisals in many fields. Willis Van Devanter Books can be seen on many weekends at the historic John Poole House which dates from the 18th century or by appointment through the week. Fortunately, the house does have a wheelchair ramp.

Call Willis today and you'll be creating culinary delights that evoke the past for dinner.

The Writer's Center

Writing & Performing Arts

4508 Walsh Street
Bethesda, MD 20815
301-654-8664
Hours: Mon.-Thurs. 10-8; Fri. & Sat. 10-5; Sun. 1-5; & during performances

"Outside of a dog, a book is man's best friend. Inside, it's too dark to read," said Groucho Marx.

As a reader or writer, your home, no doubt, is filled with many best friends in the form of books. If you want to meet some best friends in the form of humans, check out The Writer's Center.

A non-profit organization, The Writer's Center sponsors workshops, readings, seminars, panel discussions, and theater presentations which delight writers and non-writers alike. The Center publishes a quarterly literary magazine featuring poetry and essays.

At The Writer's Center, you're likely to meet writers, editors, small press publishers, and graphic artists. They all join to improve writing skills and to promote literature among the public.

Established in 1977, The Writer's Center developed a fine bookstore, The Book Gallery, filled with many pieces of literature not found in other bookstores. Among it's stock, The Book Gallery sells fiction and poetry published by small presses and more than 150 literary magazines. In addition to its regular hours of operation, The Book Gallery is open during performances conducted in the theatre of The Writer's Center.

So that you'll be able to mark your calendars and not miss a single event at The Writer's Center, they publish a bi-monthly newsletter and workshop catalogs.

The Writer's Center and Book Gallery are wheelchair accessible. They are open to the general public as well as writers of every genre and every skill level.

Yak & Yeti Books

Antiquarian-Orientalia

PO Box 5736
Rockville, MD 20855
301-869-5860
Hours: Appointment only

"We maintain the largest stock of any United States dealer of books on all subjects relating to the Himalayan region (Nepal, Kashmir, etc.), Tibet, Central Asia, and Mongolia," said Dr. Daniel W. Edwards of his business, Yak & Yeti Books.

Conducting business from a private home, Dr. Edwards sells new, used, and antiquarian books by appointment, or telephone and mail order. He does have a catalog available and will conduct appraisals on your treasured books.

Yak & Yeti Books brings you approximately 2,200 titles of books on this specialized theme. No doubt you're questioning the title of this book business. Of course, you have seen yaks at the zoo but you probably will have a tougher time tracking a yeti. It's an abominable snowman.

Zenith Comics & Collectibles

Comics

18200-P Georgia Ave.
Olney, MD 20832
301-774-1345
Hours: Mon. & Tues. 11-5;
Wed. noon-7; Thurs. & Fri. 11-8;
Sat. 11-6; Sun. noon-5

Comic books have catapulted into the realm of acceptability among book lovers: witness the critical success of Maus I and Maus II dealing with the Holocaust. At the zenith of new and used comic books, you'll find Zenith Comics & Collectibles in Olney, Maryland. From humorous to thriller comic books and from the newest releases to yesterday's favorites, this store sells them all.

So that you won't miss a single copy of your favorite comic book, Zenith maintains a subscription service and places special orders. An expert in the field, owner Louis Danoff searches for the rare and unique comic books that you request. He has conducted business since 1990.

Although there is a flight of stairs to reach Zenith Comics & Collectibles, an elevator catapults clients in wheelchairs to the second floor. Note that the elevator is not available on Sundays. Open everyday, Zenith Comics & Collectibles also sells video tapes, role-playing games, T-shirts, posters, and models. To the delight of clients, the store conducts role playing games monthly. Occasionally authors visit the store for autographing sessions.

Whether you can fly like Superman to Zenith Comics & Collectibles, beam over ala Star Trek, or zip over in Archie's hot rod, you're sure to enjoy your visit to this store.

Virginia Suburbs

APICS

Business

500 W. Annadale Rd.
Falls Church, VA 22046
703-237-8344
800-444-2742
FAX 703-237-1071
Hours: Phone and mail order only

The American Production and Inventory Control Society, Inc., (APICS) provides the resources needed to become a leader in manufacturing and business. An international organization, they offer a full range of programs and materials on the latest business management concepts and techniques. APICS was established in 1957 and continues to be a highly respected organization for both the conglomerate and small businessman alike.

APICS sponsors educational programs and certifications for integrated resource management and production and inventory management. Through APICS programs and books, you'll be exposed to leading-edge practices. They also have learning-at-home programs. Non-members are invited to order selections from a thorough catalog.

With changing technology and the ever-developing global competition, professionals in business and management need to develop the skills that APICS offers. Call their customer service toll-free number at their Falls Church headquarters.

Agribookstore, Winrock

Agriculture

Winrock, 1611 N. Kent St.
Arlington, VA 22209
703-525-9455
FAX 703-525-1744
Hours: Phone and mail order only

Agribookstore sells books devoted to the specific needs of scientists, teachers, and project managers who work for the benefit of the developing Third World. With more than 800 titles, Agribookstore carries books about agriculture and the environment. The business operates by telephone or mail order only.

Aladdin's Lamp Children's Bookstore

Children's books   126 W. Broad St.
                                       Falls Church, VA 22046
                                       703-241-8281
                                       Hours: Mon.-Sat. 10-6;
                                       Tues. & Thurs. open until 8;
                                       extended Christmas hours

When you step into Aladdin's Lamp, you'll enter a magical world of more than 15,000 children's books and memorable special events that your child is sure to enjoy. Children of all ages will find books suited just for them. If you need help, owner Alina Gawlik is certainly qualified to assist you. She was the Head of Child Services and a librarian at a suburban Washington library.

The programs presented at Aladdin's Lamp tap into the resources of the community. Artist Lorene Steinberg conducted a butterfly mask-making workshop. Author Sharon Bokoske read from her book about dolphins. A humorous poetry theater evening was conducted by local poet Kalli Dakos. Singing, dancing, and wreath-making was presented by the Polish dance troupe, Tance Polski, as an introduction to the Polish Festival of Wreaths held at the Reflecting Pool.

Aladdin's Lamp also sells a wide variety of children's gifts and, of special interest to adults, an excellent selection of Baltic amber jewelry. The store accepts telephone orders, wraps and mails items and even will deliver your purchase locally. Educators are offered special programs.

Of course, the store is stroller and wheelchair accessible. A newsletter is published three times per year announcing upcoming events. You and your little one won't want to miss a single event.

Alfa Foreign Language Books

Foreign Language   2615 Columbia Pike PO Box 4132
                                       Arlington, VA 22204
                                       703-920-6644
                                       FAX 703-521-0088
                                       Hours: Mon.-Fri. 10-6; Sat. 8-4

Alfa Foreign Language Books brings you 12-15,000 titles which are sure to fill your needs when learning a new language.

Alfa doesn't leave you alone to flounder with your studies. They also sponsor instructional classes, tutorial programs, and directed self-study programs. Audio books and video tapes assist in education. Five percent of the books in stock feature linguistics.

The store is wheelchair accessible and telephone and mail orders are accepted. Some of the books for sale are used books. Alfa Foreign

Language Books also publishes an extensive catalog of audio books in French, Spanish, Italian, German, Russian, and even Ukrainian. The audio books are cassette recordings in these foreign languages and include complete transcriptions.

Visit them or give them a call to discuss the language of your interest, whether it's a popular or obscure language.

The Almond Tree

Religious-Christian

145 W. Lee Highway
Warrenton, VA 22186
703-347-0303
800-344-0435
Hours: Mon.-Fri. 10-7; Sat. 10-6

Come to The Almond Tree and refresh your days with the Christian books and music sold in this delightful, busy store. Committed to the Christian community, bookstore manager Darrell Fletcher has access to more than 60,000 titles of books and can quickly get the books into your hands. Many titles are stocked on the bookstore's shelves. The Almond Tree also offers programs such as author autographing sessions and Bible study seminars.

Established in 1986, The Almond Tree "most definitely," according to Darrell, will mail order and special order books. He says that special orders are usually obtained within 7 days. The store has a toll free telephone number. Located in a shopping center, there is a wheelchair ramp a few doors from The Almond Tree.

The Almond Tree is a specialty store that you will want to visit when looking for religious books.

Antietam Natl. Battlefield Museum Shop

History

Echos of the Museum
6511 Sudley Rd.
Manassas, VA 22110
703-368-1873
Hours: Tues.-Sun. 10-5

Antietam National Battlefield Park commemorates the two Battles of Bull Run that brought the Civil War within reach of Washington, D.C. A small museum on the site has a short film that tell the sad story of the battles that killed so many soldiers, Union and Confederate. It is the site where Stonewall Jackson received his nickname.

The giftshop has brochures and sells guides to the eerily quiet grounds. You can also follow the instructions of an audio tape that guides you to different sites of battles. It certainly brings the Civil War to life when you retrace the actual steps of the soldiers.

The giftshop also sells video tapes, books about the Civil War and the people who fought it. Other items for sale include caps, flags, T-shirts, and children's toys from the days of the war.

The museum and shop are wheelchair accessible but most of the trails are a bit bumpy for skittish wheelchair users.

Antiquarian Tobacciana

Antiquarian-Tobacco   11505 Turnbridge Lane
Reston, VA 22094
703-435-8133
Hours: Telephone, mail order and
appointment only

While the media has given smoking tobacco the evil eye, Benjamin Rapaport takes pride in being an Antiquarian Tobaccianist and is even a member of the Pipe Smoker's Hall of Fame, inducted in 1974.

His collection of books include more than 3,500 English and foreign volumes on tobacco and related subjects. Approximately 500 volumes are included in a newsletter which also doubles as a catalog. It is available quarterly. Benjamin also conducts searches for specific titles relating to his specialty and does appraisals on your books. Telephone and mail orders are accepted.

Founding the Antiquarian Tobacciana in 1979, Benjamin clearly is an expert in his field. He is a known guest lecturer, cataloguer, and conductor of appraisals for Philip Morris Tobacco Collection, the Museum of Tobacco Art and History, Duke University Art Museum, and many others. He wrote "A Complete Guide to Collecting Antique Pipes," edited and compiled two books "A Tobacco Source Book" and "The Global Guide to Tobacco Literature," as well as writing a column for many magazines on related subjects.

If those qualifications don't impress you with his knowledge, he also is a member of American Society of Appraisers, a founding member of l'Academie Internationale de la Pipe, affiliated with global pipe clubs, and has served on the Board of Advisors for books titled "Warman's Antiques and Their Prices: and "Schroeder's Antiques Price Guide."

This guy doesn't just blow smoke at you; he really knows his stuff.

Arlington National Cemetery Bookshop

National Historic Site   Arlington National Cemetery
Arlington, VA 22121
703-557-1713
Hours: Summer: Daily 8-6:30

Just across the Arlington Memorial Bridge on 612 acres is our nation's silent testament to those in our military who served and sacrificed, Arlington National Cemetery. With precision, tombstones are arranged on the Virginia hills. Buried here are past presidents, generals, and national heros of our history.

The only way to tour the cemetery is via the Tourmobiles that are stationed at the Visitor's Center. This is also where you will find the bookstore which sells history, military, and guidebooks to Washington, D.C. Pamphlets and brochures about Arlington Nation Cemetery are also available.

In addition to the graves and the Tomb of the Unknowns (formerly known as the Tomb of the Unknown Soldier), you are invited to visit Arlington House. The house, also known as the Custis-Lee House, is the Robert E. Lee Memorial and sells books relating to the story of two great Virginia families who owned the mansion-the Washingtons and the Lees.

Arlington National Cemetery and the Arlington House are both maintained by The National Park Service. Tours and bookshops are coordinated by The Parks & History Association. Your purchases in their shops (or by mail) support future programs for park visitors.

The Associates Rare Books

Antiquarian-General   6231 Leesburg Pike, Suite LL-3
                                         Mail: PO Box 4747
                                         Falls Church, VA 22044
                                         703-578-3810
                                         FAX 703-536-3170
                                         <u>Hours:</u> Sat. 10-4 & by appointment

Originally established in 1979 as a mail order business featuring modern first edition books, the Associates Rare Books saw such an overwhelming interest in the books they opened a showroom in 1991 much to the delight of collectors.

The showroom, located across from Seven Corners Shopping Center, is open on Saturdays and by appointment. The store is wheelchair accessible. Bookcases and display cases are conducive to browsing while chairs and couches provide relaxation for long-time browsers.

"The stock," explains William Selander, owner, "is known for its excellent condition and offers the discriminating collector many interesting choices."

With approximately 5,000 titles of first editions, the topics include fiction, modern pop culture, the Vietnam War, music, poetry, ethnic studies, and alternative life styles. They also sell pop-art and Vietnam War posters and children's toys and games related to the pop culture.

The Associates Rare Books still maintains a catalog and is pleased to take orders by telephone and mail order.

If you are a book collector or new to the hobby, The Associates Rare Books is an excellent place to visit.

Audubon Prints and Books

Antiquarian, Natural History   9720 Spring Ridge Lane
                                              Vienna, VA 22182
                                              703-759-5567
                                              <u>Hours:</u> Appointment only

Whether a bird lover or not, everyone admires the works and etchings of John James Audubon. Known for his monumental work, "The Birds of America," Audubon is famous as a classical scholar in ornithology and American art.

No one in the book business knows Audubon's works like Ed Kenney of Vienna, Virginia. Ed has a fantastic collection of Audubon prints and books. His stock is limited to books by or about Audubon. A scholar himself, Ed conducts appraisals on books about natural history.

Operating from his home by appointment only, Ed also publishes a catalog and is happy to discuss your book wants over the telephone. He has been conducting business since 1974.

Book lovers who love and admire John James Audubon absolutely must contact Ed. He has all the antiquarian books and prints to delight you for years.

B. Dalton Bookseller

General   Ballston Common
                                              4328 Wilson Blvd.
                                              Arlington, VA 22203
                                              703-522-8822
                                              <u>Hours:</u> Mon.-Sat. 10-9:30; Sun. noon-5

Located in a section of Arlington that is undergoing massive rejuvenation, Ballston Commons Mall has a B. Dalton bookstore. The store, expanded to 4,600 square feet, has general interest books with excellent selections of fiction, magazines, and children's books. The store is wheelchair accessible.

B. Dalton Bookseller

General   The Galleria at Tysons II
                                              McLean, VA 22102
                                              703-821-2041
                                              <u>Hours:</u> Mon.-Sat. 10-9; Sun. noon-6

One of the more up-scale malls in the Washington area, the Galleria at Tysons II, also boasts a fine branch of B. Dalton.

The 3,000 square foot store offers a fine collection of general interest books with a slant on beautiful fine art books, decorating and gardening books, and children's books.

B. Dalton, located on the main floor near Macys, is wheelchair accessible. The mall houses many unique shops and a Ritz Carlton Hotel.

B. Dalton Bookseller

General Springfield Mall
6712 Franconia Road
Springfield, VA 22150
703-971-7010
Hours: Mon.-Sat. 10-9:30; Sun. noon-5

The grandpa of B. Dalton bookstores in the Washington area, this store has approximately 4,000 square feet. The store carries books of interest for all ages and interests.

Located on the upper level of the popular and huge Springfield Mall, B. Dalton is a full service bookstore. Park your car near Penney's and you'll be close to the bookstore. Like the mall, B. Dalton is wheelchair accessible.

B. Dalton Bookseller

General Skyline Plaza
5155 Leesburg Pike
Falls Church, VA 22041
703-820-4250
Hours: Mon.-Sat. 10-9; Sun. noon-5

Because the Skyline Mall where B. Dalton is located is near three office towers, the store stocks many computer books. They also sell general interest books.

Smaller than many B. Dalton bookstores, the store has 2,000 square feet of selling space. It is wheelchair accessible.

B. Dalton Bookseller

General 1661 Crystal Square Arcade
Arlington, VA 22202
703-413-0558
Hours: Mon.-Fri. 9-7; Sat. 10-6

If you want to do away with commuting, cars, and metros, consider moving to Crystal Square Arcade. A person can live in one of the highrises, work in another of the three towers, and shop and dine in the underground mall. Crystal City Underground has grocery stores, clothing stores, a theatre, and even a post office. Of course, you'll find B. Dalton bookstore for real entertainment. As a matter of fact, you'll find two B. Dalton bookstores in the underground.

Double the size of the smaller B. Dalton in this mall, this store is located directly on the Metro. This branch is filled with general interest books and maintains a whole "wall" of new arrivals. Because the offices are mostly staffed by military personnel, B. Dalton stocks an extensive history and current affairs departments. Be sure to check the quality selection of bargain books.

Both B. Dalton bookstores in the underground are wheelchair accessible.

B. Dalton Bookseller

General   2117 Crystal Plaza Arcade
                                             Arlington, VA 22202
                                             703-415-0333
                                             Hours: Mon.-Fri. 9-7; Sat. 10-6

The newly expanded and refinished second B. Dalton bookstore in the Crystal Plaza Arcade of the Crystal City Underground is the smaller of the two B. Dalton bookstores here. Its 2,500 square feet of selling space feature solid departments of history, biography, computer, and business. They also have terrific bargain books and a large collection of magazines.

The store is wheelchair accessible along with the many other shops you will find here.

BJ's Books

General used   381 W. Shirley Ave.
                                             Warrenton, VA 22186
                                             703-347-4111
                                             Hours: Mon.-Sat. 10-8; Sun. noon-5

"Want a cheap romance?" Beth Feagans, owner of BJ's Books, asks. One of their T-shirts claims: "Warrenton's Most Adventurous, Mysterious, Romantic store of Knowledge."

You'll find all the romance you can imagine on her bookshelves just waiting for you. At BJ's you'll find the romance books that you missed when they were first published. The good news is that they are sold here for excellent prices.

BJ's Books carries books of interest for everyone. Ninety-five percent of the books are used but she also sells some new nonfiction hardback and paperback books. Children enjoy the toy box in the back of the store while parents browse through the organized shelves. Wheelchairs and strollers have no problems in the store.

BJ's Books also carries old and new baseball cards and comic books. This means the whole family can spend time in BJ's, even with a 12-year old who has temporarily sworn off books.

Beth is also in tune with specific interests of clients and will call them when books become available in her store. When you are looking for a bookstore to hang your hat, contact BJ's Books.

Baptist Book Store

Religious-Christian

Springfield Plaza
7259 Commerce Street
Springfield, VA 22150
703-569-0067
FAX 703-569-0132
Hours: Mon., Wed., Fri., Sat. 10-6;
Tues., Thurs. 10-8

"We have a promise to God to be a Witness to the World," said Bill Hancher, manager of the Baptist Book Store.

The results of that promise are seen in the fine bookstore that has been established. In a spacious comfortable atmosphere filled with soft background music, the Baptist Book Store also has reserved a play area for children in the store.

The general interest bookstore belongs to the Baptist Sunday School Board which sponsors stores across the United States. As a service to the community, the Baptist Book Store also sells audio books, video tapes, large type print books, magazines, calendars, stationery, greeting cards, T-shirts, posters, games, and toys for children.

Special services are many: they sponsor a Birthday Club for children, book repairs, book imprinting, special orders, and charge accounts. A catalog is available for telephone and mail orders. With one step at the door, the store is available to wheelchair users with assistance. Inside, the store is completely wheelchair accessible.

Open everyday except Sunday, the Baptist Book Store is filled with gifts, books, and the most pleasant of employees to help you with your selections.

Ben Franklin Booksellers, Inc.

General

107 S. King St.
Leesburg, VA 22075
703-777-3661
800-453-4108
FAX 777-8287
Hours: Mon.-Sat. 9:30-6:30

You'll find a wealth of books available at the Ben Franklin Booksellers, Music and Frame Shop that are usually not available at other bookstores. If you visit the store or shop by their catalog, you will find the following: politics, history, literature, philosophy, fine art, architecture, foreign language, science, and music. Recently they have expanded their children's selections. They also sell musical CD's and art prints by the classical artists, the national newspaper "The New Federalist" and the magazine "EIR: Executive Intelligence Review."

The introduction of the catalog explains their purpose: "This is a unique catalogue which is striving to bring to its readers a classical tradition we believe can bring us closer to clearer thinking at a time when the literature that helped make this country a great country so many years ago has been lost, substituted for superficial publications, so varied and vast that the fundamentals of thinking can no longer take place."

All books and publications are associated and related to the beliefs of Lyndon A. LaRouche. The New Federalist newspaper carries the following quote by Ben Franklin: "Whoever would overthrow the liberty of a nation must begin by subduing the freeness of speech."

Offices and stores of the organization founded by Lyndon LaRouche can be found nation- and world-wide.

Book 'N Card

Magazines & General Interest   8110 Arlington Blvd.
Falls Church, VA 22042
703-560-6999
Hours: Mon.-Fri. 9 am-10 pm;
Sat. 9-9; Sun. 9-6

Northern Virginia's oldest independent bookstore, Book 'N Card also sells the largest number of magazines in the area. They offer more than 3,000 magazine titles, 10,000 book titles, and a number of newspapers.

Although most books and magazines are of a general theme, they specialize in mystery, science fiction, and history. Book 'N Card also place special orders. Other items for sale are greeting cards and calendars. Open everyday, Book 'N Card is wheelchair accessible.

Be sure to stop at Book 'N Card when you're looking for books, greeting cards, and magazines. Maybe their name should be Book 'N Card 'N Magazines.

Book Alcove

Used-General   2337 Hunters Woods Plaza
Reston, VA 22091
703-620-6611
Hours: Mon.-Fri. 10-9;
Sat. 9:30-9; Sun. noon-6

Book Alcove is a terrific used bookstore with three locations. The Reston location is in Hunters Wood Plaza.

Books are many and prices are exceptional. A special feature is the custom-made bookcases that are made in the Gaithersburg, Maryland location. See the write-up for that store for a detailed description of their woodwork. They also sell CD's, cassettes, records, and books on cassette tape.

When hunting used books, you can't pass by Book Alcove.

Book Ends

Antiquarian-General   2710 Washington Blvd.
                                     Arlington, VA 22201
                                     703-524-4976
                                     <u>Hours:</u> Fri.-Mon. noon-6

By buying fine antiquarian books offered at Book Ends, you will never run out of interesting books to place between book ends on your shelves. Although their stock is general interest, Book Ends offers fine selections of Americana and militaria.

Book Ends sells approximately 20,000 hard back titles and 15,000 paperback books. Owned by Janet and Mike Deatherage, Book Ends was established in 1979. Their love and knowledge of books is vast since Mike was a teacher and Janet was a librarian.

Located on the first and second floors of an old house, Book Ends is not wheelchair accessible. Give them a call and perhaps other arrangements could be made to get the books you desire into your hands.

The Book Nook—A Children's Bookstore

Children's books   10312 Main St.
                                     Fairfax, VA 22030
                                     703-591-6545
                                     <u>Hours:</u> Mon.-Sat. 10-6; Thurs. 10-8;
                                     Sept.-Jan. also Sun. 1-5

A school teacher and an editor combined their talents and interest to create The Book Nook—A Children's Bookstore. What they have created is a delightful place for children and parents alike.

Myra Strauss and Sandra Esterson sell wonderful books of all sorts for children of all ages as well as books for parents looking for suggestions about raising happy, healthy children. Teachers take note: they also have a terrific selection of professional books, puppets, and posters for the classroom. Other favorites of children, such as T-shirts and calendars, are also sold.

Knowledgeable employees can help with special orders and gift wrapping. They sponsor author visits to the delight of the authors and children. A newsletter, available upon request, informs patrons of events.

Special events abound at The Book Nook—Children's Bookstore. Story telling happens twice per month. During the summer, The Book Nook—A Children's Bookstore conduct fun arts and crafts programs during the summer. The proprietors attend school and pre-school bookfairs.

The Book Nook—A Children's Bookstore is stroller and wheelchair accessible. Everyone is sure to enjoy this bookstore. Not only do children enjoy browsing the books here, they also enjoy the play area in the store.

The Book Rack

Used Paperbacks Heritage Mall
7857D Heritage Drive
Annandale, VA 22003
703-941-6015
<u>Hours:</u> Mon.-Thurs. 11-7;
Fri.-Sat. 10-6; Sun. noon-5

"We sell our paperbacks at approximately one half the cover price," said Charlie Leach of The Book Rack in Heritage Mall.

How can they do that, you ask? The Book Rack is a used bookstore with approximately 17,500 previously read paperbacks. The store accepts trades and will accept your quality used paperbacks as trade for those you haven't read. The store also sells new recent bestsellers, Golden Books for the tots, and Cliff's Notes for the teen at an 20% discount.

"We think of the shop as a neighborhood bookstore where all members of the family can find just about any books they want, and buy them inexpensively," Charlie points out.

Located in a strip mall in Annandale, The Book Rack is wheelchair and stroller accessible. The stock is grouped by category and kept neatly organized. They specialize in fiction, romance, thrillers, and espionage.

If you're looking for something not on the shelf, a friendly employee is ready to help. New books can be ordered and used books will be searched for. You'll note above that they are open everyday.

The Book Rack, a nation-wide franchise operation, has more than 200 stores in business. Charlie and his wife, Melissa, expanded into a second Book Rack located in Fairfax. Be sure to see that write-up below this book. The Fairfax location is approximately twice the size of this location for twice the book buying fun.

The Book Rack

Used Paperbacks 9559 Braddock Rd.
Fairfax, VA 22032
703-323-0498
<u>Hours:</u> Sun. noon-5; Mon.-Wed. 10-7;
Summer: Thurs.-Sat. 10-9; Winter:
Thurs.-Sat. 10-8

Approximately twice the size of the Annandale Book Rack, the Fairfax location is estimated to hold twice the used and new paperbacks. While Charlie Leach manages the other location, his wife, Melissa, is in charge of this store which opened in January of 1993.

The two locations of The Book Rack are very similar in their stock, organization, and pleasant book browsing atmosphere. Charlie reports that the Fairfax location has been described as "like walking into a friend's living room."

Wheelchair accessible, The Book Rack is located in Twinbrooke Centre. Your entire family can enjoy book browsing here. Many of the clients have become friends with the owners because of their shared enjoyment of books.

BookHouse

Antiquarian-General

805 N. Emerson St.
Arlington, VA 22205
703-527-7797
Hours: Tues.-Sun. noon-6

Located in an old frame house with a quaint garden, BookHouse has seven rooms crammed with wonderful antiquarian quality books. Books about American history, gardening, birds and animals, architecture, ships and the sea are on the first floor. Upstairs are books about literature, foreign countries, dictionaries, philosophy, early technical books, and books for children. BookHouse has approximately 60,000 books under its roof.

Because BookHouse is an actual house, like so many homes it is not wheelchair accessible. There are four steps at the entrance. BookHouse has been located in Arlington for twenty years at the intersection of Emerson Street and Wilson Boulevard.

Bookland

General

Potomac Mills Outlet Mall
2700 Potomac Mills Circle
Woodbridge, VA 22192
703-490-5168
Hours: Mon.-Sat. 10-9:30; Sun. 11-6

Located in the same outlet mall as Books-a-Million, Bookland is a general interest discount bookstore that shares the same management as Books-a-Million (see below). They both carry the same stock.

Books Unlimited Inc.

General

2729 Wilson Blvd.
Arlington, VA 22201
703-525-0550
Hours: Mon., Wed., Fri. 10-9;
Tues. Thurs. 10-6

Not only does Books Unlimited offer you more than 5,000 titles of fiction and children's books, they also bring you calendars and greeting cards. Established in 1975, the store is accessible for everyone. Mass transit is available nearby.

Books-A-Million

General
Potomac Mills Outlet Mall
2700 Potomac Mills Circle
Woodbridge, VA 22192
703-490-3809
FAX 703-490-8580
Hours: Mon.-Sat. 10-9:30; Sun. 11-6

Books-A-Million has the books for you. Children's books, you got it. Bestsellers, they're yours. New arrivals, they're here at discount prices.

Actually, Books-A-Million is an outlet store for books. It is located in the Potomac Mills Outlet Mall. They stock books of general interest. If a book you want does not happen to be in stock, they will get the book for you and even mail it to you. The wheelchair accessible store also sells comic books, sports cards, and magazines. The store does sponsor special events such as author autograph sessions.

Just because you can't stop browsing here, doesn't mean the kids you have in tow have to be bored. They can enter "Children's World" which is filled with toys and they can play to their delight.

Books-A-Million is an Alabama based book chain that has existed since 1907. This store is affiliated with Bookland which is also found in this same outlet mall.

Borders Book Shop

General
3532 S. Jefferson St.
Baileys Crossroads, VA 22041
703-998-0404
FAX 703-998-3161
Hours: Mon.-Sat. 9-11; Sun. 11-8

As an out-of-towner looking for Borders Book Shop at Baileys Crossroads, I didn't expect it to be tucked back from the road in a strip mall. All Borders Book Shop's are well worth hunting. To help you find the store, look for the Burlington Coat Factory on the north side of Route 7. Pull into the large mall and you'll have no trouble seeing Borders.

This branch of Borders Book Shop has a large espresso bar filled with luscious treats. The labyrinth layout design of the store makes for interesting and comfortable niches. To find departments easily, artistic banners hang from the ceiling and employees are always happy to help. Borders cares about all of their customers and has a lower check-out desk which is comfortable for wheelchair using patrons.

For a more complete description and history of Borders Book Shop, see the write-up of the Vienna, Virginia, store below.

Borders Book Shop & Espresso Bar

General   8311 Leesburg Pike
                                       Vienna, VA 22182
                                       703-556-7766
                                       Hours: Mon.-Thurs. 9-10;
                                       Fri. & Sat. 9-11; Sun. 11-7

     The first time someone enters Borders Book Shop, they usually stand at the front door with their mouths wide open, in shock at the bounty of books in front of them. Whatever topic you want to read about, Borders has the book or shelf of books for you. They stock 120,000+ titles in more than 100 categories.

     Founded in Ann Arbor, Michigan, Borders Book Shop established an excellent customer service policy that holds true in every branch. Employees are well-read and enjoy nothing so much as tracking down books as if they were the hounds after the fox. If, by some wild chance, they do not have the book that you want in stock, they place special orders and quickly get the book and hold it for you.

     A diverse multitude of programs are conducted and free to the public. Included are readings, author signing sessions, musical performances, contests, story-telling, discussions, craft workshops, tea parties, mystery night detective parties, and many more. If you have an idea for a program, talk with the manager. They are always open to customer suggestions about everything in the store.

     Borders continues to expand their chain of wonderful stores. Each store has its own personality and design but they all carry vast volumes of books and deliver quality customer care. Whether you dash in and grab the book you want or spend hours relaxing on their chairs and benches and browsing through each department, Borders comes through every time.

Brentano's

General   Reston Town Center
                                       11904 Market St.
                                       Reston, VA 22090
                                       703-709-6312
                                       Hours: Mon.-Thurs. 10-9;
                                       Fri., Sat. 10-9:30; Sun. 10-6

     Reston Town Center is a lovely place to visit. Not only do they have a wonderful branch of Brentano's, they also are a host to many specialty shops, movie theaters (that sells the best popcorn), restaurants, fountains, and free musical events each weekend. The town continues to develop along a master-plan.

     Brentano's in Reston is just the place to purchase books to read while dining at a sidewalk cafe. The store has books for everyone's interests but has particularly large selections of business and computer books. Brentano's and Waldenbooks are owned by the same company. In addition to a wealth of general interest books, Waldenbooks and Brentano's sell magazines, audio and video tapes, calendars, and posters.

Special services abound at both Waldenbooks and Brentano's. Each store has the capability to track down and quickly place in the hands of customers those books in print that are not stocked in the store.

Top selling hardcover books are sold at a discount. A great way to receive an extra ten percent discount is to join the Preferred Reader Program. As a member, you are entitled to receive an extra ten percent off the price of everything in the store except magazines. So just think, for an annual fee of $10, you can purchase all the books you want at a discount including the bestsellers and even bargain books. But, Waldenbooks and Brentano's don't stop there. For every $100 worth of merchandise that a Preferred Reader customer buys, he or she receives a $5.00 store coupon.

If you're in the market for a Bible, Waldenbooks and Brentano's can have the family keepsake imprinted. Ask staff members about the details of this service.

Upon request, your purchases at Brentano's will be gift wrapped. Those people using wheelchairs or pushing strollers will be happy to learn that the store is wheelchair accessible.

Whether you live near or far from Reston Town Center, you are sure to enjoy your time here. Of course, you won't be able to resist a nice, long visit at Brentano's.

Brentano's

General

Springfield Mall
Springfield, VA 22150
703-719-5669
<u>Hours:</u> Mon.-Sat. 10-9:30; Sun. noon-5

A pleasant up-scale bookstore, Brentano's has a branch in the Springfield Mall. They carry large selections of books discussing history, military history, social science, political science, and African-American studies. The store is wheelchair accessible.

Gift wrapping of purchases is done free upon request here. The store offers many special services. To read about them, please see the write-up of the Brentano's store in Reston.

Brentano's

General

Tysons Corner Center
1961 Chain Bridge Rd.
McLean, VA 22102
703-760-8956
<u>Hours:</u> Mon.-Sat. 10-9:30; Sun. noon-5

The attractive Brentano's bookstore located in the popular Tysons Center features a large history section with sub-specialties about the Civil War and military history. They also sell many books from the expanded social science and political science departments. The store is attractively decorated and is wheelchair accessible.

Brentano's will gift wrap your purchases free. To discover other special services offered here, please see the write-up of the Brentano's store in Reston.

Brentano's

General

Fair Oaks Mall
Fairfax, VA 22030
703-591-8985
Hours: Mon.-Sat. 10-9:30; Sun. noon-6

Brentano's is an attractive bookstore that sells general interest books, with something for everyone. This location in Fair Oaks Mall has particularly large children's, science fiction, mystery, and fiction departments. They gift wrap purchases free. Read about other services offered at Brentano's by referring to the write-up of the branch in Reston.

The store is wheelchair accessible and open everyday.

Brentano's

General

Fashion Ctr. at Pentagon City
1100 S. Hayes Street
Arlington, VA 22202
703-415-4010
Hours: Mon.-Sat. 10-9:30; Sun. 11-6

Brentano's beautiful hunter green and gold blend nicely into the up-scale mall Fashion Centre at Pentagon City. While shopping here you are likely to see many military personnel who gravitate to their strong departments of social and political sections as well as their history and Civil War topics.

Brentano's offers customers free gift wrapping of purchases. For a complete description of their other special services, please see the write-up for the Brentano's store in Reston.

The store and mall are wheelchair accessible.

Burke Centre Used Books & Comics

Used & Comics

5741 Burke Centre Parkway
Burke, VA 22015
703-250-5114
Hours: Mon.-Fri. 11-8;
Sat. 10-6; Sun. noon-5

Although specific hours that Burke Centre Used Books & Comics open are listed above, you can call them. Often the store is open other hours by chance. This fine used book store has 4,000 square feet of selling space that is filled with books that will interest infants to retirees. They also sell some new titles of science fiction.

A science fiction devotee, owner Joe Gumbinger said that paperbacks, especially first edition science fiction, are becoming collectible and there are price guides for paperbacks. The reason for such interest? The artwork on science fiction covers is so spectacular and done by such fine artists that the books are increasing in value.

If you are a comic book collector, you can find all the supplies you need to preserve comic books at this store. They even conduct comic book appraisals.

Burke Centre Used Books & Comics has a second branch on Franklin Farm Road in Herndon which is smaller than this location. The Burke Centre store is wheelchair accessible. When you are in the area or are a sci-fi or comic book collector, you will surely want to visit both locations and talk with knowledgeable employees about collecting.

C & W Used Books, Inc.

Used

14587 Potomac Mills Rd.
Woodbridge, VA 22192
703-491-7323
Hours: Mon.-Sat. 10-9; Sun. 11-7

With more than 100,000 titles in 77 different categories, C & W Used Books, Inc. is a place you must visit. About half of the store are paperbacks while hardbacks take the other half. At C & W you can buy, trade, and sell quality used books.

But that's not all. They have a fine selection of used CD's, audio tapes, and comics. Children enjoy the special room devoted just to them and a huge toy box. The store is wheelchair accessible and everyone is welcome.

Capital Medical Books

Medicine

4728 Western St. PO Box 2345
Fairfax, VA 22031
703-352-8153
Hours: Telephone and mail order only

Not only does Capital Medical Books sell the latest editions of medical books available, upon request they will notify customers when updated editions of books are published. This kind of service is a tremendous aid to busy health care professionals.

They maintain approximately 1,000 titles in the store and will place special orders for other books. They also sell a selection of video tapes.

Call Capital Medical Books to talk about your book needs. All of their business is done through mail and telephone orders.

The Children's Bookshop

Children's books

5730 Union Mill Rd.
Clifton, VA 22024
703-818-7270
FAX 703-818-7387
<u>Hours:</u> Mon.-Fri. 10-7;
Sat. 10-6; Sun. noon-5

Where can your little one learn to make books an important focus of his or her life? The Children's Bookshop in Clifton. Owner Linda T. Kostrzewa conducts enchanting programs in the store which reinforce the idea that reading is fun.

In addition to authors visiting the store to autograph books, storybook characters come to life in giant size to amuse children. Storytelling time is conducted weekly. But that isn't all the store does to influence children. At The Children's Bookshop children can participate in a reading group.

A bulletin board in the store and a newsletter keeps families aware of the coming events. Other special services include ordering books not in the store, searching for titles, and gift wrapping.

The Children's Bookshop sells approximately 1,800 titles of children's and parenting books in a light, bright, and friendly bookstore which is wheelchair and stroller accessible. Also for sale are magazines and books on audio tape. While children enjoy the store, parents can browse through a fine selection of parenting books.

In business since 1989, The Children's Bookshop is a fine place to expose your children to the finest in children's literature and fun activities.

Choice Books of Northern Virginia

Religious-Christian

11923 Lee Highway
Fairfax, VA 22030
703-830-2800
FAX 703-830-0340
<u>Hours:</u> Mon.-Fri. 8:30-6; Sat. 9-1

At Choice Books of Northern Virginia, you'll choose among the approximately 1,500 Christian and Mennonite books, fiction, and self-help books. They will search for titles you want and place special orders just for you. Books on their shelves include both new and used editions of many titles.

Established in 1968, Choice Books of Northern Virginia is open everyday except Sunday. There is one step at the entrance and the store is too tight for wheelchairs to maneuver within the store. But do not fear. Friendly employees are happy to assist you while you shop.

A catalog makes telephone and mail orders easy. They also publish a newsletter three times per year.

When you're in the market for Christian and Mennonite books, make your choice Choice Books of Northern Virginia.

The Compleat Strategist

Games & Militaria

103 E. Broad St.
Falls Church, VA 22046
703-532-2477
Hours: Mon., Wed., Thurs. 11-6;
Tues. & Fri. 11-9; Sat. 10-6;
Sun. noon-6

The main focus of The Compleat Strategist is not books but they have a terrific line of books about warfare, armor, and clothing that is valuable to writers and researchers. The inexpensive over-sized paperback books describe uniforms from Samurai warriors to today's army private. They also have a small selection of books about military strategy.

The focus of the store is gaming and they sell every sort of game from traditional board games to accessories and books for elaborate Dungeon & Dragon and fantasy games.

The Compleat Strategist is wheelchair accessible and off-street parking is nearby. Be warned: it's tough to leave this store without letting the kid inside you come out and buy games. An in-store bulletin board puts gamers in touch with others interested in this hobby.

Computer Books

Computer

2030 Clarendon Blvd.
Arlington, VA 22201
703-908-0199
Hours: Mon.-Fri. noon-5; Sat. 9-noon

Have you noticed that bookstores are being overwhelmed by thick, over-sized paperback books that all try to make using computer programs easier? Have you still not found just the one you need?

Now there is one location where you can find just the right computer guidebook that speaks language you can understand. The bookstore: Computer Books.

Not only do they have how-to books, but they also sell books about programming and even a few about computer history. They also sell a few computer magazines, floppy disks, templates, and an assortment of other supplies.

Walt Belknap, owner of Computer Books always "steers someone to the right book." With the volume of books published today, it takes an expert in the field to find what you need.

Although the store is small, Computer Books is wheelchair accessible. They also place special orders and do welcome mail orders.

Don't allow yourself to get so frustrated that you throw your personal computer out the window. First, call Computer Books.

Cosmic Bookstore

Science Fiction

10953 Lute Ct.
Manassas, VA 22110
703-330-8573
Hours: Mon.-Sat. 10-8; Sun. 11-5

Since 1991, Lane Summers has had his eyes on the stars at Cosmic Bookstore and brings customers a terrific assortment of galactic and popular books. He and his staff are extremely knowledgeable about the stock of science fiction, fantasy, Star Trek, and Star Wars series that the store sells.

Cosmic Bookstore also sells a variety of books for readers of all ages. Topics include history, nonfiction, mystery, occult, Westerns, metaphysics, philosophy, and poetry. Other items sold include gaming equipment for Dungeon & Dragons, Teenage Mutant Ninja Turtles, Car Wars, and more.

Perhaps one of the more unique items sold at Cosmic Bookstore is the artwork of local artists. Lane is currently helping an underground local magazine get established.

Cosmic Bookstore is wheelchair accessible and open seven days per week. When you're looking for a unique place to shop, be sure to visit Cosmic Bookstore in Manassas. There is no place like it.

Crest Books

Used-Romance & Science Fiction

46950 Community Plaza
Sterling, VA 22170
703-450-4200
Hours: Mon.-Sat. 10-6; Sun. noon-5

The owner of Crest Books, Pattie Jacobs, knows most of her customers by their first names. Knowing her clients so well, she knows what books they like and can keep an eye out for them at the used bookstore.

Most of the books sold at Crest Books are romance and science fiction. Often customers bring books to exchange for other titles which makes for a fast turnover in stock and always interesting browsing. Pattie does place special orders for new books and even works with local schools to provide history and English books.

Open everyday, Crest Books is not wheelchair accessible due to the many steps at the entrance but give Pattie a call, she is sure to work out an alternate method of getting books to you.

Noting that Crest Books is service oriented, Pattie has been able to develop a personal, independent store that matches the needs of the community.

Crown Books

General   6025 E. Burke Center Pkwy.
Burke, VA 22015
703-239-0566
Hours: Mon.-Sat. 10-9; Sun. 11-5

All SuperCrown and Crown Books extend the same discounts and services to customers. For details, see the write-up of the SuperCrown in McLean, Virginia.

Crown Books

General   7271-A Arlington Blvd.
Falls Church, VA 22042
703-573-3500
Hours: Mon.-Sat. 10-9:30; Sun. 10-6

No doubt, you are aware that Crown Books gives you terrific discounts. See the write-up of the McLean, Virginia SuperCrown for a complete description.

Crown Books

General   9246 Old Keene Mill Road
Burke, VA 22015
703-451-0350
Hours: Mon.-Sat. 10-9; Sun. 11-5

Please see the write-up for the SuperCrown on Chain Bridge Road in McLean to read about Crown's discounts and services.

Crown Books

General   2924 Chain Bridge Rd.
Oakton, VA 22124
703-281-0820
Hours: Mon.-Sat. 10-9; Sun. 11-5

Crown Books gives you great discounts. For a complete listing of the discounts, please see the write-up of the McLean, Virginia Super-Crown.

Crown Books

General

5620-B Ox Road
Fairfax, VA 22039
703-425-2363
Hours: Mon.-Sat. 10-9; Sun. 11-5

    For a complete description of the discounts and services offered by Crown Books, please see the write-up of the SuperCrown store in McLean on Chain Bridge Road.

Crown Books

General

8365-B Leesburg Pike
Vienna, VA 22180
703-442-0133
Hours: Mon.-Sat. 10-9:30; Sun. 10-6

    Refer to the write-up for the McLean SuperCrown store to see the terrific discounts and services they offer.

Crown Books

General

21800 Towncenter Plaza
Sterling, VA 22170
703-450-6889
Hours: Mon.-Sat. 10-9; Sun. 11-5

    All SuperCrown and Crown Books extend the same discounts and services to customers. For details, see the write-up for the McLean SuperCrown.

Crown Books

General

2068 Daniel Stuart Square
Woodbridge, VA 22191
703-491-2144
Hours: Mon.-Sat. 10-9; Sun. 11-5

    Please refer to a description of Crown Books discounts and services for the SuperCrown store in McLean, Virginia.

Crown Books

General   7271-A Arlington Blvd.
                                  Falls Church, VA 22042
                                  703-534-4830
                                  <u>Hours:</u> Mon.-Sat. 10-9; Sun. 11-5

The discounts and services that Crown Books gives you are listed in the McLean, Virginia SuperCrown write-up.

Crown Books

General   11160-H S. Lake Dr.
                                  Reston, VA 22091
                                  703-620-6560
                                  <u>Hours:</u> Mon.-Sat. 10-9; Sun. 11-5

To read about the discounts and services that all Crown Books and SuperCrown offers, please refer to the description of the McLean SuperCrown.

Crown Books

General   8389 Sudley Rd.
                                  Manassas, VA 22110
                                  703-631-0409
                                  <u>Hours:</u> Mon.-Sat. 10-10; Sun. 10-6

See the write-up of the McLean, Virginia SuperCrown to read about the discounts they offer.

Crown Books

General   59-B Catoctin Circle NE
                                  Leesburg, VA 22075
                                  703-771-2585
                                  <u>Hours:</u> Mon.-Sat. 10-9; Sun. 11-5

For a complete description of the discounts and services offered by Crown Books, please see the write-up of the McLean SuperCrown in Virginia.

Crown Books

General

12492 Dillingham Square
Woodbridge, VA 22192
703-878-2550
<u>Hours:</u> Mon.-Sat. 10-9; Sun. 11-5

Please refer to the write-up of the McLean, Virginia SuperCrown for a description of the discounts and services offered at Crown Books.

Crown Books

General

4017 S. 28th Street
Arlington, VA 22206
703-931-6949
<u>Hours:</u> Mon.-Sat. 10-9; Sun. 11-5

Please refer to the write-up of SuperCrown for the McLean store for a description of the discounts and services offered at Crown Books.

Crown Books

General

6960 T Bradlick Shopping Center
Annandale, VA 22003
703-941-1458
<u>Hours:</u> Mon.-Sat. 10-9; Sun. 11-5

See the write-up of the SuperCrown store in McLean for a description of the discounts and services they offer.

Crown Books

General

7428 Little River Tpk.
Annandale, VA 22003
703-941-7318
<u>Hours:</u> Mon.-Sat. 10-9; Sun. 11-5

All SuperCrown and Crown Books extend the same discounts and services to customers. For details, see the write-up of McLean's SuperCrown store.

Crown Books

General   6011 Centreville Crest Lane
                                   Centreville, VA 22020
                                   703-968-6577
                                   Hours: Mon.-Sat. 10-9; Sun. 10-6

Please refer to the write-up for the McLean SuperCrown for a complete description of the discounts and services offered at Crown Books.

David Holloway Bookseller

Antiquarian-General   7430 Grace St.
                                   Springfield, VA 22150
                                   703-569-1798
                                   Hours: Appointment only

David Holloway, Bookseller, offers you a fine collection of books about fine art, African-American culture, modern first editions, mystery, and detective novels. The books are sold by mail order or appointment only. A catalog is published three times per year. The business was established approximately eight years ago.

Doubleday Book Shop

General   Fair Oaks Mall
                                   Fairfax, VA 22033
                                   703-273-1258
                                   Hours: Mon.-Sat. 10-9:30; Sun. noon-6

Following the example set by the Doubleday Bookshop located in Gaithersburg, this branch has moved the children's department to the front of the store. Children (and adults) are thrilled with the fine selection of books and toys sold here.

While the little ones choose books, their adults roam toward the back of the store to enjoy a full complement of general interest books. Particularly large departments include computers, business, cookbooks, fiction, mystery, and science fiction.

The large Fair Oaks Mall and Doubleday Bookshop are wheelchair accessible.

E. Wharton & Co.

Antiquarian-Classics　　　　　3232 History Dr.
Oakton, VA 22124
703-264-0129
Hours: Mail order or appt. only

An antiquarian book business of fine quality, E. Wharton & Co. specializes in women writer's 19th and 20th century first editions, most of which are fiction. But you'll also find many other special items for sale such as a signed photograph of Sarah Bernhardt and books illustrated by Childe Hassam.

How could a person part with such treasures? Owner Sarah Baldwin believes, "To part with one treasure only to find another."

Business is conducted by telephone, mail orders and by appointment. Catalogs and lists are published.

The name E. Wharton & Co., explained Sarah, reflects Mrs. Wharton who was an American novelist and short-story writer of the 19th and early 20th centuries. Her first successful publication was "The House of Mirth" published in 1905. An inscribed copy of the book which had been owned by writer and critic Leon Edel is presently available among the Edith Wharton titles offered.

There is no doubt that E. Wharton & Co. is a bookstore that will provide you with valuable assistance when developing your book collection.

Eastern Mountain Sports Inc.

Outdoor Sports　　　　　7954 Tysons Corner Center
1961 Chain Bridge Rd.
McLean, VA 22102
703-506-1470
Hours: Mon.-Sat. 10-9:30; Sun. noon-5

Eastern Mountain Sports store is a paradise for outdoorsmen. Their books all focus on outdoors sports and guidebooks.

For a more complete description, please refer to the write-up for the Gaithersburg, MD, store.

Edward N. Bomsey Autographs, Inc.

Autographs　　　　　7317 Farr St.
Annandale, VA 22003
703-642-2040
FAX 703-642-2040
Hours: Telephone, mail order, & appointment only

Ed Bomsey knows autographs, signatures, and "what-not." He collects and sells autographs by telephone, mail order, and by appointment. In business since 1976, he publishes a catalog as often as possible of items he has available.

If you want to own a little bit of history, contact Ed. You can own a signature of someone famous which will be a conversation piece for years to come.

Entremanure (see Gerachis, Andrew)

Evangelical Used Books

Used, Christian religion

1815 N. Nelson St.
Arlington, VA 22207
703-522-0596
<u>Hours:</u> Appt. only on Sat. & Sun.

With approximately 10,000 books in his basement, James I. Newman operates Evangelical Used Books by appointment or by telephone and mail order. He is available to discuss particulars of his collection during the evenings and Saturday. In business since 1978, all books focus on Christian theology and Bible reference.

Family Bookstores

Religious-Christian

Village Square Shopping Center
964 Bragg Road
Fredericksburg, VA 22407
703-786-2223
<u>Hours:</u> Mon.-Sat. 9-9

"Family Bookstores is an organization that strives to glorify God and serve Jesus Christ by the distribution of Bibles and scripture-based products through excellence in merchandising and customer service, and by responsible stewardship to the company's owners," said Lisa Eary, Copy Chief of the Marketing Department of Family Bookstores.

Serving communities for more than fifty years, Family Bookstores is the fourth largest bookstore chain in the United States. The stores sell Bibles, study guides, gift books, children's Christian books, Christian fiction, religious gifts, music, greeting cards, and inspirational books.

Family Bookstores is a Zondervan Company, a division of HarperCollins Publishers. There are seven branches of Family Bookstores in the Washington area. All of the stores are wheelchair accessible. You'll note that on Sundays, all of the stores are closed for a day of rest.

Family Bookstores

Religious-Christian   11807 Fair Oaks Mall
Fairfax, VA 22033
703-352-1489
<u>Hours:</u> Mon.-Sat. 10-9:30

Family Bookstores are a popular shops among Christians. The store in Fair Oaks Mall is wheelchair accessible. For a complete description of Family Bookstores, please refer to the write-up above for the Fredericksburg, VA store.

Family Bookstores

Religious, Christian   Manassas Mall
8300 Sudley Rd.
Manassas, VA 22110
703-330-7845
<u>Hours:</u> Mon.-Sat. 10-9:30

A branch of Family Bookstores is located in Manassas Mall and sells a variety of Christian-related items. Please see the write-up for the Fredricksburg, VA store.

Franklin Farm Used Books & Comics

Used & Comics   13340-B Franklin Farm Rd.
Herndon, VA 22071
703-437-9530
<u>Hours:</u> Mon.-Fri. 11-8;
Sat. 10-6; Sun. noon-5

A family bookstore, Franklin Farm Used Books & Comics offers something to everyone. The book departments that are particularly strong include science fiction, historical fiction, mystery, adventure, and the ever-popular cook books.

This store, a sister branch to Burke Centre Used Books & Comics, has 2,400 square feet of selling space. The Burke, VA, location is almost double the size of this store. Please see the write-up about that business in this book.

George Mason Law School Bookstore

Law College   3401 N. Fairfax Dr.
Arlington, VA 22201
703-841-2660
FAX 703-993-2668
Hours: School year: Mon.-Thurs.
8-7:30; Fri. 8-4

At the George Mason University Law School bookstore, you will naturally find books featuring law. They also have the study guides that assist students in preparing for the Law School Admission Test or LSAT. The bookstore is wheelchair accessible and will place special orders for customers.

George Mason University Bookstore

College   4400 University Ave.
Student Union Bldg 2
Fairfax, VA 22030
703-993-2665
Hours: Mon.-Fri. 9-7:30; Sat. 10-3

A four year university with an extensive graduate program, George Mason University has a bookstore that is open to the public. Most books sold are textbooks but they also sell a large volume of reference, literature, and study guides. Perhaps one of the more impressive collections they sell are books written by the faculty.

In total the bookstore carries more than 7,000 books. The store is wheelchair accessible and there are elevators in the building. Naturally, you also will be able to purchase clothes and various gifts with the George Mason University logo.

Geppi's Comic World Crystal City

Comic books   Crystal City Underground
1675 Jefferson Hwy.
Arlington, VA 22202
703-413-0618
Hours: Mon.-Sat. 10-6

Comics are hot items today and you can find approximately 150 titles of comic books at Geppi's Comic World Crystal City. Owner and comic book expert, Steve Geppi also orders special titles for customers.

All comic books he sells in the store are new books. Many comic books are of a science fiction theme. Established in 1972, Geppi's Comic World Crystal City also sell calendars, video tapes, T-shirts, posters, games, and children's toys. Located in Crystal City Underground, the store has no steps and is accessible to wheelchair users.

If comic books are your thing, you won't want to miss Geppi's Comic World Crystal City. If you can't get to Crystal City, Geppi's has a second branch in Silver Spring, MD.

Entremanure (Gerachis, Andrew)

Horticulture & Gardening

Aldie Hill, 39184 John Mosby Hwy.
PO Box 109
Aldie, VA 22001
703-327-4166
Hours: Telephone, mail order, & appointment only

Specializing in books about horticulture and gardening, Andrew Gerachis enjoys searching for the books that you want but he may not have in stock yet. Entremanure, owned by Andrew, is a new and used book business conducted by mail order or appointment.

When you're ready to grow your gardening library, call Andrew. He's ready to help you.

Grace Christian Bookstore

Religious, Christian

1102 W. Church Rd.
Sterling, VA 22170
703-430-2813
FAX 703-450-5311
Hours: Mon.-Sat. 9-6:30

Grace Christian Bookstore specializes in Christian literature, both fiction and nonfiction. Many books have been written especially for children.

As a service to customers, Grace Christian Bookstore does imprinting on Bibles making your Good Books personal heirlooms. A catalog of merchandise is published twice per year to make telephone and mail orders easier. The store also sells various Christian gifts and music recorded on cassette tapes.

The Great Commission

Inspirational

2107 N. Pollard St.
Arlington, VA 22205
703-525-0222
Hours: Mon.-Sat. 10-7

A full service non-denominational religious bookstore, The Great Commission prides itself on offering the public inspirational books. They also sell assorted gifts and greeting cards. Special orders are welcomed. A catalog is published infrequently.

The store is not wheelchair accessible due to the steps at the entrance. Owner Hanna Chang reports that they are happy to discuss books available on the telephone and mail orders to customers.

The Great Commission has inspired readers since 1983.

Great Falls Park Bookshop

National Park   9200 Old Dominion Dr. PO Box 66
                               Great Falls, VA 22066
                               703-285-2966
                               Hours: Sat. & Sun. 10-6;
                               Weekdays gift cart 10-6

When tourists visit Washington, D.C., they expect to spend their times in museums, governmental buildings, and memorials. Tourists: don't miss the spectacular parks and nature grounds surrounding the Capital. Great Falls Park in Virginia is located where the Potomac River plunges 70 feet. During the spring, the falls are so flooded that the water volume surpasses that of Niagara Falls.

The Visitor Center rotates exhibitions about nature and wildlife. Exhibits are on an upper level of the center and a ramp is available. Wheelchair users may want a bit of assistance to go up the ramp. During the week, a small gift area is open on this upper level. On weekends, a larger bookshop is open on the ground level which is accessible to everyone.

The Greenhouse Books

General   Main Street PO Box 525
                               Marshall, VA 22115
                               703-364-1959
                               Hours: Mon.-Sat. 10-5; Sun. noon-5

"The largest bookstore in Fauquier County in the western part of Virginia" is how an employee of Greenhouse Books described the general interest bookstore. Greenhouse Books does have an excellent selection of books about Virginia, its history, and the Civil War. Special orders and mail orders are welcomed.

Greenhouse Books not only sells books, but publishes them as well! The formerly out-of-print books that they publish include an 1863 diary of a soldier and many children's books.

Responsive to the community, Greenhouse Books maintains a room available for meetings, author autograph sessions, and Saturday story-telling time for children. Greenhouse Books caters to private and public school reading programs.

Located in an actual house, Greenhouse Books is wheelchair accessible through the back courtyard. The town where the bookstore calls home, Marshall, has a population of around one thousand people. Greenhouse Books is a popular store and a true convenience to local book lovers.

Habitat—National Wildlife Federation

Wildlife & Nature   8925 Leesburg Pike
                                        Vienna, VA 22184
                                        703-790-4000
                                        800-432-6564
                                        Hours: Mon.-Fri. 9-5

      Habitat, located in the Educational Center of the National Wildlife Federation, is a delightful small store in which you will find books and gifts you've never seen anywhere else. In the same building, educational programs and displays are held. The grounds have many trails guaranteed to please you and your guests. Some of the trails are even wheelchair accessible.
      Although Habitat is a small store, wheelchairs can carefully maneuver. A catalog and mail order are available.
      When travelling to this location on Leesburg Pike, keep your eyes sharp. The sign is often somewhat covered by bushes and trees. The entrance is just a driveway and the educational center and Habitat can't be seen from the street. It is located in a residential area rather than a shopping area.
      For a fuller description of items for sale in the store, see the write-up of the Habitat on 16th Street in Washington.

Hammett's Learning World

Education   Oakton Shopping Center
                                        2914 Chain Bridge Road
                                        Oakton, VA 22124
                                        703-938-0047
                                        Hours: Mon.-Thurs. 10-9;
                                        Fri. & Sat. 10-5

      With a branch in Oakton, parents and teachers can take advantage of the quality learning materials found at J.L. Hammett Company. The store is wheelchair accessible.
      For a complete description and history of J.L. Hammett Company, please see the write-up of the Gaithersburg, MD store.

Hammett's Learning World

Education   Springfield Towner Mall
                                        6420 Brandon Ave.
                                        Springfield, VA 22150
                                        703-569-2303
                                        Hours: Mon.-Fri. 10-6; Sat. 9-5

J.L. Hammett Company has many stores across the country that specialize in providing learning supplies to parents and teachers. The branch in Springfield is wheelchair accessible and located in an outdoor mall. See the complete write-up describing the business for the Gaithersburg, MD store.

The He Bookstore

Vietnamese books

6763 A Wilson Blvd.
Falls Church, VA 22034
703-532-7890
Hours: Daily 11-7:30

Because The He Bookstore sells only books written in Vietnamese, many books are imported. The categories are broad and include how to learn the Vietnamese language.

The He Bookstore is open everyday and is wheelchair accessible.

Hole in the Wall Books

Used-Science Fiction & Mags.

905 W. Broad St.
Falls Church, VA 22046
703-536-2511
Hours: Mon.-Fri. 10-9;
Sat. & Sun. 10-6

"Hole in the Wall Bookstore has the best science fiction collection in the Washington area," claims manager Scott Jones.

Inside that hole in the wall, they have more than 10,000 titles, most of which are science fiction. They also sell mystery, classics, and modern literature. Most of the books are used. Magazines sold feature science fiction and horror.

Comic books and supplies are also sold at Hole in the Wall. Scott supplies expert advice to the collector. He recommends that comic books should be kept cool, dry, and in the dark. Sunlight mars the color on the paper thus decreasing the value of the book.

The small store is not wheelchair accessible but Scott and employees will assist people climb the stairs. Established in 1979, the store does not sponsor formal programs, but Scott offers his services as a speaker to talk about "almost anything you can imagine."

If you get the chance, make Hole in the Wall Bookstore one of your stops in the Washington area. Along with your purchases, you're sure to leave with a smile.

Imagination Station

Children's books

4524 Lee Highway
Arlington, VA 22207
703-522-2047
FAX 703-527-5933
Hours: Mon.-Sat. 10-6; Sun. 11-4

If you want to interest your children in the stories that you enjoyed as a child, take them to Imagination Station. Just as you did, they'll love the thrill of flying with Peter Pan or galloping on the back of a white unicorn.

At Imagination Station, you'll find employees who can guide you to the books that are perfect for your youngster. They also sell books in foreign languages and audio cassettes. As a child of the 90's, your little one no doubt knows how to use the VCR. Imagination Station rents book-related videos.

The store sponsors a Birthday Club, author and book characters appearances, and story telling time. While you scan the parenting books, the children can enjoy themselves in the play area of the store.

Completely stroller and wheelchair accessible, Imagination Station is open everyday. They do place special orders for clients and welcome telephone and mail orders.

Your little one's imaginations will be sparked by the offerings at Imagination Station. Be careful, your imagination may take flight as well.

Immanuel Christian Bookstore

Religious-Christian

5211 Backlick Rd.
Springfield, VA 22151
703-354-5219
Hours: Mon., Thurs., Fri. 9-5;
Tues. 9-7; Wed. 9-9; Sat. 10-2;
Sun. 8:30-1:30

"We are careful about titles in our store and try to preview new materials," said Bonnie Wytsma, manager of Immanuel Christian Bookstore.

In addition to selectively choosing the books they sell, they also rent more than 600 video tapes that are all Christian films and a great resource for families with children. The rental fee is nominal.

Established in 1983, Immanuel Christian Bookstore was remodeled in 1992. A Children's Corner was added at that time. The store is completely wheelchair accessible and a comfortable, warm place to visit.

Owned by the Immanuel Bible Church, the bookstore is open everyday. In addition to Bibles, religious books, children's books, and music, the bookstore also sells audio books, video tapes, magazines, games, calendars, greeting cards, children's toys, and T-shirts.

Bonnie reported that they do place special orders often and usually are able to obtain the books in five days. As another service to the community, the bookstore maintains a bulletin board of announcements in the store.

The last word about the store from Bonnie: "Families are always welcome."

Janie's

General	10382 Willard Way Fairfax, VA 22030 703-352-8895 <u>Hours:</u> Mon.-Sat. 8:30; Sun. 8:30-6

We have "more magazines than anywhere else in Fairfax," claimed Robert Stiskin, manager of Janie's. They also have a terrific collection of general interest books.

Since they are located near George Mason University, Robert notes that they also sell items of interest to the college clientele: Cliff notes and comic books. In addition, they sell audio books, educational and game software, sports cards, and even lottery tickets. They also have a nice discount section of books.

Located in Courthouse Plaza mall, Janie's may be moving, but have no fear, it will only be a few doors down the mall. The store is wheelchair accessible.

Jeff's Baseball Corner

Used-Sports	5222 Port Royal Rd. Springfield, VA 22150 703-321-9209 FAX 703-321-8881 <u>Hours:</u> Mon.-Fri. 10-8; Sat. 10-6; Sun. noon-5

Sports fans and athletes have a place to immerse themselves in their favorite sports that lies just beyond their armchairs. Sports Etc. shares a store with Jeff's Baseball Corner in Springfield.

Combined, they offer a very extensive selection of new, used, and antiquarian books all about sports of every kind. Prices are pleasing to the buyer and discounts are offered when buying more than one title. They also have video tapes and a full line of sports cards and collector supplies for sale.

Located in a strip mall, Sports Etc. and Jeff's Baseball Corner are wheelchair accessible. For a description of Sports Etc., please see the write-up in this section of the book. Located in the same mall as Jeff's and Sports, Etc., the sports lover will enjoy "Athletic House" which sells trophies and team sportswear, and "The Ski Shak" which sells summer and winter skiing clothes and gear.

No doubt about it, if you are passionate about sports, you'll make a touchdown, a home run, and set, game, and match after reading the books offered at Sports Etc. and Jeff's Baseball Corner.

Jesus Bookstore

Religious-Christian

14214 Smoketown Rd.
Dale City, VA 22192
703-490-1070
Hours: Mon., Wed., & Fri. 10-9;
Tues., Thurs., & Sat. 10-6

Exclusively a Christian bookstore, Jesus Bookstore sells many books all written by Christian authors and Christian related items. They also sell recorded music, gifts, greeting cards, and church supplies. The store is wheelchair accessible and has a branch in Alexandria.

Jo Ann Reisler Ltd.

Antiquarian-Children's b

360 Glyndon St. NE
Vienna, VA 22180
703-938-2967
FAX 703-938-9057
Hours: Appointment only

Jo Ann Reisler knows a good children's book when she sees one. Since 1971, she has offered quality antiquarian children's illustrated books, as well as original illustrative art.

Open by appointment, Jo Ann publishes a catalog to make telephone and mail order easy. FAX her your want list and she may have the title available or can locate the title for you.

When you're in the market for antiquarian children's books, think Jo Ann Reisler Ltd.

Jolly Rogers' Comics

Comics

6503 N. 29th St.
Arlington, VA 22213
703-241-5930
Hours: Mon.-Thurs. 11-7; Fri. 11-8;
Sat. 11-7; Sun. 11-6

Superman is a hero. Superman died. Superman is alive. Who can keep up on all these changes? Jolly Rogers' Comics, that's who. You can too, if you visit the store or receive their monthly newsletter.

Open everyday of the week, Jolly Rogers' Comics carries more than 750 comic books. But there's more; the store also sells baseball cards, strategy games, T-shirts, and posters.

An expert in comic books, the owner, Thomas Mulvey, conducts appraisals, places special orders, and will search for comic books that you want. Telephone and mail orders are accepted. There is one step to enter the store but it is wheelchair accessible on the inside.

Whether you're looking for the latest on Superman or Archie and Veronica, be sure to contact Jolly Rogers' Comics.

Kramerbooks & Afterwords

General

4201 Wilson Blvd.
Arlington, VA 22203
703-524-3200
FAX 703-524-7211
Hours: Mon.-Thurs. 7-midnight;
Fri. 7am-2am; Sat. 9am-2am;
Sun. 9am-midnight

Just opened in September of 1993, this second branch of Kramerbooks & Afterwords is destined to become a welcome addition to the Washington book scene. Its other location at Dupont Circle is one of Washington's more popular book havens.

This new branch in Arlington has 10,000 square feet in the headquarters building of the National Science Foundation. This store, like the other, will be divided equally between a full-service bookstore and a cafe featuring indoor and outdoor seating, a carryout, and a bar.

Owner Bill Kramer noted that the Dupont Circle branch has grown into a 24-hour operation on the weekends and hopes that the Ballston branch will eventually support the same extended hours.

The books stocked will cover practically every category imaginable. Because of their location, the store will highlight titles of interest to scientists. With the new State Department Foreign Service campus only a mile away, the store will also offer tremendous language reference, politics, and global regional studies departments.

Kramerbooks & Afterwords doesn't skimp on special events either. They have already discussed with the Arlington County Library plans to offer a series of lectures at the Central Library which is only two blocks away from the store. They also plan to help organize a variety of reading groups on all subjects. In addition, they will conduct frequent author appearances and special events for children.

Based upon the solid reputation of the Kramerbooks & Afterwords at Dupont Circle, this new branch is sure to become another popular book haunt.

Let There Be Praise, Inc.

Religious, Christian   9 Catoctin Circle SE
Leesburg, VA 22075
703-777-6311
Hours: Mon.-Sat. 10-6;
Thurs. & Fri. 10-9

When you visit Let There Be Praise, you will praise the wealth of items available. Ninety percent of the stock is Christian books, Bibles, and study guides. They also have some classics, such as books written by Mark Twain, Charles Dickens, and more. In stock are 10,000 titles and approximately 5,000 used books. Let There Be Praise does special order new books.

Singing to the heavens is facilitated by the music cassettes, CD's and videos. The store does order sheet music. They also sell church supplies. Completely wheelchair accessible, Let There Be Praise was established in 1976. Your entire family will enjoy their visit to this nice bookstore.

Listen 2 Books

Books on cassette tape   1911 Jefferson Davis Hwy.
Arlington, VA 22202
703-415-4408
800-AUDIO BOOKS
Hours: Mon.-Fri. 10:30-6:30;
call for Saturdays

Remember how you loved bedtime stories when you were a kid? They're back. At Listen 2 Books, you can buy, rent, sell, and trade books on audio tapes.

Located in Arlington, see the write-up for the larger branch of Listen 2 Books under the Alexandria section of this book. You'll be happy when you find these pleasant stores.

MCL Associates Used Book Division

Cooking   6916 Rosemont Dr. PO Box 26
McLean, VA 22101
703-356-5979
Hours: Telephone & Mail order only

Just browsing through the MCL's Cookbook Collectors' Catalogue makes you lick your lips. The catalog is organized like a multi-course meal with headings such as Celebrating with the Seasons, Cupid in the Kitchen, Casseroles by Candlelight, Creating Memories for the Future, Opening and Closing Celebrations, Food Gifts from Your Kitchen, Celebrity Celebrating, and International Feasting.

Books sold are new, used, or rare and hard-to-find. Searches are conducted free-of-charge as outlined in the catalog. A list of cookbooks that MCL Associates would like to purchase can be found in the back of the catalog. All business is conducted by telephone and mail order. To obtain a copy of the catalog, send them $3.50.

MCL Associates have also become publishers. Their current publication is a biography of a Christian missionary titled "With Stethoscope in Asia: Korea by Sherwood Hall, M.D."

The Manuscript Company of Springfield

Antiquarian-General

PO Box 1151
Springfield, VA 22151
703-256-6748
Hours: Mail order & appt. only

If you are looking for an unusual piece to frame and adorn your walls, contact Terry Alford, owner of The Manuscript Company of Springfield. Honoring the written word from history, The Manuscript Company sells autographs, manuscripts, hand-written letters, travel diaries, and even old accounting books from the 18th to the 20th centuries.

In business since 1974, Terry reports that much of his business is conducted by telephone and mail orders. He periodically publishes a catalog. If you would like to see The Manuscript Company's collection, Terry does meet with people by appointment. He also attends many book fairs in the area.

The motto of The Manuscript Company: "We always buy as well as sell."

Middleburg Books

General

102 W. Washington St. PO Box 2258
Middleburg, VA 22117
703-687-6874
800-373-READ
Hours: Mon.-Sat. 10-5; Sun. noon-5

Want to rub elbows with Washington's well known? They often visit Middleburg Books for the charming atmosphere and terrific selection of general interest titles. Strong areas are in fiction, mystery, and children's books. They're happy to place special orders if you don't find the book to suit you. In addition to books, Middleburg Books sells greeting cards and calendars. The staff will gift wrap your purchases.

Middleburg Books has three steps at the entrance but is cozy inside once you mount the three steps. Seating is available inside for comfortable browsing. The bookstore is open daily.

Be sure to check their in-store bulletin board for notices of when authors will be visiting the store for autographing sessions. When you're in the area, Middleburg Books is a good all-around bookstore.

Mt. Vernon Giftshop

History   End of George Wash. Pkwy
                                             Mt. Vernon, VA 22121
                                             703-780-2000
                                             Hours: Mon.-Fri. 9-5:30;
                                             Sat. & Sun. 9-5:30;
                                             Nov. 1-March 1 Mon.-Fri. 9:30-4:30

"No estate in United America is more pleasantly situated than this house," George Washington wrote of his home, Mount Vernon. He lived in the beautiful white Georgian mansion from 1754 until his death in 1799.

The home and grounds have been restored and are open to visits by the public. You'll happily find a giftshop outside the main gate which, among other memorabilia, sells books about Washington, the home, the Revolutionary and Civil wars, architecture, life and furnishings of homes in Colonial America, and early American cooking. The 200 titles include some books written for children.

After strolling through the home, flower gardens, stables, small museum, and giftshop, you can walk to the family vaults where George and Martha are buried.

Natural Wonders Inc.

General   6739 Springfield Mall
                                             Springfield, VA 22150
                                             703-922-6068
                                             Hours: Mon.-Sat. 10-9:30; Sun. noon-5

Natural Wonders brings the wonders of natures to you. The stores, with four branches in the Washington area, are always busy with everyone from adults to children anxious to see and interact with their merchandise and displays.

In addition to the many books regarding nature, the environment, and wildlife, they also sell such items as Bushnell binoculars, a panorama camera, a map compass, puzzles, and everything you need when trekking into the wilds. One clever item looks like a backpack but is filled with quality items necessary for a romantic lunch in the woods. It holds long stem glassware, cloth napkins, a wooden cutting board, and whatever items you bring from your kitchen.

Natural Wonders has a toll free number that informs you about trail events that are celebrated in your area. They are a nationwide chain of stores. Located in malls nearby, the stores are all wheelchair accessible.

Natural Wonders Inc.

General   11924 U Fair Oaks
                                    Fairfax, VA 22033
                                    703-691-4793
                                    Hours: Mon.-Sat. 10-9:30; Sun. 10-6

    Located in Fair Oaks Mall, Natural Wonders is wheelchair accessible. Please refer to the fuller description above of the Springfield, VA, store.

The Nature Company

Natural History   The Fashion Centre at Pentagon City
                                    1100 S. Hayes St.
                                    Arlington, VA 22202
                                    703-415-3700
                                    Hours: Mon.-Sat. 10-9:30; Sun. 11-7

    The Nature Company at The Fashion Centre at Pentagon City is located on the ground level and, like the other branches, is a delightful, upbeat store that believes in conserving nature and wildlife.
    Please refer to the longer description of The Nature Company for the Wisconsin Avenue store in Washington, D.C.

The Nature Company

Natural History   Fair Oaks Mall
                                    Fairfax, VA 22033
                                    703-359-2924
                                    Hours: Mon.-Sat. 10-9:30; Sun. noon-6

    You won't want to miss visiting The Nature Company at Fair Oaks Mall. The family-oriented store over-flows with books and items that you won't be able to pass up.
    For a complete description of The Nature Company, please refer to the write-up for the Wisconsin Avenue store in Washington, D.C.

The Nature Company

Natural History   Tysons Corner Center
                                    McLean, VA 22103
                                    703-760-8930
                                    Hours: Mon.-Sat. 10-9:30; Sun. noon-5

    The Nature Company is a book and gift store that you absolutely cannot miss. There are four other locations in the Washington area and all are wheelchair accessible.

Please refer to the write-up of The Nature Company for the Wisconsin Avenue store in Washington, D.C.

New Leaf Bookstore

New & Used books-General

36 Main Street
Warrenton, VA 22186
703-347-7323
Hours: Mon.-Thurs. & Sat. 9-6;
Fri. 9-7; Sun. noon-4

Charlotte Mautner, owner of The New Leaf Bookstore, says that they serve a very diverse community and have many different types of books. She adds: "Our emphasis is on service--good fast service!"

A series of workshops are held at New Leaf Bookstore on the second and fourth Sundays of each month. Workshop topics include numerology, astrology, psychology, recovery, and meditation. The cost to attend is minimal and no reservations are needed. A newsletter keeps interested clients informed.

The New Leaf Bookstore sells new and used general interest books with specialties including alternative life styles, metaphysics, new age, psychology, and recovery. Don't leave the kids at home because this bookstore has books for them. In total, the store carries approximately 8-9,000 titles. They also offer audio books, magazines, newspapers, music tapes, greeting cards, posters, T-shirts, and games.

To better serve the community, The New Leaf Bookstore does place special orders, search for books, gift wrapping, and keeps an up-to-date bulletin board in the store.

Established in 1987, The New Leaf Bookstore is open everyday and is easily accessible for everyone. The comfortable store is well-lit and often plays relaxing "New Age" music. Seating within the store makes browsing enjoyable and a restroom is available to customers. Charlotte says, "We have lots of people who come in and sit and read, just for the ambiance." You're sure to enjoy it too.

Nursing Tutorial & Consulting Service Bookstore

Nursing

4542 A John Marr Dr.
Annandale, VA 22003
703-256-9854
800-US TUTOR
703-256-9894
Hours: Mon.-Fri. 8-6

How does one become a good nurse? One place that helps is Nursing Tutorial & Consulting Service Bookstore in Virginia. A WATS line and catalog make the resources they offer open to everyone across the United States.

The books sold are especially written for nursing students and the nurse practitioner in her profession. In addition to selling review books for RN and LPN State Board exams, they sell books related to nursing including: health, nutrition, psychology, recovery, cookery, education, reference, history, and even humor.

The bookstore also sells a variety of medical supplies, video tapes, review cards for nursing students, posters, calendars, games, and T-shirts. They don't discriminate here; they sell and special order medical supplies for physicians and "civilian" customers.

Nursing Tutorial & Consulting Service Bookstore goes a step farther. They have a wonderful display of historical nursing memorabilia and posters. Whether you are a nursing student or professional, you'll want to contact this specialty bookstore.

The Paschal Lamb

Religious-Christian
11194 Lee Highway
Fairfax, VA 22030
703-273-5956
Hours: Mon.-Sat. 10-6

This pleasant and peaceful place is a perfect setting for the more than 2,000 titles focusing on the Catholic religion, books about recovery, and books for children. Some books are printed in large type or are on the popular audio format. They also have a selection of magazines and newspapers as well as a wide variety of gifts.

Courteous owners who operate the store will assist you and will also conduct searches and place special orders for those books not in stock. The store maintains a bulletin board filled with announcements of interest to patrons. At times, authors visit the store and will autograph their books.

The Paschal Lamb's doors are open to everyone and is accessible to those using wheelchairs or pushing strollers. Since 1987, the bookstore has provided the best of reading material to patrons.

Pentagon Bookstore

Militaria
Pentagon Concourse PO Box 46157
Washington, D.C. 46157
703-695-0868
FAX 703-768-4086
Hours: Open by appointment only on
Mon.-Fri. 8-5; closed Federal holidays

The Pentagon is certainly one of the most recognizable of buildings in the world. Did you know you could visit a bookstore there?

The Pentagon Bookstore is open during the week by appointment only. From the Guard Station, civilian customers are escorted by a Pentagon employee to the bookstore. Customers with military identification are allowed entrance on their own. If you can't visit the bookstore, telephone and mail orders are accepted.

It's easy to guess what type of books you'll find in their bookshop: military. The approximately 10,000 books for sale also include books about aviation, nautical, and history all related to the military. Also sold are magazines, newspapers, and calendars. They do place special orders for customers. At times, authors visit the store to conduct autograph sessions.

Open since 1979, the Pentagon Bookstore has proved to be a success. As an American, you are sure to find fascinating books here.

Prince William Forest Park Shop

National Park Area

Interstate 95 at Exit 150
Triangle, VA 22172
703-221-2104
Hours: Daily 8-5

When visiting Prince William Forest Park, book lovers will enjoy a quick stop at the bookshop. They sell books about the outdoors, other National Parks, and every field guide imaginable. They sell children's books and have a delightful book about sharing nature with kids. The shop in the Visitor's Center is wheelchair accessible.

The Purple Crayon Inc.

Children's books

7515 Huntsman Blvd.
Springfield, VA 22153
703-455-6100
Hours: Mon.-Thurs. 10-8;
Fri. & Sat. 10-9:30; Sun. noon-6

Whether it is lilac, lavender, plum, pomegranate or even violet, you'll find all the shades decorating a children's bookstore named The Purple Crayon. Even the clouds suspended from the ceiling and the six-foot palm tree are purple.

"In the back of the store we have a storytelling area where kids feel comfortable enough to sprawl on the floor with their favorite book," said owner Debra Schroeder.

Established in 1991, The Purple Crayon sponsors programs to delight children. Characters come alive from the books they love and visit the store. Authors also visit for autographing sessions. Story-telling is a big hit here and they do conduct story-telling four times per month. So that your child doesn't miss one of these events, the store publishes a newsletter. A bulletin board is maintained within the store.

In addition to the 10,000 titles of books, The Purple Crayon also sells audio books, educational games, storybook related toys and calendars. Parents aren't forgotten here. Parenting books are available. Employees happily place special orders and gift wrap purchases.

Of course, The Purple Crayon is accessible to strollers and wheelchairs. There are no steps at the entrance. Seating is available throughout the store to enhance browsing the books.

Debra lives up to her philosophy about which she says: "Our philosophy is simple—a children's bookstore should cater to children and reading should be fun."

Rand McNally—The Map & Travel Store

Travel & Cartography

Tyson's Corner
McLean, VA 22102
703-556-8688
Hours: Mon.-Sat. 10-9:30; Sun. noon-6

Rand McNally—The Map and Travel Store has a location in the busy shopping area of Tyson's Corner. Manager Mike Zuber notes that this branch was established in September, 1992.

For a complete description of the stores, see the write-up for the Washington, D.C. branch.

Recreational Equipment Inc.

Recreational

3509 Carlin Springs Rd.
Baileys Crossroads, VA 22041
703-379-9400
Hours: Mon.-Fri. 10-9;
Sat. 10-6; Sun. noon-5

Recreational Equipment Inc. (REI) caters to the needs of the hiker, camper, canoeist, and climber by supplying the clothing, equipment, and books needed. For a complete description of the store, see the write-up under the branch of REI located in College Park, MD.

Reston's Used Bookshop

Used-General

1623 Washington Plaza
Reston, VA 22090
703-435-9772
Hours: Telephone or mail order only

According to their advertisements, Reston's Used Book Shop sells "paperbacks, hardbacks, rare, and not so rare" used books. Co-owners Susan Weston and Sue Schram ensure that the statement is true.

Since 1979, they have brought used general interest and children's books to the community. The store is small but Susan reports that clients "in wheelchairs have visited."

Reston's Used Book Shop accepts mail orders and will find books for clients. With comfortable music playing in the background, they also sell greeting cards and "Peaceable Kingdom" items.

Richard McKay Used Books, Inc.

Used-General   Newgate Shopping Center
                                  14114 Lee Highway
                                  Centreville, VA 22020
                                  703-830-4048
                                  Hours: Mon.-Sat. 9-9; Sun. 11-7

Richard McKay believes in recycling and carries that belief into his business, McKay Used Books.

When he began the business in 1983, he said, "The basic idea was to provide an economical way for the whole family to obtain books they wish to read, study, and enjoy. Then when they are finished, the books could be recycled so others could enjoy them."

In order to help that cycle along, books sold at McKay Used Books have incredibly good prices on top quality books. The books cover everything from ancient history to science fiction. They also sell CD's, comic books, and software.

Maintaining a stock of approximately 150,000 books, Richard estimates that the store adds approximately 30,000 books per month. Half of the books are fiction; the other half are nonfiction. McKay Used Books has become so popular that Richard has added video tapes and books on cassette tape.

Richard offers cash for books. Most books are accepted for trade credit, but McKay Used Books does offer cash for nonfiction hardback, oversized paperbacks, high demand children's preschool and beginning reading books. Talk with Richard to determine if your books qualify for cash.

Fortunately, McKay Used Books is completely accessible to everyone. Wheelchair users and stroller-pushers will be pleased to know that there are no steps at the entrance. The store maintains long hours everyday.

Richard is customer sensitive. The final paragraph in a brochure describing McKay Used Books states: "Please let us know if we can do anything to make our store better and/or more enjoyable. Thank you."

Rockaway Books

Used-General   PO Box 1508-A
                                  Woodbridge, VA 22193
                                  703-590-2966
                                  Hours: Telephone & Mail order only

Glenn and Gabrielle Goggin have to publish many different catalogs because their business, Rockaway Books sells such diverse books and merchandise.

Of major interest to book lovers, Rockaway Books specialize in vintage paperbacks from the 1940's-60's, old comics and pulp magazines such as "Weird Tales" and "Doc Savage."

Other catalogs list such items as cult movie posters and movie memorabilia, pin-up photograph of Marilyn Monroe and drawings by the artist Vargas, circus posters, programs, photographs, and postcards, burlesque pin-ups and memorabilia.

Business is conducted by mail order only. Rockaway Books was one of the first comic book businesses in the country. Contact Glenn and Gabrielle—you may have some items to sell to them. They certainly have things to sell to you.

Saludos

Spanish books   3811-I S. George Mason Dr.
Baileys Crossroads, VA 22041
703-820-5550
Hours: Mon.-Sat. 10:30-9;
Sun. 10:30-7

A store featuring books written in the Spanish language, Saludos also sells newspapers, magazines, greeting cards, and rents video tapes. Owner Janis Ashman notes that they sell general interest books from inspirational writings to works written by prize winning authors.

The store is open everyday and is wheelchair accessible. Whether Spanish is a first or second language for you, you will find books just for you at Saludos.

Scribner's Bookstores

General   The Fashion Centre at Pentagon City
1100 S. Hayes Street
Arlington, VA 22202
703-415-2005
Hours: Mon.-Sat. 10-9:30; Sun. 11-6

Located in the beautiful "Fashion Centre at Pentagon City," Scribner's Bookstore offers general interest books but has broader selections in the fine arts and literary criticism than most stores of its kind.

While shopping here, you may notice many shoppers dressed in sharp military uniforms. Many people working in the nearby Pentagon stop by to take advantage of their exceptionally complete history and current events departments. The store also sells small gift items including blank books, decorative boxes, greeting cards, and book marks.

Scribner's opened in November, 1989, when the mall opened. Managers of the store are working to establish a catalog and mail order capabilities. They also print a newsletter and sponsor author autographing sessions.

Decorated in classic hunter green with antique white and gold accents, the store has two large busts of Ernest Hemingway and F. Scott Fitzgerald. While classical or mild jazz music plays, customers can take their time browsing by relaxing on the store's benches.

Scribner's and the entire mall are wheelchair accessible. For a break in your shopping trip, stop at Scribner's for a little relaxation while you shop for books.

Sports Books Etc.

Sports

5224 Port Royal Rd.
Springfield, VA 22151
703-321-8660
Hours: Mon.-Fri. 10-8;
Sat. 10-6; Sun. noon-5

Who's on first? What's on second? The left fielder's name? The catcher's name? And tomorrow's pitching? Costello was confused by Abbott's answers. He should have gone to Sports Books Etc. where he would have gotten clear answers.

One of the few completely sports bookstores in the country, Sports Books Etc. in Springfield offers 5,000 books, 1,000 videos, numerous magazines, newspapers and audio books, and thousands of trading cards. A catalog is available for telephone and mail orders.

When Paul Haas opened Sports Books Etc. in 1984, it was the only completely sports bookstore in the world! The other all sports bookstores are now located in London, Melbourne, Milan, Vancouver and California.

Prior to getting his touchdown-idea for starting an all sports bookstore, Paul managed a tennis and racquetball club for six and a-half years. Before that he vollied cases as an attorney for the United States government.

Paul isn't the only person at Sports Books Etc. who knows his subject. Paul says, "The staff is knowledgeable - both about the products we sell and sports per se."

Open everyday, Sports Books Etc. is completely accessible whether you are a wheelchair quarterback or a stroller shortstop. If you think that only books about professional sports are found here, you're out. Categories include archery, badminton, bicycling, billiards, bodybuilding, bowling, boxing, canoeing, cheerleading, cricket, darts, fencing, field hockey, frisbee, gymnastics, horseback riding, ice skating, lacrosse, martial arts, polo, rugby, sailing, skateboarding, soccer, squash, surfing, table tennis, volleyball, and water skiing. Can you believe that this is just a partial list? Contact Sports Books Etc. for a catalog.

Sports Etc. is located in a strip mall in Springfield and shares a store with Jeff's Baseball Corner where you can buy all the sports cards ever sold and also used and antiquarian books at excellent prices.

Oh, by the way, Who's on first, What's on second and I-Don't-Know is on third. Because is in center field, Today is the catcher and Tomorrow's the pitcher. I-Don't-Give-a-Darn is the shortstop.

Storybook Palace Inc.

Children's books   9415 Old Burke Lake Rd.
Burke, VA 22015
703-425-2400
<u>Hours:</u> Mon.-Sat. 9-6

Whether your little one dreams of Cinderella's palace or the rough castle of King Arthur, Storybook Palace is the place your children will find books to keep their imagination stirred.

Books sold are geared toward youngsters from infants through teens. There is also a section of parenting books. Other items sold in the store all relate to the books. Examples are stuffed toys based upon storybook characters, cassettes telling stories, and even some project kits.

Special events are always extra-special at Storybook Palace. In addition to story-time and visits by storybook characters and authors, the store sponsors puppet shows and a variety of programs. Bedtime is a special event when children go to Storybook Palace dressed in their pajamas and toting teddy bears for a special story-time.

The bookstore is stroller and wheelchair accessible. They do publish a newsletter calendar of events and new arrival books. Since December, 1985, when it was established by Christine Bury, Storybook Palace has been a favorite of children and adults alike.

SuperCrown

General   1457 Chain Bridge Rd.
McLean, VA 22101
703-893-7640
<u>Hours:</u> Mon.-Sat. 10-9; Sun. 11-5

Situated in downtown McLean, SuperCrown has aisles comfortable for group shopping, wheelchairs, and strollers. The store has a relaxed atmosphere conducive to peaceful shopping. Every shopper enjoys the more than 50,000 titles on the shelves.

Crown Books maintains 55 very busy branches in the Washington, D.C. area. All stores stock the same fine general interest books. The difference between Crown Books and SuperCrown is merely a matter of numbers. SuperCrown stocks more than 100,000 titles. Most stores are open the same hours and all are wheelchair accessible. If they don't have a particular title in stock, employees are happy to place special orders which are quickly filled. Gift certificates are available at all branches.

When you shop at Crown Books, you know that you will be getting terrific discounts regardless of which store you visit. Crown Books shook the bookstore world in the 1970's by starting to offer discounts everyday. They are as follows: New York Times best-selling hardbacks: 40% off; all other hardbacks: 20% off; New York Times best-selling paperbacks: 25% off; all other paperbacks: 10% off; Best-selling computer books: 25% off; Audio books-on-cassette-tape: 20% off; video tapes, magazines, and CD-Rom: 10% off. Crown Books also have tables with stacks of hardback books that are greatly discounted and are sold for $1.00-$5.00.

With headquarters in Landover, Maryland, Crown Books and SuperCrown can be found nationwide. Everyone knows of the fine reputation of Crown Books. Find the branch closest to you.

SuperCrown

General
6286 Arlington Blvd.
Falls Church, VA 22044
703-534-4830
Hours: Mon.-Sat. 10-20; Sun. 10-8

For a description about the discounts offered by Crown Books, please see the write-up of the McLean store. You'll want to take advantage of the discounts after making your selections from more than 30,000 titles.

SuperCrown

General
6758 Springfield Mall
Springfield, VA 22150
703-313-8370
Hours: Everyday 10-midnight

Located on the Loisdale Road side of Springfield Mall, SuperCrown has 18,000 square feet filled with more than 100,000 titles of books. In addition to full shelves of books, they sell magazines, audio books-on-cassette-tape, children's videos, book lights, book marks, and even CD-Rom interactive disks.

Children won't want to leave this SuperCrown. After choosing their purchases from the large children's book section, they can play in the castle, stroll down the yellow brick road which is underneath a rainbow, or curl up and read underneath one of the tiny trees.

To read about their terrific discounts offered at SuperCrown and Crown Books, please refer to the write-up of the McLean store.

SuperCrown

General
9508 Main Street
Fairfax, VA 22031
703-425-9188
Hours: Mon.-Sat. 10-10; Sun. 10-8

All SuperCrown and Crown Books extend the same discounts and services to customers. SuperCrown stores offer more than 50,000 titles sure to interest everyone. For details, see the write-up for the store in McLean, Virginia.

SuperCrown

General

13005 Lee Jackson Mem. Hwy.
Fairfax, VA 22033
703-378-2052
<u>Hours:</u> Mon.-Sat. 10-10; Sun. 10-8

Visit the renovated Greenbriar Towncenter and you can enjoy the SuperCrown located there. Greenbriar Towncenter is located on Route 50 between the city of Fairfax and Dulles Airport.

At the SuperCrown, you'll enjoy the comfortable browsing while resting on the store's many benches. In addition to the approximately 100,000 general interest titles, they also have a number of specialty areas such as African American studies, computer books, cookbooks, and children's books. It's easy to quickly slip into SuperCrown to grab a bestseller or to leisurely browse through all of the books.

For a description of the discounts and services, see the write-up of the McLean store.

SuperCrown

General

6758 Springfield Mall
Springfield, VA 22150
703-313-8370
<u>Hours:</u> Mon.-Sat. 10-9; Sun. 11-5

Located on the Loisdale Road side of Springfield Mall, SuperCrown has 18,000 square feet of book shopping delight. In addition to full shelves of new books, they sell magazines, audio books-on-cassette-tape, children's videos, book lights, book marks, and even CD-Rom interactive disks.

Children won't want to leave this SuperCrown. After choosing their purchases from the large children's book section, they can play in the castle, stroll down the yellow brick road which is underneath a rainbow, or curl up and read underneath one of the tiny trees.

To read about their terrific discounts offered at SuperCrown and Crown Books, please refer to the write-up of the McLean, Virginia store.

Thyme Books

General

1 Loudoun St. SW
Leesburg, VA 22075
703-777-5277
<u>Hours:</u> Mon.-Sat. 10-6; Sun. noon-5

Inside 1,500 square feet of an old building, Thyme Books sells general interest and some children's books that are sure to keep pleasing the reader in times to come. They also sell some used paperbacks.

Special orders and book searches are no problem for Mark Sharples, owner of Thyme Books. The store sponsors author autograph sessions and special workshops for teachers.

Thyme Books is unfortunately not wheelchair accessible. The store was established in the early 1970's.

Toy Corner Book Dept.

Children's books

2952 A Chain Bridge Road
Oakton, VA 22124
703-255-3232
Hours: Mon.-Sat. 10-6;
Thurs. until 8; Sun. noon-5

Just mention toys and you'll see a child's eyes light up. When you take your little one to Toy Corner, you'll also find a good selection of books guaranteed to keep that sparkle alive for many years to come. The store is stroller and wheelchair accessible.

Truro Episcopal Church Bookstore

Religious-Christian

10520 Main St.
Fairfax, VA 22030
703-273-8686
FAX 703-591-0737
Hours: Mon.-Thurs. 9:30-4:30;
Fri. 9:30-7:30; Sat. 10-2; Sun. 9-2

In a warm and inviting atmosphere, Truro Episcopal Church Bookstore sells approximately 4,500 titles including books for children. Some books are in audio form and printed in large type. The bookstore places special orders. At times, authors conduct autographing sessions.

Open everyday, Truro Episcopal Church Bookstore also sells a variety of quality gift items as well as calendars, greeting cards, video tapes, and T-shirts.

Since 1976, the bookstore has supported the ministry's message of Christ. The doors are open to everyone and wheelchair accessible, too.

Universal Chinese Bookstore

Chinese books

6763 Wilson Blvd.
Falls Church, VA 22034
703-241-7070
Hours: Daily 10:30-8

If you are looking in Washington for books written in Chinese, head for Universal Chinese Bookstore. Most books are imported. The stock is all of a general interest theme.

The entrance is wheelchair but aisles may be crowded at times.

W.B. O'Neill Old & Rare Books

Middle East & Eastern Med.

11609 Hunters Green Ct.
Reston, VA 22091
703-860-0782
FAX 703-620-0153
Hours: Telephone, mail order, &
Appointment only

"This is the only book business in the USA specializing entirely on the countries of the Eastern Mediterranean and Middle East, with a special focus on Modern Greece, Cyprus and Turkey," said Bill O'Neill, owner of W.B. O'Neill Old & Rare Books.

Bill is happy to meet with you by appointment to discuss his collection of new, used, and antiquarian books that are for sale. He also expertly performs appraisals. A catalog is available for telephone and mail orders.

While Bill was in the Army for 32 years, he spent most time as an Area Specialist/Linguist in the part of the world relative to the books he sells today. His work revolved around NATO assignments culminating in his serving as Senior NATO Officer in Greece and liaison to the CINC Greek Armed Forces.

Prior to entering the service, Bill worked in an antiquarian book business as an apprentice in New York's Brick Row Book Shop.

Today, Bill is always pleased to find just the books that clients need and want in this highly specialized field. When you're looking for an expert in the Eastern Mediterranean and Middle East field, be sure to contact W.B. O'Neill Old & Rare Books.

WETA Learningsmith

General

Tysons Corner Center
1961 Chain Bridge Rd.
McLean, VA 22102
703-556-0200
Hours: Mon.-Sat. 10-9:30; Sun. noon-5

WETA Learningsmith is "a general store for the curious mind," according to their catalog. The store is a must visit. In addition to selling books they have hands-on interesting and unique items for all ages.

Examples are a children's herb kit that allows the child to grow different herbs. The kit includes seeds, growing pots, soil, instructions, and recipe cards. Sim Ant is a software program that allows you to experience life as an ant by invading the homes of humans, fighting for the queen and colony, and defending your home from enemy ants. They sell things like 3-dimensional puzzles, The Audubon Society field guides, map puzzles, weather tracker's kits, video tapes, audio tapes, and a wide collection of books and activity kits such as "The Why Book of Golf," "Watercolor for the Artistically Undiscovered," "The Physics of Baseball,"

"The Kids' Book of Fishing," "The Original Bug House Kit," and so much more.

Learningsmith stores are a chain that is slowly expanding across the country. Wherever a branch opens, it's a big hit. People have enjoyed the stores so much that they spend hours investigating their offerings.

The WETA Learningsmith in Tysons Mall is wheelchair accessible. In July, 1993, a second branch opened in Georgetown Park Mall.

Waldenbooks

General   Manassas Mall
                                   8300 Sudley Road
                                   Manassas, VA 22110
                                   703-368-8366
                                   <u>Hours:</u> Mon.-Sat. 10-9:30; Sun. noon-6

Only four miles from the Manassas battlefield, Waldenbooks has a large collection of books relating to the Civil War and life at that time in our country's turbulent history.

Waldenbooks is located in Manassas Mall and is wheelchair accessible. Refer to the write-up for the Brentano's store in Reston for details of the many services offered to customers at Waldenbooks and Brentano's.

Waldenbooks

General   6725 Springfield Mall
                                   Springfield, VA 22150
                                   703-971-9443
                                   <u>Hours:</u> Mon.-Sat. 10-9:30;
                                   Sun. noon-6

If you think that every chain store is just like another, visit Waldenbooks in the Springfield Mall. They sell a general stock but specialize in science fiction.

This branch sponsors reading and writing groups and hosts authors who autograph their books while in the store. Waldenbooks is definitely wheelchair accessible and has a book for you, no matter what your interests are.

For a more detailed description of the services Waldenbooks and Brentano's offer to customers, please refer to the Brentano's store in Reston.

Waldenbooks

General

Ballston Commons
4238 Wilson Blvd.
Arlington, VA 22203
703-527-2442
Hours: Mon.-Sat. 10-9:30; Sun. noon-6

When you're on a heavy-duty shopping trip to Ballston Commons in Arlington, Virginia, you must take a few minutes to stop at the Waldenbooks store located there. They offer more than 15,000 books and have something for everyone's interests. The manager notes that they have particularly strong selections in fiction, romance, science fiction, books written in Spanish, and children's books.

Waldenbooks has been of service to the community in this mall for the past eight years. The store is wheelchair accessible.

Please see the write-up for the Brentano's store in Reston to read about all the special services that Waldenbooks and Brentano's offer to customers.

Waldenbooks

General

Tysons Corner Center
1961 Chain Bridge Rd.
McLean, VA 22102
703-893-4208
Hours: Mon.-Sat. 10-9:30; Sun. noon-5

At Tysons Center in McLean you'll find a Waldenbooks that has a particularly strong collection of children's books as well as fiction, romance, and science fiction departments. The store is located in a mall and is wheelchair accessible.

Please see the write-up for the Brentano's store in Reston to discover the wonderful special services that both Waldenbooks and Brentano's offers you.

WaldenSoftware

Computers

Tysons Corner Center
1961 Chain Bridge Rd.
McLean, VA 22102
703-760-8947
Hours: Mon.-Sat. 10-9:30; Sun. noon-5

In addition to selling software, WaldenSoftware sells the latest in computer books and magazines and even publishes a quarterly newsletter to keep clients aware of happenings in the field. Open everyday, WaldenSoftware is accessible to all.

Before you throw your computer across the room in frustration, take a trip to WaldenSoftware. They'll help you find the right book which will clearly lead you down the path to harmony with your computer; after all, computers are our friends, right?

WaldenSoftware

Computers   Manassas Mall
                                     8300 Sudley Road
                                     Manassas, VA 22110
                                     703-361-1702
                                     <u>Hours:</u> Mon.-Sat. 10-9:30; Sun. noon-6

Computer books and magazines are featured at WaldenSoftware in Manassas alongside a wide range of software. Computer buffs and computer illiterates can both find what they need here.
This branch is wheelchair accessible.

Wild Bird Center

Ornithology   5765 S. Burke Centre Pkwy.
                                     Burke, VA 22015
                                     703-323-7898
                                     FAX 703-323-7899
                                     <u>Hours:</u> Mon.-Sat. 10-6; Sun. noon-5

For a complete write-up of The Wild Bird Centers, please refer to the Cabin John, MD store.
The franchise of The Wild Bird Center in Burke is wheelchair accessible.

Wild Bird Center

Ornithology   141 Church St. NW
                                     Vienna, VA 22180
                                     703-938-5788
                                     <u>Hours:</u> Mon.-Sat. 10-6; Sun. noon-5

Located in Vienna, The Wild Bird Center is a part of the franchise which has its headquarters in Cabin John, MD. Please refer to the description written about that store.
Please note that the Vienna Wild Bird Center is not wheelchair accessible. There are three steps at the front door, but employees are willing to help. Call them ahead of time.

Wild Bird Center

Ornithology

Glen Shopping Center
4220 Merchants Plaza
Woodbridge, VA 22192
703-878-6688
Hours: Mon.-Fri. 10-7; Sat. 10-6;
Sun. noon-5

Located in Glen Shopping Center, the Wild Bird Center is wheelchair accessible. This location sponsors a concession at the Mason Neck State Park in Lorton, Virginia.

For a complete description of the popular stores, please refer to the write-up for the Cabin John, MD store.

Words of Wisdom Books & Gifts

Religious-Christian

4209 Annadale Ctr. Dr.
Annandale, VA 22003
703-256-3005
Hours: Mon.-Sat. 9:30-5:30

Words of Wisdom owner Evangeline Nicholson has brought fine Christian books to people of all ages for the past twenty years. Words of Wisdom also sells a complete stock of musical CD's, cassettes, song-books, and family video tapes.

Bible imprinting is free when you purchase your Bible at Words of Wisdom. The store also places special orders.

Although the actual store is small, it is wheelchair accessible. When words of encouragement and spirituality escape you, visit Words of Wisdom to fill that gap inside you.

Indexes

Alphabetical Index of Stores

Alphabetical Index of Stores

Index of Stores by Specialty

Alternative Life Styles
Aquarius Metaphysical Center	*Alexandria*
Associates Rare Books, The	*Virginia*
Book 'N Card	*Virginia*
Cardinal Images	*Alexandria*
Lambda Rising Inc.	*Washington*
Lammas Books	*Washington*

Agriculture
Ag-Connection Bookstore	*Washington*
Agribookstore, Winrock	*Virginia*
Pierce Mill, Rock Creek Park Shop	*Washington*

Americana
Antietam Natl. Battlefield Museum Shop	*Virginia*
Antiquarian Bookworm	*Maryland*
Arts & Industries Building	*Washington*
Bartleby's Books	*Washington*
Blue & Gray Books and Prints	*Alexandria*
BookHouse	*Virginia*
Continental Divide Trail Society	*Maryland*
Daughters of the Am. Rev. Museum Shop	*Washington*
Decatur House Shop	*Washington*
Donna Lee's Books	*Alexandria*
Ford's Theatre Museum Bookshop	*Washington*
Frazier's Americana	*Maryland*
Frederick Douglass Home Bookshop	*Washington*
Fuller & Saunders Books	*Washington*
Greenhouse Books, The	*Virginia*
Hearthstone Bookshop	*Alexandria*
Jefferson Memorial Bookshop	*Washington*
Jennie's Book Nook	*Alexandria*
Lincoln Memorial Bookshop	*Washington*
Mail Order Division--Parks & History Assoc.	*Washington*
National Archives Museum Store	*Washington*
National Museum of American History	*Washington*
National Portrait Gallery Bookshop	*Washington*

261

Old Print Gallery, The	*Washington*
Pierce Mill, Rock Creek Park Shop	*Washington*
Q. M. Dabney & Co.	*Maryland*
T.A. Borden	*Maryland*
This 'N' That Antiques	*Maryland*
Tower Bookshop (Old Post Office Tower)	*Washington*
Travel Books & Language Center Inc.	*Maryland*
Washington Monument Bookshop	*Washington*

Antiquarian

All Books Considered	*Maryland*
Antiquarian Bookworm	*Maryland*
Antiquarian Tobacciana	*Virginia*
Ashe & Deane Fine Books	*Maryland*
Associates Rare Books, The	*Virginia*
Audubon Prints and Books	*Virginia*
Bartleby's Books	*Washington*
Bonifant Books	*Maryland*
Book Cellar, The	*Maryland*
Book Ends	*Virginia*
BookHouse	*Virginia*
Children's Book Adoption Agency	*Maryland*
Continental Divide Trail Society	*Maryland*
David Holloway Bookseller	*Virginia*
Doris Frohnsdorff	*Maryland*
E. Wharton & Co.	*Virginia*
From Out of the Past	*Alexandria*
Georgetown Book Shop	*Maryland*
Jennie's Book Nook	*Alexandria*
Jo Ann Reisler Ltd.	*Virginia*
Joshua Heller Rare Books, Inc.	*Washington*
Kay's Bookshelf	*Alexandria*
Lambda Rising Inc.	*Washington*
Logic & Literature	*Washington*
Manuscript Company of Springfield, The	*Virginia*
Old Hickory Bookshop	*Maryland*
Old Mill Books	*Alexandria*
Old Print Gallery, The	*Washington*
Old World Mail Auctions	*Maryland*
Oscar Shapiro	*Washington*
President's Box Bookshop, The	*Washington*
Q. M. Dabney & Co.	*Maryland*
Quill & Brush Bookstore	*Maryland*
Samuel Yudkin & Associates	*Washington*
Scavengers of Georgetown	*Washington*
Steven C. Bernard First Editions	*Maryland*
T.A. Borden	*Maryland*
Voyages Books & Art	*Alexandria*
W.B. O'Neill Old & Rare Books	*Virginia*
Washington Cathedral Bookshop	*Washington*

Architecture

Arts-Fine

Schweitzer Japanese Prints Inc.	*Maryland*
T.A. Borden	*Maryland*
Voyages Books & Art	*Alexandria*
William F. Hale Books	*Washington*

Arts-Performing

Backstage Books & Costumes	*Washington*
Book Niche & Capital Comics Center, The	*Alexandria*
Kennedy Center for the Performing Arts Shop	*Washington*
Writer's Center, The	*Maryland*

Arts & Crafts

Daugh. of the Am. Rev. Museum Shop	*Washington*
Elegant Needle, The	*Maryland*
G Street Fabrics Book Dept.	*Maryland*
Indian Craft Shop	*Washington*
Textile Museum Shop	*Washington*

Autographs

E. Wharton & Co.	*Virginia*
Edward N. Bomsey Autographs, Inc.	*Virginia*
Manuscript Company of Springfield, The	*Virginia*
Waverly Auctions Inc.	*Maryland*

Books-On-Cassette-Tape

A-Z Used Books	*Maryland*
Agape Christian Bookstore	*Washington*
Alfa Foreign Language Books	*Virginia*
Antietam Natl. Battlefield Museum Giftshop	*Virginia*
Aquarius Metaphysical Center	*Alexandria*
Arawak Books	*Maryland*
Audubon Naturalist Bookshop	*Wash & MD*
Baptist Book Store	*Virginia*
Bay Books, Inc.	*Maryland*
Book Fair, The	*Maryland*
Book Nook	*Maryland*
Bookstall, The	*Maryland*
Cardinal Images	*Alexandria*
Children's Bookshop, The	*Virginia*
Encore Books	*Maryland*
Heaven Christian Gift Store	*Maryland*
Icon & Book Serv. Monastary of Holy Cross	*Washington*
Immanuel Christian Bookstore	*Virginia*
Iranbooks Inc.	*Maryland*
Kennedy Center for the Performing Arts Shop	*Washington*
Lambda Rising Inc.	*Washington*
Liberty Library	*Washington*
Listen 2 Books	*Alex & VA*
Middleburg Books	*Virginia*

Business & Management

Children's

Middleburg Books	*Virginia*
National Air & Space Museum Bookshop	*Washington*
Nature Company, The	*Wash & VA*
Pierce Mill, Rock Creek Park Shop	*Washington*
Purple Crayon Inc., The	*Virginia*
Rock Creek Park Nature Center Bookshop	*Washington*
Ship's Store	*Washington*
Storybook Palace Inc.	*Virginia*
Sullivan's Toy Store	*Washington*
Takoma Kids	*Maryland*
Thyme Books	*Virginia*
Tower Bookshop (Old Post Office Tower)	*Washington*
Toy Corner Book Dept.	*Virginia*
Toys...Etc. Book Dept.	*Maryland*
Tree Top Toys Inc. Book Dept.	*Washington*
Truro Episcopal Church Bookstore	*Virginia*
WETA Learningsmith	*Wash & VA*
Washington Cathedral Bookshop	*Washington*
Why Not	*Alexandria*

Classical Studies

Ashe & Deane Fine Books	*Maryland*
Book Niche & Capital Comics Center, The	*Alexandria*
Bridge Street Books	*Washington*
Capitol Hill Books	*Washington*
Chapters	*Washington*
Cleveland Park Bookshop	*Washington*
E. Wharton & Co.	*Virginia*
Folger Shakespeare Library Shop	*Washington*
Old Forest Bookshop, The	*Washington*
Quill & Brush Bookstore	*Maryland*
R. Quick, Bookseller	*Maryland*
Vertigo Books	*Washington*

Colleges/Universities

Gallaudet University Bookstore	*Washington*
George Mason Law School Bookstore	*Virginia*
George Mason University Bookstore	*Virginia*
George Washington University Bookstore	*Washington*
Georgetown Univ. Law Center Bookshop	*Washington*
Georgetown Univ. Leavey Center Bookshop	*Washington*
Georgetown Univ. Medical Bookstore	*Washington*
Howard University Bookstore	*Washington*
Univ. of District of Columbia Bookstore	*Washington*
Univ. of Maryland Book Center	*Maryland*

Comics

Aftertime Comics Inc.	*Alexandria*
Another World	*Washington*
BJ'S Books	*Virginia*

Blue Beetle Comics & Baseball Cards — *Maryland*
Book Niche & Capital Comics Center, The — *Alexandria*
Books & Comic Outlet — *Maryland*
Burke Centre Used Books & Comics — *Virginia*
Closet of Comics — *Maryland*
Collectors World — *Maryland*
Comic Classics — *Maryland*
Comics Center & Book Niche — *Alexandria*
Cosmic Bookstore — *Virginia*
Franklin Farm Used Books & Comics — *Virginia*
Geppi's Comic World Crystal City — *Virginia*
Geppi's Comic World of Silver Spring — *Maryland*
Janie's — *Virginia*
Jolly Rogers' Comics — *Virginia*
Zenith Comics & Collectibles — *Maryland*

Communications/Writing

Alexander Graham Bell Association — *Washington*
NTL Institute Book Department — *Alexandria*
Professional Book Center — *Alexandria*
Tools of the Trade-Books for Communicators — *Alexandria*
Writer's Center, The — *Maryland*

Computers

Capitol College Bookstores — *Maryland*
Computer Books — *Alexandria*
Maryland Book Exchange — *Maryland*
National Air & Space Museum Bookshop — *Washington*
Professional Book Center — *Alexandria*
Reiter's Scientific & Professional Books — *Washington*
Reprint Bookstore — *Washington*
Tools of the Trade-Books for Communicators — *Alexandria*
WaldenSoftware — *Alex & VA*

Cooking

Arawak Books — *Maryland*
Beautiful Day Bookstore — *Maryland*
Blue Nile Books — *Washington*
Book Nook — *Maryland*
Chapters — *Washington*
Cricket Bookshop — *Maryland*
MCL Associates Used Book Division — *Virginia*
Mt. Vernon Giftshop — *Virginia*
Pierce Mill, Rock Creek Park Shop — *Washington*
R. Quick, Bookseller — *Maryland*
Recreational Equipment Inc. — *MD & VA*
Sakura Books & Food — *Maryland*
Smile Herb Shop — *Maryland*
Sutton Place Gourmet Inc. — *Wash, MD & Alex*

| Willis Van Devanter Books | *Maryland* |

Economics

Book Market	*Washington*
Brookings Institute Bookshop, The	*Washington*
International Monetary Fund Bookstore	*Washington*
Professional Book Center	*Alexandria*
Sidney Kramer Books, Inc.	*Washington*
World Bank Bookstore	*Washington*

Education

Hammett's Learning World	*MD & VA*
Kenilworth Aquatic Gardens Shop	*Washington*
Liberty Library	*Washington*
NTL Institute Book Department	*Alexandria*
Pierce Mill, Rock Creek Park Shop	*Washington*
Pursell's Church Supply Inc.	*Washington*

Electronics

| Capitol College Bookstores | *Maryland* |
| Reiter's Scientific & Professional Books | *Washington* |

Environment

Agribookstore, Winrock	*Virginia*
Am. Society of Landscape Architects	*Washington*
Audubon Naturalist Bookshop	*Wash & MD*
Beautiful Day Bookstore	*Maryland*
Glen Echo Park	*Maryland*
Habitat--National Wildlife Federation	*Virginia*
Kenilworth Aquatic Gardens Shop	*Washington*
National Museum of Natural History	*Washington*
Nature Company, The	*Wash & VA*
One Good Tern Ltd.	*Alexandria*
Pierce Mill, Rock Creek Park Shop	*Washington*
Recreational Equipment Inc.	*MD & VA*
Rock Creek Park Nature Center Bookshop	*Washington*
Wild Bird Center	*MD & VA*
Wild Bird Center and Absolutely Bats!	*Maryland*

Ethnic Studies

Ambia, Inc.	*Washington*
Anacostia Museum	*Washington*
Arawak Books	*Maryland*
Associates Rare Books, The	*Virginia*
Bethune Museum & Archives Shop	*Washington*
Cheshire Cat Bookstore	*Washington*
Chuck & Dave's	*Maryland*
David Holloway Bookseller	*Virginia*
Howard University Bookstore	*Washington*

Latin American Books	*Washington*
Martin Luther King, Jr. Library Giftshop	*Washington*
Pierce Mill, Rock Creek Park Shop	*Washington*
Professional Book Center	*Alexandria*
Pursell's Church Supply Inc.	*Washington*
Pyramid Bookstore	*Wash & MD*
Reprint Bookstore	*Washington*
Revolution Books	*Washington*
Scottish Merchant, The	*Alexandria*
Taj Book Service	*Washington*
Thistle & Shamrock Books	*Alexandria*
Vertigo Books	*Washington*
W.B. O'Neill Old & Rare Books	*Virginia*

Foreign Language

A Likely Story Children's Bookstore	*Alexandria*
Alfa Foreign Language Books	*Virginia*
Arawak Books	*Maryland*
Book Cellar, The	*Maryland*
Cheshire Cat Bookstore	*Washington*
Children's Bookshop, The	*Virginia*
Editorial El Mundo	*Washington*
Fairy Godmother-Children's Books & Toys	*Washington*
Georgetown Univ. Leavey Center Bookshop	*Washington*
Ginza Things Japanese	*Washington*
He Bookstore, The	*Virginia*
International Language Center	*Washington*
Iranbooks Inc.	*Maryland*
Islamic Center Shop	*Washington*
Kulturas Books & Records	*Washington*
Lado International Books	*Washington*
Latin American Books	*Washington*
Literal Books	*Washington*
Map Store Inc., The	*Washington*
Rand McNally - The Map & Travel Store	*Wash, MD & VA*
Revolution Books	*Washington*
Sakura Books & Food	*Maryland*
Saludos	*Virginia*
Scottish Merchant, The	*Alexandria*
Tempo Bookstore	*Washington*
Travel Books & Language Center Inc.	*Maryland*
Travel Merchandise Mart	*Washington*
Universal Chinese Bookstore	*Virginia*
Victor Kamkin Inc.	*Maryland*
W.B. O'Neill Old & Rare Books	*Virginia*

Gardening & Landscaping

Am. Society of Landscape Architects	*Washington*
Beall-Dawson House Giftshop	*Maryland*

BookHouse	*Virginia*
Chapters	*Washington*
Entremanure (Gerachis, Andrew)	*Virginia*
Kenilworth Aquatic Gardens Shop	*Washington*
One Good Tern Ltd.	*Alexandria*
U.S. National Arboretum	*Washington*
Washington Cathedral Bookshop	*Washington*

Genealogy
Hearthstone Bookshop	*Alexandria*
Jennie's Book Nook	*Alexandria*
National Archives Museum Store	*Washington*

Government
Capitol Gift Shop, The	*Washington*
Farragut West Bookstore	*Washington*
International Monetary Fund Bookstore	*Washington*
Liberty Library	*Washington*
Library of Congress Shop	*Washington*
Q. M. Dabney & Co.	*Maryland*
U.S. Government Printing Office Bookstore	*Wash & MD*

Health & Nutrition
Beautiful Day Bookstore	*Maryland*
Betz Publishing Co., Inc.	*Maryland*
Blue Nile Books	*Washington*
Cardinal Images	*Alexandria*
NTL Institute Book Department	*Alexandria*
Nursing Tutorial & Consulting Service Bookstore	*Virginia*
Smile Herb Shop	*Maryland*
This is the Place	*Maryland*
Yes! Bookshop	*Washington*

History
Alphaville Bookshop	*Maryland*
Antietam Natl. Battlefield Museum Giftshop	*Virginia*
Antiquarian Bookworm	*Maryland*
Arawak Books	*Maryland*
Arlington Natl Cemetery Bookshop	*Virginia*
Arts & Industries Building	*Washington*
Associates Rare Books, The	*Virginia*
Beall-Dawson House Giftshop	*Maryland*
Bethune Museum & Archives Shop	*Washington*
Blue & Gray Books and Prints	*Alexandria*
C&O Canal National Historic Park	*Maryland*
Calvert Marine Museum Shop	*Maryland*
Capitol Gift Shop, The	*Washington*
Capitol Hill Books	*Washington*
Clara Barton National Historic Site Bookshop	*Maryland*

Supreme Court Giftshop	*Washington*
Thistle & Shamrock Books	*Alexandria*
Tower Bookshop (Old Post Office Tower)	*Washington*
U.S. Holocaust Memorial Museum Shop	*Washington*
W.B. O'Neill Old & Rare Books	*Virginia*
Washington Monument Bookshop	*Washington*
Woodlawn Plantation Museum Shop	*Alexandria*
Woodrow Wilson House Gift Shop	*Washington*
World Bank Bookstore	*Washington*

Home Builders
Home Builder Bookstore	*Washington*
National Building Museum Shop	*Washington*

Imported Books
Antiquarian Tobacciana	*Virginia*
Arawak Books	*Maryland*
Cheshire Cat Bookstore	*Washington*
Ginza "Things Japanese"	*Washington*
He Bookstore, The	*Virginia*
Hillwood Museum Gift Shop	*Washington*
Latin American Books	*Washington*
Mystery Books	*Washington*
Sakura Books & Food	*Maryland*
Saludoes	*Virginia*
Thistle & Shamrock Books	*Alexandria*
Vertigo Books	*Washington*
Victor Kamkin Inc.	*Maryland*
International Affairs	
National Archives Museum Store	*Washington*
Professional Book Center	*Alexandria*
Sidney Kramer Books, Inc.	*Washington*
Vertigo Books	*Washington*

Law
George Mason Law School Bookstore	*Virginia*
Georgetown Univ. Law Center Bookshop	*Washington*
Howard University Bookstore	*Washington*
Leonard S. Blondes Used Law Books	*Maryland*
Lerner Law Book Co., Inc.	*Washington*
Library of Congress Shop	*Washington*
Professional Book Center	*Alexandria*
Q. M. Dabney & Co.	*Maryland*
Supreme Court Giftshop	*Washington*
Washington Law Book Co., Inc.	*Washington*

Magic & Occult
Aquarius Metaphysical Center	*Alexandria*
Cardinal Images	*Alexandria*

Dream Wizards	*Maryland*
John C. Rather: Old & Rare Books	*Maryland*
Rosey Cross	*Washington*

Maps, Antique

Map Store Inc., The	*Washington*
National Gallery of Art Bookstore	*Washington*
National Geographic Society Store	*Washington*
Old Print Gallery, The	*Washington*
Old World Mail Auctions	*Maryland*
Pursell's Church Supply Inc.	*Washington*
Rand McNally - The Map & Travel Store	*Wash,*
	MD & VA
Waverly Auctions Inc.	*Maryland*

Medical

Capital Medical Books	*Virginia*
Foundation Bookstore	*Maryland*
Georgetown Univ. Medical Bookstore	*Washington*
Liberty Library	*Washington*
Nursing Tutorial & Consulting Service	*Virginia*
Old Hickory Bookshop	*Maryland*
Professional Book Center	*Alexandria*
Reiter's Scientific & Professional Books	*Washington*

Metaphysical/New Age

All Books Considered	*Maryland*
Aquarius Metaphysical Center	*Alexandria*
Blue Nile Books	*Washington*
Cardinal Images	*Alexandria*
Divine Science Metaphysical Bookstore	*Washington*
Dream Wizards	*Maryland*
Rosey Cross	*Washington*

Military

Air, Land & Sea	*Alexandria*
All Books Considered	*Maryland*
Antietam Natl. Battlefield Museum Giftshop	*Virginia*
Arlington Natl Cemetery Bookshop	*Virginia*
Book Ends	*Virginia*
Compleat Strategist, The	*Virginia*
Eastern Front Military Distributors	*Alexandria*
Frazier's Americana	*Maryland*
Fuller & Saunders Books	*Washington*
Georgetown Book Shop	*Maryland*
Ground Zero Books Ltd.	*Maryland*
Liberty Library	*Washington*
Marine Corps Museum Shop	*Washington*
National Intelligence Book Center	*Washington*

Olde Soldier Books, Inc.	*Maryland*
Pentagon Bookstore	*Virginia*
Q. M. Dabney & Co.	*Maryland*
Rock Creek Bookshop	*Washington*
Ship's Store	*Washington*
W.B. O'Neill Old & Rare Books	*Virginia*

Music

Alphaville Bookshop	*Maryland*
Associates Rare Books, The	*Virginia*
Backstage Books & Costumes	*Washington*
Ben Franklin Booksellers, Inc.	*Virginia*
Book Stop	*Alexandria*
Family Bookstores	*Maryland*
Gospel Notes Records & Books	*Maryland*
Immanuel Christian Bookstore	*Virginia*
Oscar Shapiro	*Washington*

Mystery

Book Niche & Capital Comics Center, The	*Alexandria*
David Holloway Bookseller	*Virginia*
Hole in the Wall Books	*Virginia*
Mystery Books	*Washington*
Mystery Bookshop: Bethesda	*Maryland*
Schweitzer Japanese Prints Inc.	*Maryland*
Steven C. Bernard First Editions	*Maryland*

National Historic Site

Antietam Natl. Battlefield Museum Giftshop	*Virginia*
Arlington Natl Cemetery Bookshop	*Virginia*
C&O Canal National Historic Park	*Maryland*
Capitol Giftshop, The	*Washington*
Calvert Marine Museum Shop	*Maryland*
Clara Barton National Historic Site Bookshop	*Maryland*
Daugh. of the Am. Rev. Mus./Continental Hall	*Washington*
Kenilworth Aquatic Gardens Shop	*Washington*
National Aquarium Giftshop	*Washington*
National Shrine of the Immaculate Conception	*Washington*
The Octagon Museum	*Washington*
Pierce Mill, Rock Creek Park Shop	*Washington*
Supreme Court Giftshop	*Washington*
Tower Bookshop	*Washington*
Washington Cathedral Bookshop	*Washington*
White House Historical Assoc., The	*Washington*
Woodrow Wilson House Gift Shop	*Washington*

Nature/Natural History

Am. Society of Landscape Architects	*Washington*
Audubon Naturalist Bookshop	*Wash & MD*

Nautical & Aviation

Newspapers

Orientalia

Yak & Yeti Books — *Maryland*

Ornithology

Audubon Prints and Books	*Virginia*
BookHouse	*Virginia*
Habitat--National Wildlife Federation	*Wash & VA*
Natural Wonders Inc.	*MD & VA*
Nature Company, The	*Wash & VA*
Old Print Gallery, The	*Washington*
One Good Tern Ltd.	*Alexandria*
Recreational Equipment Inc.	*MD & VA*
Wild Bird Center	*MD & VA*
Wild Bird Company & Absolutely Bats!	*Maryland*

Parenting

A Likely Story Children's Bookstore	*Alexandria*
Cheshire Cat Bookstore	*Washington*
Children's Bookshop, The	*Virginia*
Fairy Godmother-Children's Books & Toys	*Washington*
Purple Crayon Inc., The	*Virginia*
Storybook Palace Inc.	*Virginia*
Tree Top Toys Inc. Book Dept.	*Washington*

Philosophy

All Books Considered	*Maryland*
Alphaville Bookshop	*Maryland*
Aquarius Metaphysical Center	*Alexandria*
Catholic Univ. of America Bookstore	*Washington*
Islamic Center Shop	*Washington*
Kulturas Books & Records	*Washington*
Logic & Literature	*Washington*
Newman Bookstore	*Washington*
Smile Herb Shop	*Maryland*
Yes! Bookshop	*Washington*

Photography

Book Alcove	*MD & VA*
Bookworks/Washington Project for the Arts	*Washington*
Corcoran Museum Shop, The	*Washington*
National Gallery of Art Bookstore	*Washington*

Poetry

Alphaville Bookshop	*Maryland*
Arawak Books	*Maryland*
Ashe & Deane Fine Books	*Maryland*
Associates Rare Books, The	*Virginia*
Chapters	*Washington*
Kulturas Books & Records	*Washington*
Natl Museum of Women in the Arts Shop	*Washington*

Rampant Lion, The	*Washington*
Reiter's Scientific & Professional Books	*Washington*
Tempo Bookstore	*Washington*
University of Maryland Book Center	*Maryland*
Washington Law Book Co., Inc.	*Washington*

Religion--Buddist
Vihara Book Service	*Washington*

Religion--Christian
Agape Christian Bookstore	*Washington*
All Books Considered	*Maryland*
Almond Tree, The	*Virginia*
Ark & The Dove	*Alexandria*
Baptist Book Store	*Virginia*
Book Nook	*Maryland*
Books For Growing	*Washington*
Catholic Univ. of America Bookstore	*Washington*
Choice Books of Northern Virginia	*Virginia*
Cokesbury Virginia Theological Seminary Book Service	*Alexandria*
Divine Science Metaphysical Bookstore	*Washington*
Evangel Temple Bookstore	*Maryland*
Evangelical Used Books	*Virginia*
Family Bookstores	*Alex,*
	MD & VA
Gospel Notes Records & Books	*Maryland*
Grace Christian Bookstore	*Virginia*
Great Commission, The	*Virginia*
Heaven Christian Gift Store	*Maryland*
Icon & Book Serv. of Monastary of Holy Cross	*Washington*
Immanuel Christian Bookstore	*Virginia*
Jacob's Well Christian Books	*Maryland*
Jesus Bookstore	*Virginia*
Jesus Bookstore of Mount Vernon	*Alexandria*
Jesus' Bookstore Inc.	*Maryland*
Let There Be Praise, Inc.	*Virginia*
MCL Associates Used Book Division	*Virginia*
Maranatha Christian Bookstore & Supply	*Alexandria*
Metropolitan Baptist Bookstore	*Washington*
National Shrine of the Immaculate Conception	*Washington*
Newman Bookstore	*Washington*
Olive Branch, The	*Maryland*
Paschal Lamb, The	*Virginia*
Pursell's Church Supply Inc.	*Washington*
Rejoice Christian Store	*Maryland*
Rock Uniform & Christian Bookstore	*Washington*
Saint Paul Book & Media Center	*Alexandria*
Swann's Religious Gifts	*Maryland*
This is the Place	*Maryland*
Truro Episcopal Church Bookstore	*Virginia*

Washington Cathedral Bookshop	*Washington*
Way of the Cross Ministry Book & Bible Store	*Washington*
Words of Wisdom Books & Gifts	*Virginia*

Religion--Jewish
All Books Considered	*Maryland*
B'nai B'rith Klutznich National Museum Shop	*Washington*
Book Fair, The	*Maryland*
Jewish Bookstore of Greater Washington, The	*Maryland*

Romance
Book Nook	*Maryland*
Book Rack, The	*Virginia*
Crest Books	*Virginia*
Silver Spring Books	*Maryland*

Science
Alphaville Bookshop	*Maryland*
Ben Franklin Booksellers, Inc.	*Virginia*
Betz Publishing Co., Inc.	*Maryland*
Calvert Marine Museum Shop	*Maryland*
Foundation Bookstore	*Maryland*
Logic & Literature	*Washington*
Professional Book Center	*Alexandria*
Ptak Science Books	*Washington*
Reiter's Scientific & Professional Books	*Washington*
Rock Creek Park Nature Center Bookshop	*Washington*

Science Fiction & Fantasy
Aftertime Comics Inc.	*Alexandria*
Book Niche & Capital Comics Center, The	*Alexandria*
Book Nook	*Maryland*
Cosmic Bookstore	*Virginia*
Crest Books	*Virginia*
Dream Wizards	*Maryland*
Geppi's Comic World Crystal City	*Virginia*
Geppi's Comic World of Silver Spring	*Maryland*
Hole in the Wall Books	*Virginia*
National Air & Space Museum Bookshop	*Washington*
Robert A. Madle Sci-Fi-Fantasy Books	*Maryland*
Silver Spring Books	*Maryland*
Steven C. Bernard First Editions	*Maryland*
Yesterdays Books	*Washington*

Smithsonian Institution Museum Shops
Anacostia Museum	*Washington*
Arthur M. Sackler Gallery	*Washington*
Arts & Industries Building	*Washington*
Freer Gallery of Art	*Washington*

Hirshhorn Museum & Sculpture Garden	*Washington*
National Air & Space Museum	*Washington*
National Museum of African Art	*Washington*
National Museum of American Art	*Washington*
National Museum of American History	*Washington*
National Museum of Natural History	*Washington*
National Portrait Gallery	*Washington*
National Zoological Park	*Washington*
Renwick Gallery	*Washington*

Social Services
Sidney Kramer Books Inc.	*Washington*

Sports
Eastern Mountain Sports Inc.	*Alex & VA*
Georgetown Book Shop	*Maryland*
Jeff's Baseball Corner	*Virginia*
Old Print Gallery, The	*Washington*
Recreational Equipment Inc.	*MD & VA*
Scavengers of Georgetown	*Washington*
Spinnaker & Spoke	*Alexandria*
Sports Books Etc.	*Virginia*
Woodlawn Saddlery Ltd.	*Alexandria*

Technology
Foundation Bookstore	*Maryland*
Pierce Mill, Rock Creek Park Shop	*Washington*
Ptak Science Books	*Washington*
Reiter's Scientific & Professional Books	*Washington*

Travel & Tourism
Map Store Inc., The	*Washington*
National Geographic Society Store	*Washington*
Old Mill Books	*Alexandria*
One Good Tern Ltd.	*Alexandria*
Rand McNally - The Map & Travel Store	*Wash,* *MD & VA*
Reprint Bookstore	*Washington*
T.A. Borden	*Maryland*
Travel Books & Language Center Inc.	*Maryland*
Travel Merchandise Mart	*Washington*
W.B. O'Neill Old & Rare Books	*Virginia*

Used
A-Z Used Books	*Maryland*
Adams Bookstore	*Washington*
Air Land & Sea	*Alexandria*
All Books Considered	*Maryland*
Alphaville Bookshop	*Maryland*

Rockaway Books	*Virginia*
Samuel Yudkin & Associates	*Washington*
Second Story Books & Antiques	*Wash & MD*
Silver Spring Books	*Maryland*
Steven C. Bernard First Editions	*Maryland*
Stewart's Used Bookstore	*Maryland*
T.A. Borden	*Maryland*
Taj Book Service	*Washington*
This 'N' That Antiques	*Maryland*
Thyme Books	*Virginia*
Voyages Books & Art	*Alexandria*
Waverly Auctions Inc.	*Maryland*
Well Read Books	*Maryland*
Zenith Comics & Collectibles	*Maryland*

Washington Touring Books

Arlington National Cemetary/Arlington House	*Washington*
Capitol Gift Shop, The	*Washington*
Clara Barton National Historic Site Bookshop	*Maryland*
C & O Canal Natl. Historic Park	*Maryland*
Ford's Theatre Museum Bookshop	*Washington*
Fort Washington Park	*Maryland*
Frederick Douglass Natl. Historic Site	*Washington*
Fuller & Saunders Books	*Washington*
Glen Echo Park	*Maryland*
Great Falls Park Bookshop	*Virginia*
Hearthstone Bookshop	*Alexandria*
Jefferson Memorial	*Washington*
JFK Center for the Performing Arts	*Washington*
Lincoln Memorial	*Washington*
Martin Luther King, Jr. Library Giftshop	*Washington*
National Archives Museum Store	*Washington*
National Building Museum Shop	*Washington*
News World	*Washington*
Newsroom	*Washington*
Old Post Office Tower Bookshop	*Washington*
Pierce Mill/Rock Creek Park	*Washington*
Prince William Forest Park Shop	*Virginia*
Recreational Equipment Inc.	*Virginia*
Sewell-Belmont House	*Washington*
Sidney Kramer Books, Inc.	*Washington*
Supreme Court Giftshop	*Washington*
Travel Books & Language Center Inc.	*Maryland*
Washington Monument Bookshop	*Washington*
Woodrow Wilson House	*Washington*

Women's Studies

Cardinal Images	*Alexandria*
Lammas Books	*Washington*
National Woman's Party Gift Shop	*Washington*

Zoology/Animals

BookHouse	*Virginia*
Habitat--National Wildlife Federation	*Washington*
National Aquarium Giftshop	*Washington*
National Zoological Park Bookstore	*Washington*
Natural Wonders Inc.	*MD & VA*
Nature Company, The	*Wash & VA*
Old Print Gallery, The	*Washington*
Prince William Forest Park Shop	*Virginia*